No Problem, Mr. Walt

A MEMOIR OF LOSS, BUILDING A BOAT, REBUILDING A LIFE, AND DISCOVERING CHINA

By Walt Hackman

No Problem, Mr. Walt: A Memoir of Loss, Building a Boat, Rebuilding a Life, and Discovering China

Print Edition Version 1.1

The author has tried to recreate events, locales and conversations from his memories of them. To maintain their anonymity, in some instances the names of individuals have been changed; as well as some identifying characteristics and details such as physical properties, occupations and places of residence.

ISBN 978-0-9964755-3-2
The Library of Congress Cataloging-in-Publication Data is available.

Address all correspondence and order inquires to publisher:
Publish Authority, Newport Beach, CA, U.S.A.
www.PublishAuthority.com

Cover design by: Raeghan Rebstock
Edited by: Gordon Jackson
Illustrations by: Ron Pastucha
Photographs by: Walt Hackman, author

To the memory of my son Wally.

". . . forgetting seems to take the longest time."

Willie Nelson, "Forgiving You Was Easy"

"The journey of a thousand miles begins with a single step."

Lao Tzu 6th Century BC

CONTENTS

ACKNOWLEDGEMENTS

The usual acknowledgments page in a book is devoted to a long list of people who assisted the author with the arduous task of accomplishing a near impossible mission of converting blank paper into a story. This book is different: I wish to acknowledge all the people who helped me convert an idea into a Chinese junk, thereby enabling me to write this true story.

A NOTE ON ROMANIZATION

The conversion of Chinese words into the Western alphabet is called, "Romanization": a convoluted process that evolved over many years. In writing this book, I used two systems: the *pinyin* and Wade-Giles. Where possible, I have used the Chinese standard *pinyin* system for the transliteration of Chinese names of people (including divine beings), places, dynasties, books, Chinese words, and concepts. The other system I used was the older Wade-Giles system, the more traditional Romanization most Westerners are accustomed to. I used both systems because many of the older traditional names and places would be more familiar to the reader. The first time a traditional name is used, the *pinyin* name follows in square brackets. As an example, Hong Kong will appear "Hong Kong [Xianggang]." Most people in America can't even pronounce the *pinyin* name and sure as hell won't know where it is. This is because *pinyin* has a phonetic convention and does not represent English pronunciation. Both names will appear in the book only once.

In cases where I use *pinyin,* it is without reference to the other system. In the back of the book, I've provided a list of all the people (including divine beings), places, dynasties, books, Chinese words and concepts that appear in the text. I have added dates, titles, and so forth for reference.

To make the system of names just a little more confusing, there is one final thing to know about Chinese personal names. In China, a name is written with the last (surname or family) name first and the first (given) name next. For instance, Xi Jinping, the Paramount Leader of the People's Republic of China, would be addressed as President Xi, not President Jinping. Now you know why they called me "Mr. Walt."

Walt Hackman

BALLAD OF THE VOYAGER

Ocean voyager, on heaven's wind,
In his ship, far wandering
Like a bird, among the clouds,
Gone he will leave no trace.

Li Po [Li Bai] (701–762)

PREFACE

Scan the Hong Kong harbor. Crammed stem to stern on its sparkling waters are hundreds of ships and boats—big and small, old and new, with listing masts and soaring funnels. There are luxurious yachts and rust-laden container ships, pleasure craft, fishing skiffs and tugboats. But here and there, dotted amongst them all, you still see a few traditional Chinese junks plying the harbor much as they have for many hundreds of years. China has eighteen thousand miles of coastline, along with thousands of miles of canals and rivers where junks can still occasionally be seen. In the US, though, there are only a few, all imitations of the original . . . except one:

The *Mei Wen Ti.*

The fifty-four-foot-long *Mei Wen Ti* is presently berthed in Los Angeles Harbor in sunny Southern California. Built completely by hand in the early 1990s in an ancient shipyard not far from Shanghai, the *Mei Wen Ti* is the only authentic wooden junk of its kind and size in America.

How the Mei Wen Ti got there is part of what this book is about. The journey of building the Mei Wen Ti began in a way I never expected, nor would I wish on my worst enemy. To say it's the story of a journey I never, ever thought I would take is an understatement.

Looking back, I now realize I had daydreamed about living on a boat for a long time, but I certainly didn't think it would ever happen. By the end of the 1980s I had a wonderful family, a mortgage, an MBA, and owned an art gallery and a computer maintenance company. I was president of the Old Pasadena Business and Professional Association, and I volunteered with the Flying Samaritans, a non-profit organization that provides health care for the underserved in Mexico. I was a busy man and the dream seemed impractical and remote. When the daydream popped in my head, I'd push it back down. And then came the worst day of my life.

In April 1989, my son, Wally, was indiscriminately murdered by a complete stranger. After that dark day, my life seemed to have lost its moorings. Blurred by grief and sorrow, I was sure life as I had known it was over. I lost interest in my businesses and stopped flying to Mexico with the Flying Samaritans. My son's death and my divorce a short time later left me with some big decisions to make.

Here I was at fifty-five years of age, thoroughly set adrift. One day I sat pondering where to live and what to do when I remembered how Wally, my daughter Lynn and I had laid down blue masking tape outlining an early sketch of a Chinese junk on the showroom floor of the art gallery. Thinking of how our lives had changed in an instant and remembering how enthusiastic Wally had been that day, I thought, why not, finally, pursue my dream? Why not live on a boat? But not just any boat: I wanted something unique that honored Wally's memory and our times together. Having looked for boats around Southern California, I had come to realize that nothing could compare to the Chinese junk we laid out that day. So, I got back in touch with a modern-day China trader I had met, and the adventure began. This book tells the story of that adventure, which I have come to view as Wally's parting gift to me.

While the narrative is woven around my experiences during the construction of the *Mei Wen Ti*, it is also a journey of discovery. And it is more: a travel book, a memoir, a little history, and a first-person account of life in an ancient land. The story alternates between California and China while the junk is constructed.

It's about China today and about ancient China. It's about understanding the difference between fighting and singing crickets, enjoying breakfasts of *congee* and green tea, discovering the Eight

Immortals, walking the streets of Shanghai at daybreak, riding in a Red Flag limousine, learning the proper way to eat dim sum (the chicken feet dish must precede the sweet bean wontons), and how ordinary Chinese citizens work and play. But mainly this story is about the people and experiences I encountered during the construction of the junk, and the new path my life took in the process.

"Mei wen ti" means "no problem" in Chinese. I chose this playful yet sarcastic name because no matter what I asked during the beginning of this tumultuous two-year process of building the junk, that's what the Chinese answered. This beautiful and unique vessel's birth, however, was anything but unproblematic, as you will see.

MAP OF EASTERN CHINA

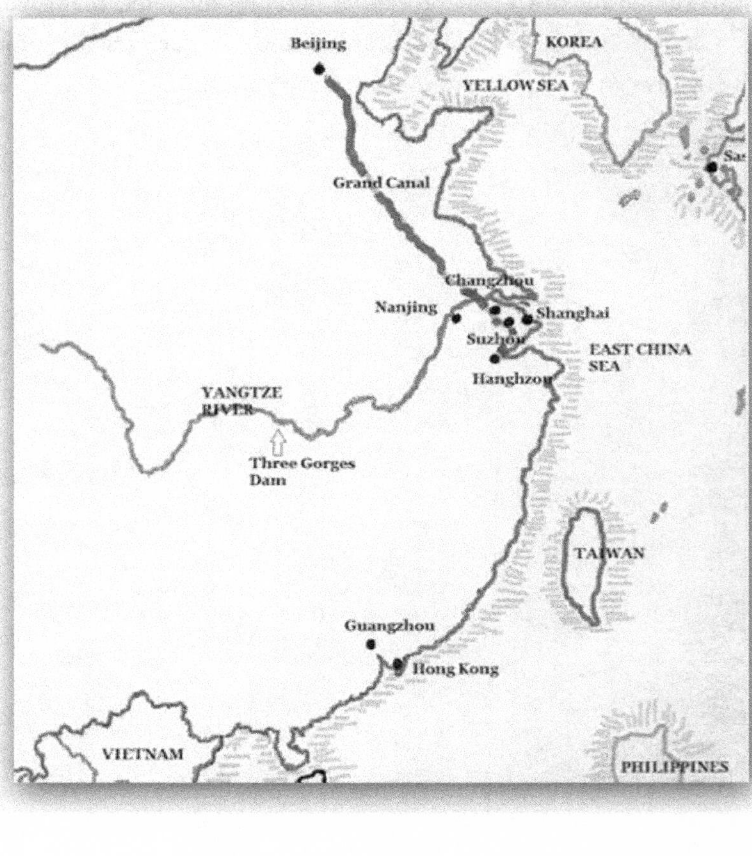

CHAPTER ONE

A NEVER-DEPARTING SHADOW

IT WAS 1993 and one of those beautiful sunny December days you get as a bonus for living in Southern California. I was walking down the edge of the pier toward berth 243 in Los Angeles Harbor; ahead of me was the super-sized container ship *Express Heaven*, piled high with shipping containers, waiting to be unloaded. A squawking seagull took flight from a piling as I reached the ship and turned to walk up a long steep aluminum gangway to the main deck.

As I reached the top of the gangway, one of the ship's officers said, "Good morning, how can I help you?"

"I'm the owner of the Chinese junk up forward that you just brought in from Hong Kong," I replied, "and I've stopped by to find out when it is scheduled to be off-loaded into the water."

As he shuffled through papers on a clipboard, he said, "Doesn't look like the shipping documents have shown up yet. We can't unload it into the water without all the proper paperwork."

I was disappointed, but not surprised. "I'll fax the import-export company in China and see what happened."

"If there is a delay in getting the documents, we will unload your boat onto the pier," he continued. "This ship must clear the berth on schedule. If they have to unload your boat onto the pier, they will charge you to lift it and set it in the water later."

"I understand. Thanks for your help." I turned to leave and saw the junk sitting up forward on the main deck, dirty but in one piece. The large canvas covers supported with large bamboo poles that the Chinese had used to protect her during shipping were torn and hanging down. "*Mei wen ti*" ("no problem"), I thought as I set off to track down the missing paperwork.

The paperwork didn't arrive, so several days later I went back to the pier to watch the junk being unloaded. It was lifted skyward by one of the immense gantry cranes along the pier next to the *Empress Heaven*. The crane looked like a monster from a Star Wars movie. I watched the junk rising from the deck as if taking flight. The junk hung suspended in mid-air for just a moment and then the big crane started slowly moving it toward a predetermined spot on the pier. From the crane operator's perspective at the top of the crane, it must have looked about the size of a loaf of bread. As I stood looking up at it, the tiger head painted on the bow of the Mei Wen Ti was getting bigger and bigger. How relieved I felt now that its long journey was nearly over.

After it was placed on the pier, a crew of longshoreman disconnected it from the crane. After a few minutes, I walked over to look at it. I hadn't seen it for about five months. As I approached the junk, a longshoreman in khakis and a hard hat walked up next to me and stood quietly looking up at the junk.

After a while, he said, "What a great boat; are you the owner?"

"Yeah, my name's Walt, and it's a Chinese junk," I responded.

"I thought so," he responded. "They call me Duke. I helped get her lifted from the main deck onto the pier. I knew the *Empress* was in here from Hong Kong [Xianggang]. Where in China did your junk come from?"

"It came from a small boatyard near Shanghai, not far from the Yangtze River [Chang Jiang]," I said, as I started walking slowly around the junk.

Duke joined me as I inspected the hull for any signs of damage from the long trip and all the handling. The Chinese had built a cradle at the boatyard and secured the junk in the cradle, and then towed the junk down the Yangtze River to Shanghai. In Shanghai, it was loaded onto the main deck of a small cargo ship. The cargo ship took it about 800 miles south down the coast of China to Hong Kong. It was unloaded, and after a short stay, it was loaded as deck cargo on the *Express Heaven* for its long trip across the Pacific.

"Mind if I ask you a question?" Duke said.

"No," I replied, anticipating he was going to ask how much it cost.

"How can I get one of these?" he asked, as if he thought all I did was look in some gigantic Chinese catalog under "J" and order one.

"Well," I said, "It's kind of a long story—a very long story."

* * *

That story has its genesis in a series of hard knocks I received on the way to the "good life" in 1989–90. So as not to make this a story about my misfortunes, I thought I would condense them into a small part of the book, up front, and then get on with the front story.

The story is not about the vicissitudes of my former life, but about rebuilding my life while on a journey to build a boat and discover China. This is what happened.

I once had a great wife, two wonderful kids, a fine house, a nice car, a master's degree, two businesses, great father- and mother-in-law, friends, and a long list of other privileges and possessions. Efficiency, punctuality, achievement, and success were all important.

Somewhere along the way two things happened that changed the course of my life completely and unexpectedly: my son Wally found drugs, and my wife Diane and I slowly started falling out of love (not necessarily in that order). The two problems got worse as time went by: I'm not sure if they were connected, and I suppose I'll never know. The drugs and all its aftershocks took their toll on the whole family, and our daughter Lynn left home to start a happier new life of her own. Diane and I buried ourselves in the businesses.

When it looked like Diane and I were headed for a separation, I decided it was time to start thinking about a place to live. I thought about this for days. After going through a long list of possibilities, I finally decided: I would live on a wooden boat. Why a wooden boat? I believe a wooden boat has a distinctive feel and personality and after many years of use they even have their own smells from cooking, diesel fuel and the smell of the waters they had explored. And so, I find that wooden boats are warmer and more inviting - like a home. And a home is what I needed. I had often thought about living on a boat, and this was the perfect opportunity. It would certainly allow me to get out of the area and live at the beach. So why not finally pursue my dream?

Having decided to live on a wooden boat I wanted to find one that was unique and signaled a fresh start. I spent weeks looking at boats up and down the coast that were within my budget but just couldn't find the right one. I was determined to keep looking, and then a simple question to a real twentieth century China trader did it. I asked him about wooden boats in China, and before I knew it, I had made contact with an ancient boatyard in the eastern coastal province of Jiangsu in the People's Republic of China. The boatyard still built and repaired wooden fishing boats. They said they could build me a wooden boat, and after sending me several rough sketches, I decided to concentrate on a type of boat called a Chinese junk. I later found to my chagrin the boatyard had not built one since the 1940s and it was a more difficult project than either I or the boatyard believed it would be. But, our mutual enthusiasm for the project at this stage made such practical concerns seem superfluous.

Then one day I went to work, a day like any other day, and everything changed in an instant when I was informed by two Los Angeles police detectives that my son had been murdered. My life fell apart as I lost all interest in the businesses and everything else. It wasn't long before my marriage fell apart also; it was just a long time coming. Our son's death and the subsequent separation end this short back story for now, but now you understand why my life needed rebuilding.

After Wally's death, I decided I needed some kind of mental therapy. The personal devastation murder brings to the victims it leaves behind cannot be explained. I now shunned all graphic depictions of murder by not going to movies or watching television. It has become the staple of our news and entertainment industry, and it's pervasive in our society. I've come to believe that those in the mass-media business have bred insensitivity about murder while providing no understanding about what it does to those who remain. A long time ago Mark Twain wrote that experiencing the death of a loved one is like experiencing your house burning down; it takes years to fully figure out what you have lost.

I first tried going to meetings of Parents of Murdered Children with Diane, but for me it made things worse. While getting my master's degree at Pepperdine University, I had spent a third of the time in a behavioral block, so my next thought was to see a psychiatrist. But after a lot of soul-searching I decided not to take that path. I knew the solution was deep within me, and I would have to discover how to find it on my own.

One day while I was in The Bodhi Tree bookstore on Melrose Avenue in West Hollywood, I walked past a bulletin board and noticed a flier for a Buddhist temple advertising an upcoming meditation class.

But what caught my attention was the opening line of the *Dhammapada*, spoken by the Buddha 2,500 years ago.

> *We are what we think.*
> *All that we are arises with our thoughts.*
> *With our thoughts we make the world.*
> *Speak or act with an impure mind*
> *And trouble will follow you*
> *As the wheel follows the ox that draws the cart.*
> *We are what we think*
> *All that we are arises with our thoughts.*
> *With our thoughts we make the world.*
> *Speak or act with a pure mind*
> *And happiness will follow you*
> *As your shadow, unshakeable.*[1]

Since I was sure my current mental condition was mind-made, and I had no other option, I enrolled in the beginner's meditation class. I did not join to better understand Buddhism, but instead to see if, through meditation, I might in some way learn to overpower the darkness that had taken over my mind. The first thing I was told: "In meditation one seeks to gain nothing."

The temple, with its burning incense, ringing gongs, and scriptures I did not understand, provided me with an urban environment where complete seclusion was possible. After I learned the basic techniques of meditation I found myself going as often as possible; I usually stayed about an hour. After several months my cushion seemed softer as the discomfort of sitting on the floor with legs folded became easier. At the rate an iceberg melts, my mind started to become calmer. I found the experience to be more practical than religious, but I could only attribute my slow progress to the meditation. The only "religious" thing I learned was, "In walking, just walk. In sitting, just sit. Above all, don't wobble."

It is said that the journey of a thousand miles begins with a single step. Taking it one step at a time, I found a little happiness and peace of mind started to follow me like a never-departing shadow.

CHAPTER TWO

THE CHINA TRADER

***China in the Twentieth* Century**

I think it is safe to say that the average American may suffer a bit of historical amnesia regarding China's recent history. Therefore, I have decided to start in the next chapter with the last Emperor Pu Yi in the early 1900s, and present the reader with a brief history up to the present; these bits of history will be presented at the beginning of each chapter. If you understand China's recent past, it will be easier to understand references to history in the story, and easier to understand present-day China.

I UNLOCKED ONE side of the old double door and walked in. The building had once been an indoor car showroom back in the 1920s, where shiny Dorts and Paiges had once been displayed for sale. Now Old Town Pasadena was undergoing a renaissance, and I had converted the front area, where cars once sat, into a large art gallery. The rear area of the building had been made into an immense picture-frame shop. Many a Rose Parade float had been reflected in the building's windows over the years as they passed down Colorado Boulevard; now there was a two-foot-high signature of an artist sprawled in orange cursive across the window. Smiling to myself, I turned on the gallery lights then walked back to the frame shop and turned on the rest of the lights.

It was early, and none of the employees had arrived yet. I walked into my office, which had more than likely been the garage manager's office back when Babe Ruth was slugging homers. It had glass windows all around to allow the boss to see everything that was going on out in the garage. I turned on my computer and opened the price list I had been working on. Tonight I had a new show opening, and I needed to finish up all the pricing of the artwork hanging in the gallery before another busy day started.

That evening, an hour or so after the show opened, the gallery was humming with people walking around looking at Clint Sloan's work and drinking Chardonnay. This was Clint's first show, and his small watercolors were selling well. We had sold several of the pieces to people who had walked into the place the day before while we were setting up the show.

Walking toward the back area where we were serving wine, I ran into a friend, Henry, who owned a store a few blocks away. "What a great show," he said. "I didn't know Clint was such a good painter. What the hell is he doing working for you as a picture framer?"

Clint had worked for us for several years as a picture framer here in Pasadena and for our other business, as well. I had not seen Clint's work until just recently, but when I had, I knew I needed to talk him into having a show.

"If this show is any indication, he probably won't be working here for long," I said as I poured myself another glass of wine. "What brings you out tonight?"

"I'm here with a couple of friends who are up front. We just finished dinner next door at Barney's, saw all the people, and decided to drop in," he said. "Hey, here they come. I'll introduce you."

As they walked up, he said, "Don and Mei, I'd like you to meet Walt Hackman. He owns this joint and is the president of the merchant's association here in Old Town Pasadena." Don and I shook hands as Henry continued. "Don here is a China trader, and Mei is a Chinese doctor. Don is looking into purchasing some things for me in China."

"Glad to meet you," I said. "What exactly does a China trader do?"

"You tell me what you need in China, and I find out how to get it," he answered as he took a long sip of his wine. "That's all I do. When we're in the States, Mei here practices a little Chinese medicine from her small office in our home in Hollywood. When I go to China, she comes along and translates. I don't speak Chinese; it's too damn difficult to learn."

"Yes," Mei said. "I practice Traditional Chinese Medicine. It part of Chinese culture—much different Western medicine. I do acupuncture and herbology for people - my office."

"I spent several years in Japan when I was in the Navy, so I know a little about Eastern medicine. China is a place I have always wanted to visit," I said.

The four of us talked for a few more minutes, and then I excused myself and headed back toward the gallery to talk with customers and try and sell some artwork.

Day by day, the guilt, confusion, and anger over my son's death and the impending end to my marriage kept me driving over to the Buddhist temple in West Hollywood to sit on my cushion and meditate and "seek nothing." For me, the meditation was in no sense religious, though it is usually thought of as such. I think most people associate meditation with saintly or holy people, as I once did before I came to believe that daily life is the working material of meditation and that it wasn't about what I gained, but about what was diminished; namely the guilt, anger and confusion.

I didn't tell anyone I drove all the way over to West Hollywood to sit in a Buddhist temple. How could I explain it to anyone? Most would perceive the whole process as idolatry or some form of mysticism. As the days turned into weeks, I continued to meditate, and happiness and peace of mind started to slowly, oh-so-slowly, overpower the darkness that had taken over my mind and my life.

Still, I had good days and bad days. Diane and I decided to divorce and go our separate ways; I had seen it coming for a long time and done nothing about it. Since Wally's death, I had slowly lost interest in everything - my marriage, the house, the businesses, everyone's opinion and advice. Efficiency, punctuality, achievement, and success were no longer important. It's hard to be a good husband when you don't care much about anything.

I started to believe things would get better if I kept sitting. I also thought that as soon as the divorce, selling the house, the businesses, and all the other associated garbage was finished, things would get better, and I would find a new direction. Perhaps a life-changing event would point my life on a new bearing.

There had been times in my life when events had set a completely new direction to my life. Sometimes they were planned and sometimes they weren't. One of the unplanned kind happened to me when I was nineteen years old while in Navy boot camp in San Diego.

"What are we standing in line for?" I asked a fellow recruit.

"Beats the heck out of me," he replied, as we moved ahead slowly in the line.

After about a half an hour, I found myself at the head of the line, standing outside a small office, wondering what the hell was going on. The door flew open, and a recruit came rushing out and headed down the hall. I heard, "Next!" before I had chance to ask him what was happening inside.

When I walked into the small office, I saw a salty First Class Petty Officer sitting behind an old wooden desk that took up about half the office. "Close the door and sit down!" he barked. I closed the door and slid into the wooden folding chair in front of his desk.

He asked my name and serial number while looking at some papers on his desk. Without looking up, he inquired, "What do you know how to do?"

"Do?" I replied. "You mean like occupation as a civilian?"

"Yeah, what do you know how to do?" he said much louder, looking straight at me.

"Well, I'm sure not going to tell him I can cook," I thought. I had been employed in restaurants since I was sixteen and had worked my way up from dishwasher to fry cook. *"This little meeting must have something to do with my future job in the Navy—careful what you say."*

"Nothing," I replied. "I was a student in high school."

"Come on, help me out. What do you know a little about?" he said, getting impatient.

"Well, I worked with a mining engineer when I was in high school, and I know a little about surveying," I replied.

"Fine, surveyor is a Seabee rating." Seabees are the construction battalions of the Navy who build shore-based facilities, roads, and airfields in time of war. "But we don't need any of those," he said. "What else?"

"Well, when I was in high school I took a lot of drafting and while I worked with a mining engineer, I learned to draw maps."

"Good, but draftsman is another Seabee rating, and we don't need any of those, either." He scratched a note on his papers. "One more and we're done." He looked up at me, waiting.

"That's it," I said. "I don't know how to do anything else."

"Well, we need three choices," he said as he threw a thick book across the desk to me. "Pick something."

The book listed every rate (occupation) in the Navy and was pretty dense. As I thumbed through it, he sat staring at me like I was holding up his life or something.

"C'mon, I got a long line of people outside waiting!" he yelled.

I had no idea what to pick and stopped turning the pages when he started yelling. I turned the book around so he could read it and said, "How about this?"

He looked at the page, scribbled something down on his paper, and said, "Good choice, we need those. That's all. NEXT!"

I went out the door thinking I had come out the winner in our little encounter. I had kept my culinary skills a secret and was not going to be a cook in the Navy. At that point what I did wasn't important to me; I just wanted to see the world. I quickly forgot the whole episode, but little did I know I had just made a decision that would result in a monumental life-changing event which would set a new direction to my life that would last for decades.

Sometime later, toward the end of boot camp the Chief Petty Officer in charge of the company got us all together one day behind the barracks.

"Now listen up!" he yelled. "I have some important information here I need to read." He proceeded to read off a name and then a ship or shore station where the person was to report after boot camp. When he got to the H's, he yelled, "Hackman, Walter B., IC Class A School, and San Diego, California."

"What did he say?" I thought. *"What the hell is IC Class A School? I don't want to go to school."* After the chief had finished, I went over and asked him what kind of school I was going to. He said it was Interior Communications Electrician School, and it was right there on the base in San Diego. The page I had stopped on that day had landed me in a school I didn't want to attend. I had joined the Navy to see the world, not to go back to school.

Being sent to that school allowed me to attain the rank of Interior Communications Electrician First Class (the highest rank possible) before I was discharged, and that was just the beginning of a lifetime involved with things electrical or electronic. I have often wondered what rate was on the next page.

Clint's show turned out to be a huge success. We sold every piece in the gallery, about twenty-five pieces. I continued to drive to the Buddhist temple in West Hollywood to sit on my cushion as my marriage proceeded slowly toward dissolution. On weekends, I looked at boats. Then something happened.

I was in Barney's restaurant one afternoon having a beer at the bar, waiting for my lunch to arrive. Since it was a little early for lunch, there were only a few other people at the bar. The manager was standing at the end of the bar talking with the bartender.

"Hi, Walt," I heard from behind. I turned and Don, the China trader, was standing behind me. "Mind if I sit down?" he asked. "I have an appointment with your pal down the street after lunch."

"No, not at all," I said as he slid onto the stool next to me.

The bartender came over and handed him a menu. Don ordered a beer and started looking at the menu. When the bartender returned with the beer, Don ordered pastrami on rye with fries.

"Mei and I really enjoyed ourselves when we were over here last time," he said. "How is the show going?"

We talked about the show, Old Town Pasadena and then we started talking about his adventures in China as we ate our lunch. I got around to telling him I was going through a divorce but didn't mention Wally's death. I never did. After lunch, as we parted, we agreed to meet after work for "a cool one."

Later that day, just as I was closing the small pull-down windows in the gallery using a long pole hook, Don walked in and started looking around the gallery. "How long you been doing this?" he asked.

"Too long." It had been a long day, and I was ready for a cold beer.

We walked next door to Barneys, sat at the end of the bar, and ordered a beer.

"So what are you going to do once you get divorced?" he asked.

"I've been working on that for a long time, and I have decided to move down to the beach and live on a boat," I said. "I have been looking for an unusual boat, but just haven't been able to find anything I like.

Do they still make wooden boats in China?"

"I'm not sure, but I think they still do. I know this old Chinese guy who once worked in a boatyard near Changshu [Changzhou]. I've had him help me on several jobs. I'll ask him; he would know. Tell you what: on my next trip to China I'll check it out. Give me a fax number and if I find out anything, I'll fax you."

We talked for a while longer, I gave him my fax number, and then we went our separate ways.

I forgot about our discussion, until one day, a couple of months later, I received a fax at the gallery from Don saying he was back in China and had learned of a boatyard that made wooden fishing boats. He said they could make me a fishing boat or an old-style Chinese junk. They asked him to find out what kind of boat I wanted. After reading his message, I sent him a fax saying that I did not want a fishing boat, but that I would think about the Chinese junk and get back to him in a few days.

I started looking in books for anything about Chinese junks, but all I found were scant references and historical material. I did find out that Chinese junks date way back in Chinese history. The breakthrough came when I found a large book in an old bookstore titled, *The Junks & Sampans of the Yangtze*, by G.R.G. Worchester. Mr. Worchester had worked for the Marine Department of the Chinese Maritime Customs Service during the early part of the twentieth century. His boss released him from duties as a River Inspector to allow him to spend eight years researching the people, customs, and boats along thousands of miles of the Yangtze River. He produced a book full of details about Chinese junks. Just the book I had been looking for. I bought the book for $68.95 and started reading about the wonderful wooden boats that Marco Polo first described around 1295, and that Worchester saw during his thirty years of service in China. When I got to page 29 I read:

> *When a man decides to build a junk he is not confronted with any difficulty in choosing his design; that*

> *was decided for him centuries ago, for certain types are proper to certain districts. Some slight modifications are permitted to meet peculiar requirements, but these are in no way allowed to interfere with the essential design, which is scrupulously adhered to.*[2]

The more I read the book, the more I began to think that maybe the answer to finding a good live-aboard boat was to build a junk with some slight modifications to fit my requirements.

In late September of 1990, I sent Don a fax to ask him to inquire about the ballpark price for building a forty-five-foot junk. I asked him to have them send a rough sketch to show me the basic design.

We began trading fax messages, and I wrote a two-page basic requirements paper that I sent to him. As we traded information and sketches, I zeroed in on a junk that was fifty-four feet long and had a beam (width) of fourteen feet. The Chinese wanted to use a fishing boat hull designed centuries ago. The plan was to add two marine diesels and make some other modifications to meet my requirements.

On October 29, 1990, I sent Don a fax that read, "I think we are close enough for now on the price. We now need the layout drawings to go over together. Following that, I will try and go with you on your next trip to China."

I had started down the path of another life-changing event - one more significant than the one I picked out of a book way back when I was a boot in boot camp.

CHAPTER THREE

BEFORE THE FIRST TRIP

China in the Twentieth Century - The Last Emperor

In 1644, the Manchu army crossed China's northern border and overthrew the Ming Dynasty (1368–1644 AD) which had ruled China for about 275 years. The Qing (Manchus) Dynasty (1644–1911 AD) had reigned for over 260 years when the Dowager-Empress Tzu His [Ci Xi] got sick and died in 1908. Before her death, she chose two-year-old Pu Yi to be the next emperor. The young boy moved into the Forbidden City in Beijing as the new emperor under the tutelage of his father, Prince Chun, and a large staff of eunuchs. The dynasty at the time of Tzu His's death was corrupt, ineffectual, and weak. With a feeble national government, China's historical check on provincial autonomy started to disintegrate, and the independent militarists or warlords started gaining power.

IT WAS A warm spring evening in Hollywood. I was headed down Santa Monica Boulevard on my way to Don's house in my not-so-new Ford Ranger pickup truck. Don and Mei had invited me over for dinner and to talk about the project.

In this part of Hollywood, there were lots of small dingy strip malls, dirty cars, neon signs, and a lot of not-so-well-dressed people. As I approached Don's street, I noticed the large well-lit liquor store he said would be at the corner of his street when he gave me directions to his house. As I turned the corner from the brightly lit boulevard and headed down the dim street, I noticed a woman wearing a short black dress standing on the corner. She gave me a glance that was all too recognizable in Hollywood. *Was that a hooker I saw on the corner? I think it was,* I thought as I looked out into the night for any sign of their house number. I spotted it, pulled up in front, and parked.

Before I got out of the truck, Don came out and yelled, "Hey! It's better to pull back into the driveway." Looking around at the neighborhood I took his suggestion without asking why. You would never know this part of town wasn't far from the legendary Hollywood and Vine.

Their house was probably built in the '30s and had a large front porch where people once sat back when Hollywood was safe and sane, before air conditioning.

"I think that's a hooker down on the corner," I said as I got out of the truck, pointing back toward the corner.

Don's face agreed with this conclusion. "There's usually more," he said. He smiled, turned, and headed back into the house.

Their house had a homey, well-used appearance. Don slouched back down on a big couch, watching something intently on television. "Grab a beer," he said, pointing toward the kitchen without looking up.

I walked into the kitchen, where Mei was busy cooking something on the stove. I said hello and headed for the refrigerator for a cold beer.

"How you, Water?" she said.

"Great! What are you cooking?" I asked as I opened a beer and took a long swallow.

"Of course, family Chinese dinner," she said without looking back.

"I sure would like you to teach me a bit of Chinese cooking," I declared, looking over her shoulder.

"It Szechwan [Sichuan] style food and much known for spicy flavor," she said.

As I stood there watching, she gave me a few pointers about making family-style Chinese food. She told me there was no main dish; that was why she was preparing three dishes, all considered equal in importance. She said that the cook, not the diner, cuts and seasons the food. That's why there is no knife used with chopsticks, and why I should go easy on the soy sauce.

Pointing to the dish she was cooking, she instructed, "When cook a dish, ingredients combined, not alone." She stirred a vegetable dish together with chicken and peppers.

After our little discussion about cooking, I started feeling the heat from the chilies she was cooking. "Thanks for the lesson. I think I'll keep Don company so you can finish up," I said, and I headed for the living room.

"Look around," Don said. "This show will be over in a few minutes."

Right off the living room was a bedroom that had been converted into a doctor's office for Mei. On the walls were several large Chinese posters: one depicting the channels carrying the "vital force" and another showing the hundreds of points where a patient might be pricked with very fine needles during acupuncture. On the walls were official-looking certificates Mei had earned over the years; most were in Chinese. Around the room, I saw Chinese medical paraphernalia and rows of bottles filled with herbs, bark, and other materials for prescriptions. The room smelled like the Chinese stores I had visited in Chinatown—a smell like no other. Mei later told me that the rows of bottles contained ingredients for medicines to be served as stews she called "soups." There can be up to twenty ingredients in a Chinese stew; I'll tell you more of what I learned about Chinese medicine later in the book.

On the other side of the house was a master bedroom that contained modern Chinese furniture with a bathroom that had fixtures and tile from long ago. The third bedroom had been converted into Don's office. It contained a small desk and chair, and files spilled everywhere. Unfolded and thumbtacked to the wall was a large map of China. The workhorse of the office was an old fax machine, standing ready to send and receive messages. A long fax message from far-off China hung out the back awaiting Don's attention (I know because I peeked).

After Don finished watching TV and Mei finished cooking, we sat down to a wonderful family-style Chinese meal of three dishes and rice. As she said, "No main dish."

It wasn't long before all the bowls on the lazy Susan were empty and the dinner had turned to talk about our upcoming trip to China.

"I have some business in Shanghai and Beijing in about three months, maybe late July through mid-August," Don said over the clatter of Mei picking up the dishes. "If you can get your act together, we can stop in Shanghai, and then go to the boatyard for a few days. You can see what you think, and then we can all go up to Beijing and maybe get in some sightseeing." He made it sound as simple as going down to the corner liquor store.

"I can't wait to talk to the boatyard, and I would love to see Shanghai and Beijing," I said as I got up and headed to the refrigerator to get us each another beer.

"You will like China too much and have dinner my Shanghai parents," Mei said as she unloaded the dishes into the sink.

Over the next hour or so the three of us talked and talked about the trip and, specifically, what I should get done before leaving. We decided I needed to write something that outlined all the requirements; the Federal Express would send this document about a month before our meeting. The Chinese would translate the document into Chinese, study it, and then be able to discuss building the junk with us.

As we were about to wrap it up, Don asked, "How is the boat going to get to California?"

"I promise to work out a solution," I replied. Little did I know how important Don's question would turn out to be.

The next week I started working on how we would get the junk to California. Not realizing the difficulties involved, I jumped right in. After a little study, I resolved to ask the Chinese if I could get some of their crew and take the junk down the coast of China to Hong Kong, resting every evening along the way. I thought this might be a once-in-a-lifetime trip, stopping in small seaports along the coast. Once we reached Hong Kong, I would have it loaded as deck cargo on a container ship, vessels that are capable of carrying deck cargo as well as containers above and below the main deck. Once the junk got to Los Angeles Harbor, it would be unloaded with one of the huge dockside gantry cranes that are used to unload container ships. I began calling shipping companies.

Next I started working on preliminary specifications that would give the Chinese the specifics about what I wanted. I began with information Don had brought back from his last trip to China, along with information I had obtained by fax from the boatyard. At this point I knew they planned to use a fifty-four-foot junk (fishing boat-hull design) that had been designed long ago when junks were still kings of the seas in China. The junk would need to be modified to accommodate two marine diesel engines, which old-time junks never had.

The research and writing of the design requirements continued week after week, and I wasn't getting any answers from the shipping companies. The document at this point was short on details; it mainly outlined what I wanted on the junk.

I called Don and brought him up-to-date on the tasks we had decided I needed to address. I said I thought I was about half way through the requirements, but was having trouble getting a handle on the shipping.

"Taking the junk down the coast to Hong Kong sounds feasible to me. I'd say let's go with that plan for now; we can always change later. Just keep working on the requirements so we can get a draft copy sent out in June. If you can do that, we got it made. Hey, I gotta go, so you gotta excuse me. Call me next week." Click.

As the weeks rolled by, I started making noticeable progress on the requirements. There was nothing new regarding shipping the junk; it seemed like getting a price to ship the junk as deck cargo was going to be a problem.

When I had finally finished all my work, we had another fine Chinese family-style dinner and a meeting afterward. I got to talk with Mei for a little while about cooking before the meal. Afterward, I showed them the six-page document I had completed. They thought it was more than enough information and detail to allow the boatyard to quote a price to build the junk. Since I was not having any luck solving the shipping problem, we decided to ask the Chinese to figure in the shipping cost. We then started making plans for the upcoming trip. As Don had mentioned earlier, he had other business in China, so we planned to fly into Shanghai and have dinner with Mei's parents. The next day the boatyard would drive over and pick us up. After the meetings, we would return to Shanghai and fly up to Beijing for Don's business meeting and then get in a little sightseeing. We were ready to go.

As I backed out of their driveway and headed toward the luminous boulevard, I couldn't help but think about the adventure I was about to embark upon. As I turned the corner from their hazily lit street onto the boulevard, I noticed that the woman wearing a short black dress was no longer on the corner. It was just another early summer evening in Hollywood.

CHAPTER FOUR

SHANGHAI - FIRST TRIP

China in the Twentieth Century - The Republic

The year was 1912. Pu Yi, Prince Chun, and all the others inside the Forbidden City in Beijing lived in a make-believe world totally separated from the world outside the huge walls around them—much as China had been doing for centuries. Outside, a new republic was being formed, and one of the Republican's goals was to rid China of the foreign rule of the Manchus. It wasn't long before the young emperor abdicated and China's ancient system of government was thrown into the trash can of history.

During this period, the Western trading nations and the Japanese controlled large parts of China and tried their best to uphold the corrupt foreign Manchu Dynasty to protect their own extraterritorial rights, garrisons, gunboats, and unequal treaties.

SHANGHAI IS GOING through an enormous metamorphosis. Once known as the Pearl of the East and widely regarded as the financial center of China, it is, in modern times, the city that has been chosen to drive China's new economic progress. It all started after Mao's death in 1976, when Deng Xiaoping rose to power and said, "To get rich is glorious." Deng Xiaoping is sort of the George Washington of modern China. He immediately started removing the roadblocks that had held back the Chinese economy and initiated a massive program of market reforms. His actions are responsible for the booming city I encountered when Don, Mei, and I arrived in Shanghai on a hot July day in 1991. We were on our way to our first face-to-face meeting at the boatyard outside Changshu (Changzhou) to talk about building the junk.

We had just landed at the Shanghai Airport; it was sweltering, noisy, and packed with people. I was soon to learn that everything in Shanghai was sweltering, noisy, and packed with people. The airport personnel wore army-type uniforms, and the airport colors were drab, giving the place a military feeling. It took way too long to get the luggage off the plane and into the airport, but I noticed all the Chinese passengers waited patiently; they have learned how to accept inconveniences gracefully. It is best not to have a tight schedule when traveling in China. We spent no time at all getting our passport stamped and getting through customs—the Chinese didn't seem interested in what we were bringing in.

When we got out of the airport headed toward where the taxicabs were all lined up, Mei stopped and said, "Wait back here, I get cab."

"What is this all about?" I asked Don as I set my bag down.

"Oh, you will learn," he said, dropping his bag next to mine. "Everything costs more if you are a foreigner."

Soon Mei waved for us to join her in the taxi at the head of the line. She had determined the route and that the cab had a working meter. The cab driver put our luggage in the trunk as we jumped into the hot cab for a ride to the Hengshan Hotel.

The cab driver was a small, serious man who didn't say much. I think Mei had pissed him off. He wore a short-sleeve white shirt that had been washed a thousand times and had Mao's picture proudly displayed on his sun visor. Next to Mao's picture was one of the 1960s revolutionary hero Lei Feng. If you see a photo of a soldier with a boyish smile in your travels to China, it is sure to be this dead soldier, hailed as a model of charity. A well-worn copy of *Quotations from Chairman Mao Zedong* was stuck next to the driver's seat. It was required reading not too long ago.

The cab was old and small and smelled like the inside of an ashtray. The windows were open, and the breeze felt good, once we got rolling. The city has the same polluted air as Los Angeles on a bad air day, only humid. The humid breeze didn't last long once we hit the traffic outside the airport and began a slow crawl, inching along narrow streets, dodging people, bicycles, and all sorts of three- and four-wheeled vehicles. The driver chain-smoked cigarettes and drank green tea from a fruit jar as he zigzagged in and out of traffic.

As we approached the area around the Hengshan Hotel, the streets were lined with large, old trees that almost reached across the street to touch each other. I was surprised at the number of people I saw sweeping the streets with large straw brooms. It seemed like every person works, so this might be their answer to welfare.

Mei and Don stayed at the Hengshan Hotel every time they were in Shanghai, so those at the front desk knew them by sight.

"Good see you, Mister Don and Doctor Mei," the old clerk exclaimed as he dealt us registration cards to fill out. The countertop was well-worn gray marble.

"And who you?" he asked, watching me fill out my registration card.

"My name is Walt Hackman, and I have stopped here on my way to Changshu to see about building a wooden boat." I filled out the registration card and handed it back.

"Welcome, Mister Walt, glad stay here," he said as he handed me an antique door key, the old-fashioned metal kind that fit into a hole beneath the doorknob. This was the first time someone addressed me as Mr. Walt, and it wouldn't be the last. In China, a name is written with the surname first and the given name second. But like almost everything in China, that isn't always the convention.

The old hotel looked as if it had been remodeled many times over the years. All the furniture in the lobby was threadbare. The original brick building dates back to when this was the French section of Shanghai before the Communists came to power in 1949.

When we got to the elevator, I pushed the button. The moving arrow above the door indicated that the elevator was slowly moving down. When it arrived, I opened the timeworn, accordion-style door, and we all got in.

As we rode up to the third floor, Mei said, "My family expect us to dinner this evening; let's meet lobby at six."

"See you then," I replied.

We planned to spend just one night in Shanghai before leaving for Changshu the next morning. Mei's parents, her brother, his wife, and small daughter lived in an old section of the city. Since we had planned to visit them, I'd brought over a couple of small gifts.

My room was plain and drab; the bed was about two inches too short, but, all in all, it wasn't a bad place to stay. I hung my clothes on old wooden-style hangers inside a standing wooden closet and put my other things inside a more modern Chinese-style dresser.

I looked out the only window at a park across the street. It was full of people walking, doing *tai chi,* and sitting on benches talking. Several games of mah-jongg were in process. There was even an older couple dancing to music I couldn't hear; as if they were in a beautiful ballroom.

I went back down to the small bar I had noticed off the lobby when we arrived. When I walked in, it was empty except for the bartender, who was looking at a small television set behind the bar. The picture wasn't good; I thought it might be a Chinese TV. He turned down the volume as he rose from his stool.

"Welcome," he said, "What can I get?"

I gazed at every brand of alcohol you could think of. However, the labels looked worn. *Can the Chinese counterfeit booze?* I wondered.

"A Tsingtao beer," I replied as I sat down at the bar. Tsingtao (pronounced "ching-dow") is a German-style pilsner I always ordered when I went to Chinatown in Los Angeles. I didn't know the names of any other Chinese drinks.

The bartender brought me a large bottle of Tsingtao beer at room temperature and set it on the bar with a small glass.

"You vacation here?" he asked as he wiped off the bar with a dry rag.

"No," I said, "I'm here for a day, and then I'm leaving for Changshu."

"Could be Changsha?" he replied.

"No, I am going to Changshu,"

"Not much visitors go Changshu; it is, what you say, much manufacturing."

Before this trip to China, I had been reading everything I could get my hands on about China. I had read that Changshu was not a tourist destination, but was an industrial city of over a million people, located in Jiangsu Province about seventy miles northwest of Shanghai, along the mighty Yangtze River, upriver from the never-ending outskirts of Shanghai. Changsha is the capital of Hunan, a province in south-central China where Mao Zedong began his career and, therefore, has become a fading tourist destination.

As I picked up my glass and poured my beer, the bartender returned to his stool and went back to watching his program; the show seemed to be a Chinese war movie. I began to watch, and noticed there were two types of characters in the film: they were either good-looking young Chinese men with short haircuts and attractive young women both dressed in plain peasant clothing; or short, fat officers and mean-looking soldiers in disheveled uniforms. It finally dawned on me that the film he was watching depicted the struggle between the Communists and Chiang Kai-shek's Army before their defeat by the Communists and their withdrawal to Formosa (Taiwan). In the movie, it looked as if the last of Chiang's troops were selling their arms to the Reds and crossing over to join them, to the dismay of the regiment's portly officers. I knew that what remained of the old Kuomintang army was now living out their lives on Taiwan. The movie he was watching reminded me of the old B-Class cowboy-and-Indian westerns I had watched as a kid. You always knew who won. This was much the same; only the Chinese good guys didn't ride white horses.

It was about six o'clock as I drank the last of my beer. I paid the tab, said good evening to the inattentive bartender, and walked out into the lobby to meet Don and Mei. "*Oh well,* I thought, *come to think about it, those old westerns I used to watch weren't much better.*"

CHAPTER FIVE

DINNER IN OLD SHANGHAI

China in the Twentieth Century - Dr. Sun Yat-sen

One of the first people to try and "mount the dragon's back" after Pu Yi was Dr. Sun Yat-sen [Sun Zhongshan], the Republican leader from the south who had formed the National People's Party, or Kuomintang (KMT) [Gua Min Dong]. The party was dedicated to the overthrow of the Manchu Dynasty, land reform, and the establishment of a democratic republic. Sun's movement grew between 1905 and 1912. After a successful revolt by imperial army troops, the Republic of China was established, and Dr. Sun was made the provisional president in 1912.

AS YOU WALK down the sidewalks of this city that was built on the trade of gambling, smuggling, prostitution, kidnappings by secret Triad organizations, opium, and even cricket fights, it's hard to believe it could be safe to walk anywhere; but it is. (When traveling in any country, I always try and remember that there are scammers everywhere.) We headed toward Mei's parents' home located in one of the old sections of Shanghai.

The tree-lined streets around the hotel gave way to streets without vegetation. These streets gave way to smaller and narrower streets filled with people. As we approached Mei's parents' house, the streets were narrow and crowded with whole families trying to escape the heat. Small tables, stools, and chairs were set up everywhere along the narrow sidewalks and the sides of the street. We walked past loud groups of men playing card games, past people eating and women talking and cooking on small charcoal stoves that filled the air with smoke. There were children playing and street merchants selling. The sound of Chinese music mixed with TV continued block after block. A thin gray haze hung in the streets between the old buildings that lined the streets. Laundry hung out many of the windows.

Just before we got to Mei's parents' house, we passed an old man sitting on a small stool selling Tsingtao beer out of a large wooden box. He was watching some excruciating Peking opera on a small TV set perched on top of another empty wooden box. There is nothing that looks and sounds more Chinese than Chinese opera. The heroines are graceful impersonators with falsetto voices that are superimposed over head-rattling percussion instruments. "*I'm going to buy some beer to take to dinner,*" I thought as I turned around and walked back. While listening to some male princess attack my ears, I pointed at his box full of large bottles and gave him a hand signal for three. Mei negotiated the cost; I got the beer and paid the bill. Since there was usually no tipping (or a city called Tipping) in China at the time, I leaned down and held out my hand for the change. I rushed to catch up with Don and Mei as they made their way down the crowded street.

Mei's dad was waiting beside an old green door that had been propped open with a rock. He seemed glad to see all of us. Their small charcoal brazier sat outside the door on the sidewalk, smoking away, getting hot along with hundreds of others in the neighborhood. After meeting him, I went inside and met the rest of Mei's family. The family was glad to see Mei and a long, loud, continuous conversation started immediately. The apartment was old and consisted of only two small rooms, with the cooking area in one corner of the smaller room. There was an old piece of screen-covered furniture for holding fresh food, which indicated that they probably shopped every day. On top sat a small statue of Kuan Yin [Guanyin], the Goddess of Mercy. (You will see this statue everywhere you go in China.) A small pot with sand sat next to the statue and held several joss sticks that sent a thin stream of smoke toward heaven. Next to the only window was a small bamboo birdcage with a small songbird inside.

As the talking died down, I brought out the gifts I had brought over on the plane. I gave Mei's parents a succulent plant in a small ceramic pot; they thought it was a nice gift, but I'm not sure people keep live plants in their homes in China, and their small place had no yard. I gave Mei's niece a children's dictionary. The young girl said in broken English, "I prize it." She continued, "It better than teacher's." It contained a lot of pictures of things she had never seen. Like many families in Shanghai, the family was having her study English so she could get an important job someday.

The women returned to the small kitchen area to continue preparing the dinner. When I tried to walk into the smaller room to see what they were preparing, the top of my head brushed along the top of the ceiling, and I had to stoop to walk around. The women thought it was funny, and I guess it was. After banging my head on their ceiling, I realized that many things were made for a country of shorter people: all the steps were too close together and not wide enough for my feet, and all the beds were too short for my long legs. I later found out the ceilings in the buses were too low, and the seats in planes, trains, and buses were too close together. Maybe that's one reason the Chinese stared at me; I looked like a giant in a country designed by and for shorter people.

In Chinese cooking, almost all the time is spent in the preparation. As the women were finishing up the preparation, the rest of us went outside with the masses to drink the Shanghai-temperature beer I brought. Since I had already had a beer at the hotel, it wasn't long before I needed to go to the bathroom. I trotted back in the small apartment, but couldn't locate the bathroom.

Don saw me looking around and said, "It's down at the end of the block. Give me a second and I will go with you."

As we walked down the street, Don said, "Public toilets are common all over China, so you need to start carrying a small roll of toilet paper in your back pocket." As we walked into the large reeking restroom, I was confronted with open holes in the floor and a latrine against one wall. There were times when the cultural difference hit me right in the face; this was one of those times. Above the door going in I noted the Chinese character for "man" so I would know which side to enter in the future. On our way out I noticed a sign on the wall in Chinese; underneath, in English, it said, "Please Keep Cleaning." On the way back, I drew the Chinese character for man in my notebook and wrote "= man" next to it for future reference.

When we got back, the small cook stove that sat outside was glowing red-hot. Mei's sister-in-law set out two plates of room-temperature food that had been prepared earlier and went outside and began cooking the next course. We each took a plate and a pair of chopsticks and gathered around the small table; some of us standing and others sitting. I took a small amount from each of the first two plates and began eating. Before I had finished, the next course arrived piping hot. This continued unending for quite some time. I managed to try some of each dish. About the time I started to get full, I was handed a soup bowl full of rice. The cook came in and started eating. Shortly after that, they presented me with a bowl of chicken soup with a chicken leg in it. I said I was way too full, which they took as a compliment to the cook. I'm sure the family only ate this amount of food on special occasions and to them that day was special.

As the meal progressed, every time someone raised a glass and shouted "*Kan pei*!" we all tossed our beer down. By the time the dinner was over, I was stuffed, and all the beer was gone. We talked a little longer and then headed back toward the hotel. As we walked past the public toilets, I reminded myself that a "sit-down" toilet really is a luxury.

The next morning I met Don and Mei in the hotel restaurant for breakfast. Mei and Don ordered croissants and tea. I decided to try a Chinese-looking breakfast I had noticed several Chinese people eating as we walked into the dining room. When it came my turn to order, I pointed to the nearby table, and said, "That." It was there I learned that short English sentences work best in China. It turned out to be a bowl of *congee*, some fermented tofu, a small serving of dark leafy greens, a steamed roll (*baozi*), and green tea. *Congee* is a thin rice gruel that resembles porridge. This breakfast had pungent flavors and was a surprise of tastes, none of which I had ever experienced before—especially at breakfast—and a Chinese breakfast is surely an acquired taste. The recipes for this breakfast can be found in Chapter Twelve.

I picked up my chopsticks and started eating my breakfast. While they ate, Don and Mei engaged in a heated exchange about something. "*I wish they would settle such matters in private,*" I thought as I noticed others in the dining room starting to look our way. Don had a bad habit of disparaging people in public. "*I hope his temper doesn't get us in hot water down the road.*"

After breakfast we waited in the lobby to be picked up; the boatyard had made arrangements for a vehicle to transport us about seventy miles to Changshu. The boatyard was located a short distance outside Changshu. This transportation arrangement became common practice on every other trip to China.

After a short wait, a well-used airport-type van arrived. An older Chinese man and a young driver hopped out of it. The smiling older man was introduced to me as Mr. Wen. I didn't meet the driver but thought of him as Mr. Kamikaze after driving with him for several hours. Mr. Wen had short, jet-black hair. He was missing a few teeth, and the remainder were stained from a lifetime of smoking. He wore a short-sleeve white shirt and faded green shorts, and his shoes had open toes that showed dark brown socks. After the short introduction, Mr. Wen and the driver helped load the suitcases.

As we pulled out into the noisy Shanghai traffic, Mei said, "We work Mr. Wen other times."

Don and Mei had worked with Mr. Wen on other small projects in the past. In the course of the conversation, I found out Mr. Wen had worked almost all his life at the boatyard where the meeting was to be held. I learned he was retired and lived with his extended family in Changshu. I had no idea then, as we discussed this unremarkable man that he was to play a major role in building the junk.

As we headed away from the hotel, I looked out the window at all the Shanghainese also headed down Hengshan Road. It was obvious there were not many privately owned vehicles alongside. This is rapidly changing with the introduction of capitalism. The average person gets around on the city's crowded bus system or by China's most popular means of transport: the bicycle. Shanghai's streets are a congested and confusing mix of pedestrians, bicycles, buses, old trucks, and other vehicles such as three-wheeled bicycles and pedicabs. (As opposed to rickshaws, pulled by a person on foot, pedicabs are human-powered by pedaling.) The number of pedestrians is huge, and many of the lanes are railed off for bicycles only, making the streets incredibly narrow. The trip moved slowly along, as I look ahead for the outskirts that never came. It is hard to imagine that the traffic can get any worse in Shanghai than it already is, but that is going to be the price of more capitalism and progress. Creeping along in the traffic, I looked out the van window thinking, "*This is Los Angeles in another few years.*"

CHAPTER SIX

IS THIS THE BEGINNING OR THE END?

China in the Twentieth Century - General Yuan Shikai

If the Western powers couldn't have the Manchu Dynasty, they put their money on the military chief of the country, General Yuan Shikai. Lacking foreign support, Dr. Sun stepped down and accepted Yuan as president. Yuan was the next leader to "mount the dragon's back" for a short ride. In 1915, he decided to nix democracy and become the first emperor of a new, short-lived dynasty. The provinces were controlled by army strongmen who were loyal to Yuan.

THE TRIP FROM Shanghai to Changshu was lengthy and stifling. It was, as the bartender in Shanghai had said, "Not many tourists and a lot of manufacturing." The van dropped us off at the Yushan Hotel, a more modern-looking building than the Hengshan Hotel in Shanghai. It was situated at the foot of picturesque Yu Mountain, which I was told is the only local tourist attraction. I learned later that China has many more famous mountains than Mount Yu.

The next morning, Mr. Wen and Mr. Kamikaze picked us up in the same van for the trip to the boatyard. After a fast but uneventful journey, we pulled up outside the sea fishery company's facility, located along a canal that flows into the mighty Yangtze River. All the buildings in the complex were built long ago. The meeting was held in their main office building, which sat apart from the boatyard. When we got up to the second floor, from the windows we could see many wooden fishing boats grouped together down below, along the bank of the canal. Several wooden fishing boats were in the boatyard being worked on and one new boat under construction could be seen.

The room where the meeting was to take place was a large office with no desks or conference table; instead, many chairs were grouped in a half-circle around a long, low table with bowls on top containing bananas. On one of the walls was a high serving table that held tall metal thermoses of hot water for tea. Mr. Wen, using Mei to translate, introduced us to those in the room. We met Mr. Ru, the naval engineer who would be working on the project, and his assistant Mr. Tao. We met the head guy Mr. Li and several of his associates from the sea fishery company and boatyard, along with some supervisory people from the boatyard. Finally, there were several people from one of the province's import-export companies who would handle the contractual matters and the shipment of the junk.

After tea, bananas, and a lot of talking, the chairs were gathered into a loose circle and the meeting started. An executive with the company, dressed in a short-sleeve shirt with no tie and a pair of wash-and-wear short pants, gave a talk about the company in Chinese with Mei acting as interpreter. It seemed to take a lot of Chinese talking to make a few short sentences in English, and I wondered what was lost in translation. He said they did three things: fishing, constructing new wooden fishing boats, and overhauling and repairing fishing boats. They had been doing these things for generations. Next, Mr. Li from the boatyard gave a short speech about building wooden fishing boats. He said that the basic design for the junk was based on a fishing boat whose construction had followed the same pattern for over a thousand years. Mr. Li suggested we adjourn the meeting to walk down and look at one of the recently completed eighty-foot fishing boats.

The sights in the boatyard were amazing. We walked past two teams of men transforming trees into perfectly square wooden beams with nothing more than a short ax and a long wooden plane. These planes were of the type that hadn't been seen or used for generations in the United States. A man on each side of the tree would take a chop with a small ax, followed by the man on the other side. After a short time, they would stop and plane. This went on all day long until two perfectly square beams were produced. I know because the next day I stood at one end and sighted with my eye right above the cut surface; it was perfectly flat and square all the way down. It was as if it had come out of a huge modern electric wood planer

We walked past an area where men were hand-sawing large trees. The two-man crew, one on a platform above the tree and one standing below, used an elongated steel saw with a handle at each end to cut a large trees into planks. In the back of the area, a man squatted down, making a bucket out of scrap wood.

Further on, an older timber fishing boat was having several planks replaced. A small crew of caulkers were crouching underneath, pounding hemp covered with a white caulking compound into the spaces between the planks. The ancient Chinese character for caulking was once discovered carved into an ancient turtle shell, proving that this is indeed an age-old Chinese trade.

We finally arrived at the new wooden fishing boat parked on the canal. Walking across the thin gangplank, I noticed that the water in the canal was the color of a cup of coffee with cream. There was another older fishing boat tied outboard of the new one with tires hanging in between. The new boat had a raised, pointed bow and a traditional fishing boat stern. The person in charge of the construction said the junk would be built using the same basic construction methods, which hadn't changed since the junks were built long ago. Because the boat was new, it had a new clean wood smell and look. *"I'm so thankful God didn't make trees out of fiberglass,"* I thought, as I smelled the camphor wood soon after stepping inside the boat. In building it, they didn't use sandpaper on any of the planking, so you could see the faint plane marks if you looked close. The sanitation system was a wooden bucket. The single locally built diesel engine was similar to a large, old-style British tractor engine, and was noisy when they fired it up. The quarters for the crew were quite small, and I noticed how short the wood bunks were. The electrical system was basic: the only electronics equipment aboard was a VHF radio. The boat looked strongly built, and I thought to myself then that they would have no problem building the junk, but what about all the things we specified for inclusion on the junk that were not on this boat? The sanitation system must be more than a wooden bucket. Oh, well, I was sure it would become clear later. As we walked off the boat, someone said, "Lunch."

This was the first of dozens of lunches I was to eat with various people from the boatyard over the course of the time the junk was being built and tested. After trudging down a dirt alley for approximately a block, we came to a two-story, unpainted wooden building. The building looked similar to the ones you see along the main street in an old western movie. I think the restaurant was part of the sea fishery company because we never ate anywhere else. The Chinese were the first at many things in history, and the Chinese restaurant predates anything else that might be called a restaurant in Western culture. We all went upstairs and sat around a large, round, wooden table for the first of many fine meals I was to eat in this modest establishment. The room was warm, so I plopped next to a window and ordered a beer. (I was beginning to acquire a taste for room-temperature beer.) Lunch usually lasted an hour or so, and the food was always a treat for me.

After lunch the meeting continued. Mr. Ru, the naval engineer, talked about his background as a professor at Shanghai Tiao Tung University. He said he would be providing engineering assistance to the boatyard, and that his assistant, Mr. Tao, would enjoy doing some translating to practice his English skills. As we finished lunch, Mr. Ru said we were welcome to visit him at the University in Shanghai. Don and I assured him we would.

The next person to speak was Mr. Chao from the import-export company. He talked about what an import-export company does: they would handle the contract, financial matters, parts shipments into China, and the shipment of the junk to California.

By early afternoon, we finally got to the meat of what we had come all this way to find out. Could the Chinese, using the design document I had written several months earlier, build and deliver a Chinese junk? A simple enough question.

Mr. Ru had translated copies of all the available paperwork into Chinese and said the boatyard had spent many hours going over everything.

We began with the principal dimensions of the junk. It was to be 54 feet in length with a beam of about fourteen feet. The draft (the depth of water the junk draws) was about three feet. We then proceeded with a discussion of the hull construction, fittings, and general equipment that would be provided on the delivered junk. As we marched down the list of requirements one at a time, I was astonished there were so few questions, and nothing seemed to be a problem. "*Mei wen ti,*" they would tell Mei; no problem. I felt uncomfortable inside; unlike most American business meetings, there were no questions and not much dialog. I thought to myself, "*Why aren't there more questions?*"

During a break in the meeting, Don said, "Need to hit the head?"

I looked over at him. "Sure."

We got up and walked downstairs, toward the back of the building. We stepped outside, and there, along the back of the structure, was a ten-foot uncovered latrine built up against the back of the building.

As we stood there, I said to Don, "Something is wrong. There just aren't enough questions."

"Maybe they don't have any questions," Don responded, sounding positive.

"That's what bothers me," I said while I buttoned my pants up. We headed back upstairs to the meeting. Continuing through the requirements, they would constantly tell Mei, "*Mei wen ti.*" We finally came to the Yanmar marine diesel engines that were to be used. I had expected there would be questions since the engines were Japanese, and I was sure they had never seen one. They indicated immediately there was an issue that needed to be resolved with the engines, but the problem, however, was there was not enough money in their estimate to purchase the engines, build the boat, and ship it to Los Angeles. "*That* is *a problem*!" I thought as I looked across the table at Don, who was staring back at me in disbelief.

CHAPTER SEVEN

SAVING FACE

China in the Twentieth Century - WWI

As the world rushed off to war in 1914, Japan saw an opportunity to strengthen her position in China by declaring war on Germany and seizing German territory in China. In 1915, the Japanese made a series of demands that Yuan was forced to accept. During this period, China was trying to organize a republic and gain political stability; several tried to ride the dragon, but China was a republic in name only.

AS WE HEADED back to the hotel, I told Don we had two major problems that were about to derail the project: the first was specifications and the second, their cost estimate.

"I'm sure I didn't do that good a job writing the design requirements; they need to be more detailed. There should have been a lot more questions and discussion. As for their original price, we will just ask for another estimate," I said.

"Regarding the specs, maybe they are a lot smarter than you give them credit for," he responded.

"I'm sure they are smart, but there are a lot of things on this boat we didn't see on that fishing boat."

"Well, I can tell you this from spending years over here doing business: the Chinese don't want to lose face. They also worry about the face of others," he said.

"That's it, Don!" I cried. "They don't want us to think they don't understand by asking questions. They don't want to say, 'Hey, wait, I don't understand this, this part of the requirements needs clarification,' because it would make them look bad, or me look bad since I wrote it, and then someone would lose face."

"Well, what do we do about that?"

"I don't know, but I *do* know its an extremely important cultural issue. But what worries me most is, can they install the engines and everything else correctly?"

"What should I do?" That night at the hotel I began to think. "*Maybe the best thing to do is just to quit and go back home.*" That evening after dinner, I went to Don's room to discuss the project. Mei was sitting on the bed reading a Chinese newspaper.

"I'm absolutely positive they can build the junk. The problem is, I'm not sure they have the expertise to install the engines and other systems properly. I think getting a new price is a separate issue that is easily resolved; we either buy it, or we don't. Even though the Chinese manufacture almost everything for the States, the Chinese parts I saw on the fishing boat were totally unsatisfactory to me. We sure as hell can't use a wooden bucket for a toilet. And finally, this issue of face must be taken seriously," I said.

"Well, you're the guy with the master's degree. I'm sure you can figure it out," Don grinned as he flopped into the chair next to me.

"We emphasize efficiency and directness in speech, but they seem to emphasize indirectness in business dealings. It seemed that form is more important than content."

"Well, I can tell you for sure after spending a lot of time in China, that the indirectness you are seeing is frequently used as a strategy to avoid loss of face of another or oneself."

"I think you're right. It seems better to avoid a topic than ask questions that might cause embarrassment for Mr. Ru, the boatyard, or me."

Mei had been listening and chimed in. "If Mr. Ru or the boatyard lose face you will lose respect of all others. This extremely important, keep face in front of foreigner."

After further discussion, with no resolution of my misgivings, I said I would meet them for breakfast at seven o'clock the next morning and returned to my room.

I couldn't sleep, so I picked up a book on the *Tao Te Ching* (pronounced "dow deh jing") I had brought with me. The *Tao* is a classic manual on the art of living written by Lao-Tzu, the founder of Taoism. It says when you are in tune with the Way, things go as they are intended to go. It is different from our belief that we must be in charge of everything.

I had been thinking nonstop about ways to change, remake, or reshape the project, but to no avail. The Way of the Tao means that those who understand it try to get "in the flow" instead of making things into something else. It was time to stop thinking about what they could and could not do. What could *I* do? I went to sleep that night thinking, "*What can I do*?"

The next morning, after a quick Chinese breakfast with Don and Mei and a fast ride to the boatyard, I found myself again in a meeting. Not knowing what else to do, I went back to the engines where we had left off the day before when the meeting broke off; I was determined not to lose my temper or put anyone on the spot as we continued. Just as in our last meeting, everyone was polite and courteous. We learned that the engineering work necessary to determine the size of the engines had not been completed. However, based on preliminary information they had from Yanmar, they were sure their original cost estimate for the engines and accessories was too low, and they were not prepared to come up with another total price at this time. Now what? I needed more time to try and salvage things.

I said that since we came here to discuss the specifications, not the price, we should proceed with our discussion of the requirements. Everyone agreed. After leaving the engines, we went to the "Other Requirements" portion to start discussing the junk power system.

As I picked up my paperwork and turned to the section, the solution dawned on me. During the next break in the meeting, I looked over at Don and nodded toward the latrine.

We got up and walked downstairs and outside as we had done many times during the long meetings. As we stepped up to the latrine, I turned to Don and said, "I figured it out. It's easy."

"What, taking a piss?" he responded with a big smile.

"No," I said. "Getting the project moving without anyone losing face."

After we finished, we stood at the door leading back into the building for a few minutes while I explained the plan.

"We increase the information in the design document and then specify in the contract that the junk must comply with all our requirements. We can put a big section in to cover the engines and associated parts. We will supply most of the parts and even the engines and all the accessories if necessary. I propose we jump in and give them information they didn't even know they needed. What the hell, if they don't need it, nothing's lost. It's our documentation, and we're the buyer, we can put anything in it. The beauty of the solution is that it is kind of Chinese," I said. "What do you think?"

Don took my hand and shook it enthusiastically. "You sure about this?" he said, trying to absorb what I had just said.

"Yeah, I'm sure, but I want them to give us a price for the boat with engines they purchase. What do you think of my ideas?"

"I guess I'm happy if you're happy." He shrugged.

As we headed back into the meeting, I knew I would need to work on the idea a bit before presenting it. "*Tonight, after the meeting*, I thought, *I'll make a plan out of these early ideas.*"

The meeting shifted to a discussion of the interior requirements, starting with the forward cabin. By the end of the day, we had finished with the interior requirements without many problems.

The next day, we continued through the last page of the specifications with few comments. *Mei wen ti.* During the meeting, I had taken notes on a yellow tablet to document all the problems and changes we had agreed to.

When we had finished with everything, they all seemed pleased that the ordeal was over. They had maintained surface harmony while I boiled inside at their indirectness. After coming all the way to China, I didn't even know the total cost of the junk.

It was time to reveal the plan I hoped would save the project, solve my problems of getting the equipment installed correctly, get the engine problem resolved, and at the same time maintain harmony and face. I didn't want Mr. Ru or the boatyard to think I didn't have confidence in them.

"Well, here we go," I thought as I started to roll out my plan for Mei to translate. "I am pleased we got through everything with only one major problem, and I am sure the engine size and cost will be determined soon. After seeing the fishing boat, I have decided I want to use American systems design and parts on the boat. To do this, I will need to get the various systems designed that we have just discussed to American standards and develop parts lists for all the systems. I can't do that by myself." Then I proceeded to tell them what I had told Don: I planned to hire a marine engineer to help me. He would design all the systems using American parts and supply detailed parts lists and drawings for all the systems. We would also provide information to help with the installation of the engines. All these new data were to become part of a new revised design requirements document.

"When the marine engineer has finished the design and parts information, I will rewrite the specifications to add more design information and indicate every part that I will supply. If we can get them cheaper, we will also supply the engines and all the accessories. We will have to agree on a new price after the detailed requirements are completed." After speaking, I could see from facial expressions around the room that I had succeeded. What Mei had said earlier was still running through my brain. "*If Mr. Ru* or the boatyard *loses face; you will lose the respect of all the others."* Mr. Ru and most of those present had a big smile on their faces. "*We're started*," I thought.

As we were picking up our things to leave, I remembered something else I wanted to say before we left. "Before we say goodbye, I wish to say a few final words. I came to China hoping you could build the junk and I am now going home knowing from this visit and our discussions that you can build it once we resolve a few problems. Also, I have decided on an appropriate name for it." As I paused and looked around, the room was silent in anticipation of some enlightened name soon to be uttered. "I have decided to name the junk '*Mei Wen Ti*.'" They all smiled or laughed and thought it was a good Chinese name. Little did I know at that time that the project would have as many ups and downs and twist and turns as the Great Wall of China.

CHAPTER EIGHT

JUNKS IN CHINESE HISTORY

Followings Yuan's death in 1916 the Dragon had a long list of temporary riders. Li Yuan-hung, Feng Kuo-Chang, Hsu-Shih-Chang, Zhou Ziqi, Lin Yuan-hung, Zhang Shaozeng, and on and on and on. Had the Western Powers gotten behind Dr. Sun Yat-sen maybe China would have taken a very different path..

AFTER DON LOCATED a boatyard that said they built wooden boats and could build an old-style fishing boat, I began researching junks. This chapter presents an overview of what I learned about junks down through Chinese history.

In the late nineteenth century, some peasants in Hunan Province unearthed what they thought were dragon bones. The farmers sold them to local practitioners of Chinese medicine, who ground the shells and bones into a fine powder they used in various potions. In 1899, a scholar determined there was ancient writing on the turtle shells and ox bones that could be dated to the Shang Dynasty (1766–1122 BC). During the Shang period, turtle shells and ox bones were used to foretell the future. A question would be engraved on the shell or bone, and the surface was heated until it cracked. The patterns formed by the cracks were thought to divulge the divine answer from ancestors or gods.

Among the thousands of ancient markings were found the characters for a boat, propelling a boat with an oar, and caulking the seams in a boat. The old "dragon bones" are the earliest reference to boats, and they show that China has had a long tradition of wooden boat building.

I was surprised to learn Chinese junks were built for coastal sea-going trade as far back as the Southern and Northern Dynasties period (420–589 AD) and that by the Tang dynasty (618–907 AD) junks were sailing as far as India and the Persian Gulf.

So it wasn't surprising to find that Marco Polo wrote about junks in the thirteenth century in his book *The Travels of Marco Polo.* Marco gave a fairly detailed description of the junks he saw when traveling around China during the reign of the Yuan (Mongol) Dynasty (1280–1368 AD).

He said that the junks used by the merchants were built of fir timber and had a single deck. The hull was double-planked, fastened with iron nails, and caulked inside and out with a material make of quicklime and oil. This caulking material, along with hemp strands, was pounded into the cracks to seal the junk. Below the deck, the junk was divided into compartments, the number determined by the junk's size. The bulkheads or divisions were made with thick planks forming athwartship watertight compartments inside the hull. These divisions prevented water from passing from one compartment to another in case of a leak. The craft he described had four masts and sails; the number of masts and sails varied according to the size of the junk.

The junks Marco wrote about were new to him but had been around for about 800 years by the time he reached China. The great Khan, who ruled China at that time, had thousands of junks built for battles in Japan, Vietnam, and Java, as well as for carrying grain and tribute north to the capital via the Grand Canal.

During the early part of Ming Dynasty (1368–1644 AD) junk building continued. The old designs were radically altered in the early 1400s when the emperor ordered a fleet of large ocean-going junks built. Some of the fleet of over sixty vessels were large junks reported to be approximately 400 feet in length, with a beam of approximately 120 feet. To give you some idea of how big that was, these large junks were about the same beam and about half the length of the *RMS Queen Mary* launched in 1934.

In 1405 Admiral Cheng Ho [Zheng He] set sail from Nanjing with a total force of over 27,000 men bound for India. Their priceless cargo consisted of silver, gold, teas, silks, porcelains, and other exotic goods. With this cargo traveled a formidable army, along with the necessary food and water for extended periods at sea. The purpose of this and subsequent voyages was to show the flag, as well as to barter and trade: they wanted everyone to know that the "center of the world" was in Beijing. Admiral Cheng stopped along the way to make visits as an emissary of the Dragon throne, to barter and trade, and to collect all types of tribute—exotic plants and animals like zebras and giraffes were brought back from Africa.

The fleet made seven voyages with varying numbers of junks and crew, visiting Siam (now Thailand), India, Arabia, and East Africa. This exploration took place sixty years before the first Portuguese explorer,

Bartolomeu Dias, showed up in the same part of the world, having traveled around the tip of Africa from Europe. The Chinese were not land-grabbers and did not strive for a large empire on which the sun never set. It was all right that there were other kings, but when they came to China, they knew they were "vassal kings." China's defense strategy was to have friends to provide peripheral padding against barbarian enemies.

The early Ming (1368–1644 AD) emperors had, by the early 1400s, amassed a fleet of thousands of junks, many of them used for coastal defense and protection against pirates. China had the most powerful navy on earth. So what happened to the greatest navy the world had ever seen?

To understand what happened to the fleet, we need to look at a chain of events that could only have been set in motion by the Chinese god of fire. In addition to the vast navy the Emperor was building, he decided to construct a gigantic new palace in Beijing that was named the Forbidden City. The Emperor had completed repair and extension of the Grand Canal to allow supplying his new capital from the south, which had a longer growing season than in the north. By 1421, when the Forbidden City was completed, it seemed as if the glory and prosperity of the Ming was going to last for a thousand years. But then the gods stepped in and changed things. Without warning, lightning struck the new palace, setting it ablaze, and it was heavily damaged.

Thinking the gods were angry, the Emperor stopped all voyages of the large sea-going junks and suspended all foreign travel. Was the destiny of the Chinese navy going to be decided by lightning? The emperor shifted his attention to domestic matters, intrusions and other problems on the northern border. While on an expedition to the north, however, the Emperor died of illness. Zhu Di was buried in an elaborate tomb about twenty miles northwest of Beijing, in an area later to be known as the Ming Tombs. (During the project to build the junk I went to Beijing and visited the tombs, and I'll tell you all about them later in the story).

His son Zhu Gaozhi and his Confucian advisors thought the empire's strength and prosperity was in the land, not the sea, since most of the population was farmers, just as they are nowadays. The ban on maritime trade and voyages of the sea-going junks was continued. Also, there were prohibitions against repairing the existing fleet as well as against future building of any more large junks. So the great fleet of large sea-going junks was left to rot away, unused, while the Ming concentrated on domestic issues, unaware of what was happening in the rest of the world. They thought all was well behind the Great Wall with the Grand Canal to ensure safe transport of supplies north by fleets of junks.

By the early 1500s, the Chinese Navy was down to one-tenth of the early Ming size. It was a capital offense to go to sea in a junk with more than two masts without special permission. A ruling in 1525 authorized the destruction of many of the larger classes of junks. China had entered a xenophobic, isolationist phase similar to the one that closed Japan for centuries. The Navy and Chinese-borne overseas trade was gone. However, it wouldn't be long before the Celestial Kingdom would be plagued by illegal trade, thousands of pirates, and a swarm of unwanted foreign visitors.

China's isolationist policies continued for centuries, during which the emperors saw no reason to import manufactured goods from the "barbarians." On the other side of the world, small European countries like Portugal were expanding into empires that stretched around the world, building better ships and better armaments. A collision of cultures was about to happen.

The first Europeans that arrived in China were regarded as little better than the Japanese pirates who plagued the coast of China. The Chinese wanted to control the Europeans, but now they did not have a strong enough navy to do so. The door was opened just a little in 1577 when the Emperor agreed to let the Portuguese establish a trading base at Macao. The Portuguese settlement there fast became the Western trade center in the Far East.

The British didn't show up until the mid-nineteenth century, followed by the French, Dutch, Spanish, Japanese, and Russians; eventually the Americans showed up. America would join the others with gunboats and garrisons in the race for extraterritorial rights and unequal treaties. The Chinese navy and their small fleet of wooden junks were ineffectual, and there was no system of customs to control illegal imports. It wasn't long before the Qing (1644–1911 AD) emperors were losing battle after battle against almost everyone because of inferior naval vessels and armaments. China got opium and the British got Hong Kong in 1840. The Summer Palace was burnt down in 1860, and another unequal treaty was signed. Even the small vassal kingdom of Japan easily smashed their navy and took a chunk of territory in 1895. Still another unequal treaty was signed after the Boxer Rebellion (1899–1901). The visitors now held territorial concessions in all major Chinese ports, and the Chinese paid heavily for parking their massive junk fleet and not keeping up with the progress of shipbuilding and military technology. The emperors of the Celestial Empire had been wrong: the empire did not have all things in prolific abundance.

After the arrival of all the modern navies of the world, the Chinese junk continued to be a part of Chinese society, but it was relegated to the backwaters of history. When World War II ended, junks continued to carry cargo up and down the coast of China, along the rivers and thousands of miles of canals covering the eastern part of China, but they were slowly replaced with workboats powered by gas or diesel engines. In the canals, the workboats pulled long strings of cargo barges. The sails on existing junks were replaced with engines. These boats and barges, for the most part, carried much the same cargo that junks had transported for the past 1,600 years.

CHAPTER NINE

THE YANTZE AND THE GRAND CANAL

China in the Twentieth Century - May Fourth Movement

The first mass movement in modern Chinese history occurred in 1919. On May 4, thousands of Beijing students gathered in Tiananmen and protested the awarding to Japan of the former German leasehold in Shandong Province that happened at the Versailles Peace Conference following World War I. There were other grievances against foreign imperialists' privileges and the Japanese demands. Demonstrations and strikes soon spread to Shanghai and over a hundred other cities, and a boycott of all Japanese goods was declared. The government suppressed all discussion at the demonstration and arrested many students. This was the first in a long series of demonstrations that would be held in Tiananmen through the years.

MEI, DON, AND I sat on a plane at the end of the runway in Shanghai, waiting to take off, me in the window seat and Mei sitting next to me. She and Don were in a quiet conversation I couldn't hear. It seemed like just the other day when I was having dinner at their house that Don had said, "If you can get your act together, we can stop in Shanghai and then we can all go up to Beijing and maybe get in some sightseeing." Well, we had seen Shanghai and were now on our way to Beijing.

The trip to Shanghai was a wonderful experience, and it gave me a chance to see firsthand China's explosive growth. There is no doubt in my mind that this growth will continue as long as the rest of the world, especially America, measures success by stock prices and last quarter's financials, continues to invest billions of dollars in China, educates thousands of Chinese in American colleges, and continues trying to reform our traditional market economy by exporting jobs (with a little help from Don). I'm sure the Communist Party's successes have many economists scratching their heads, wondering how this is possible. My take on it is pretty simple: Chinese government incentives, no unions, cheap labor, few environmental controls, and lots of help from Uncle Sam. In this respect, China at present is a bit like America a hundred years ago.

I'm sure the folks on Taiwan and many politicians in America are worried about the changing global balance of power and trade. China's successes are not limited to the economy. Shanghai is full of bustling streets, friendly people, and an impressive skyline. It is a clean and safe city (at least the streets are clean and safe; the air and water are neither) that boasts great food, a lively culture, and plenty of wonders to see. What you see in Shanghai seems to fly in the face of all the critics and skeptics; however, the explosive growth I noticed in Shanghai is moving at a much slower rate out in the countryside.

As the jet engines revved up, I got the uneasy feeling I always get just before taking off or landing. After a few minutes, we were airborne and headed toward Beijing; the flight time was about two hours. I looked out the window as the plane banked and gained altitude heading north. Through the light haze, I saw many lakes, waterways, and the mighty Yangtze River [Chang Jiang] flowing out into the South China Sea. It is the largest river in China and stretches about four thousand miles, flowing east from the far-off Himalayan Mountains. Where it hits the sea, you can't see across it, and it produces a huge silt plume that extends miles out into the ocean.

The river and all the waterways below created Shanghai. Shanghai, like several other large cities, including Canton [Guangzhou] in the south near Hong Kong, grew up over the years as sea trade and commerce were fed by thousands of junks, launches, and ships from the interior. Shanghai's potential as a port was recognized by the imperialist powers back in the nineteenth and early twentieth centuries, when unfair treaties were negotiated with China to expand trade. At the end of the Opium War in 1835, the British got a large pile of cash, Hong Kong, and the right to trade in five treaty ports, including Shanghai and Canton. The volume of trade exploded. To give you an indication, by 1935 well over seventy-seven thousand junks cleared customs in Shanghai. There remains but a fading shadow of this once-mighty fleet of junks still making their way among the boats and ships in the bustling port.

Foreigners forced treaty after treaty on China after the British opened it, and soon, foreigners were no longer subject to Chinese law, so they set up their own laws, courts, and police. Later, they forced the Chinese to allow them access to the interior and opened the Yangtze River to navigation by foreigners.

To cruise up the Yangtze is much different from what it was many years ago when junks ruled the Yangtze. Since junks had no engines, the ones going west required manpower to pull them upriver in the area that was once called the Three Gorges. The men in a tracker gang could number in the hundreds, depending on the size of the junk, time of year, and the weight of the cargo. Each man in the gang would be connected to a large hawser by a small long rope; the rope was attached to a sling the tracker wore over his shoulder, and the end of the hawser was firmly attached to the junk. The trackers formed long lines along the shore and, using brute force pulled the junk through the rapids.

The mighty river has now been tamed by a public works project on a scale with the Great Wall and the Grand Canal. The marriage of the old Three Gorges to the biggest dam in the world has transformed the river and the lives of millions of people that live along its path. The project dates back to 1919 when Dr. Sun Yat-sen proposed construction of a dam in the Three Gorges to make better use of the water resources and improve navigation. Nothing happened for years and then, in 1956, Chairman Mao wrote the following verse titled "Swimming."[3]

Great plans are afoot:
A bridge will fly to span the north and south,
Turning a deep chasm into a thoroughfare,
Walls of stone will stand upstream to the west
To hold back Wushan's clouds and rain
Till a smooth lake rises in the narrow gorges
The mountain goddess if she is still there
Will marvel at a world so changed.

Mao chased one crazy idea after another following the writing of the poem and the dam got no further than his verse. Then, in 1980, Deng Xiaoping, who took over the leadership of China after Mao's death, pledged his support, and the project finally got more traction. After years of planning, engineering and resettlement studies, meetings, and volumes of speeches, construction finally began in the early 1990s. The lake Mao had envisioned in his poem finished rising in 2009, and China now has a shipping route from Shanghai back into China—fifteen hundred miles. The old tracker's routes and many other historical sites are hundreds of feet under the new lake formed by the biggest dam in the world. (I sure hope the concrete dam is constructed better than their concrete apartment houses.)

Many of the waterways that created Shanghai still carry goods from the hinterland to Shanghai via a vast network of creeks and canals. Those of Venice are world-famous but don't begin to compare with China's vast system: long before Christ, the Chinese were building canals for transport.

West of Shanghai is the world's largest canal, the Grand Canal [Da Yunhe]. When Marco Polo was in China (1275–1292) he traveled throughout many parts of China, and later wrote about his adventures. In his book, he described the Grand Canal and the vast amount of cargo that was transported north to the capital on a canal system that was already ancient when Polo first saw it.

The Grand Canal as we know it was, in large part, the creation of the Sui Dynasty (589–618 AD). They had millions of people digging for about ten years to create a canal system that connected the lower Yangtze region (present-day Hangchow) to the capitals of that period. In addition, they dug a link about four hundred miles north (near present-day Beijing) to radiate power outside the district; this link did not function in the winter because of low water and ice. At this time, the Grand Canal was approximately fourteen hundred miles long and was in service up until the Mongol conquest. It was also the main route for shipping tax grain from the south to the capital in the north. The grain tax was collected for at least 4,000 years, providing the bulk of imperial China's government revenues.

The Mongol conquest led to the establishment of the Yuan Dynasty in 1280 AD. The Mongols formed their capital in the area of present-day Beijing. This necessitated abandoning part of the old canal system and building a major link that took them about ten years to complete. The "new" section of the canal allowed them to link Beijing, in the north, with Hangzhou, in the south, a distance of approximately 1,100 miles. This canal system would remain in service after the fall of the Yuan Dynasty, all through the Ming (1368–1644 AD) and Qing (1644–1911 AD) dynasties, until there was no longer an emperor to receive the tribute. During this long period, thousands upon thousands of junks carried grain and tribute to the capital, dynasty after dynasty.

Like the Great Wall, some of the northern sections of the Grand Canal have fallen into disrepair and are inaccessible to boats, and has over time becoming little more than an aqueduct. The more southern parts of the canal, from Hangzhou North to Jining, are still navigable and annually carry vast amounts of bulk cargo. The map in the front of the book shows the path of the Yangtze River, the location of the Three Gorges Dam, and the path of the Grand Canal.

I glanced over and saw that Don was taking a nap as we started our descent into Beijing. The city is about the same latitude as Washington, DC, so I expected more of the hot, humid, rainy weather we experienced in Shanghai. Looking out the window, I noticed the sky around Beijing was darker than the worst day I had ever seen in Shanghai or back home in Los Angeles. When you see China's air pollution firsthand, you understand why air pollution is a pressing problem for a society that uses coal for energy, charcoal for cooking, and gasoline for cars and trucks. As the plane dropped down into the haze, the sunlight disappeared, and grayness surrounded the plane as if we were flying into an eighteenth-century mill town. As I looked out the window into the man-made discoloration, it made me think of a new ending for Mao's swimming poem:

The mountain goddess if she is still there
Would cringe at a world so changed.

Don woke up as the plane's tires hit the runway. We were in Beijing—the trio had landed.

CHAPTER TEN

BEIJING, KIDS, AND PEKING DUCK

China in the Twentieth Century - The Warlords

The old empire dissolved into smaller constituencies, most of them controlled by warlords with their own armies, agendas, and taxes. These warlords, numbering in the hundreds, dominated politics from 1916 to 1928. There was a breakdown of government at the national level as chronic warfare, and disorderly conditions prevailed all over China. The dragon ran wild, and a unified republican government was not to be. Forming a republican government has never been easy; nor is it always successful..

SURE ENOUGH, THE hot, humid weather had preceded us. If you go to Beijing in the summer, you will understand why the imperial court built the Summer Palace a little northwest of the city. The city that day was topping 100 degrees; the average temperature in July and August is a bit over 90 degrees.

Getting from the airport to central Beijing is easily done by taxi. After collecting our luggage, we trooped out to the taxi line and Mei went ahead as usual to talk to the taxi driver. Having ridden in a few taxis by this time, I had come to believe that most taxi drivers were relatively honest. However, since these taxis use meters, Mei would discuss the route to the hotel to make sure we didn't take the scenic route. As in most places in the world, the rate depends on the type of taxi being used: nicer cars costs more. Don had warned me never to go with any of the "bastards" that cruise around the airport because they are price gougers.

The driver opened the trunk, and we put in our luggage. As I got in the front seat of the cab, I looked at the meter to make sure it wasn't running (remember, I said *most* drivers were honest). The cab smelled like a combination of garlic, Chinese food, and cigarette smoke. The driver slapped the meter, and we were off on another adventure.

Like many cab drivers in Shanghai, ours was a small, serious man who wore a white short-sleeve shirt with a pack in the pocket. He chain-smoked cigarettes, spat out the window, and drank green tea from a jar as he zigzagged through traffic. Chinese taxi drivers are the most aggressive you will ever meet, so be prepared. I saw a picture of Mao clipped to the visor, but no picture of Lei Feng, the soldier with a boyish smile from the 1960s who is still thought of by older Chinese as a model of charity. Lei Feng seems to represent the traditional morality of the Chinese people: love for the young, respect for the old, pleasure in helping others, selflessness, solidarity, and harmony. Most Americans don't know who Johnny Appleseed was, and it won't be long before you won't see Lei Feng's picture when you get into a taxi in China.

The driver's attempt at conversation with me was a complete failure. After his first sentence I didn't know what he had said or how to reply, so I smiled and started looking out the window.

If you don't speak Mandarin, it is a good idea to carry around a notebook that has Chinese characters next to various words and phrases. I learned to carry such a notebook back in the 1950s when I was in the Navy traveling around Japan all by myself. Here, I usually got Mei or a hotel employee who spoke English to write down the Chinese name of the hotel, destinations, foods I liked, and anything else I needed to communicate to people while traveling without a translator.

The cab pulled up in front of an inauspicious hotel on a narrow street and double-parked, just like they do in Boston—to hell with everyone else. Since we were on a budget, Don had booked us into an obscure hotel whose name I don't remember. The cab driver opened the trunk and stood there waiting for us to hoist out our own suitcases.

"Don't tip him," Don advised as we grabbed our luggage. Tipping is not expected and in most cases not deserved. As I stood with the bags, Don went back to get a receipt and pay for the cab. I had learned to always get a receipt; there is a huge fine for taxi drivers who take advantage of their passengers.

We agreed to meet later for dinner, so I was on my own for a few hours. I decided to take a walk and see a little of Beijing. Heading away from the hotel, I soon found myself in an older area of the city. Like Shanghai, new skyscrapers, high-rise apartment houses, and other expensive developments are rapidly changing Beijing. Swaths of the city that are laced with alleys (hutongs) and courtyard houses are being torn down to make way for the new Beijing that is rising. Fortunately, the government is preserving some areas of the city where you can still see the old alleys and courtyard houses. It's a shame so much of the city must be torn down to make way for more people. Not so slowly, China's population is moving from the country to the city: Beijing's population is about twenty-one million and growing. While writing this chapter, Los Angeles's population just crested four million; and has more people than twenty-six states. The LA population was about one hundred thousand in 1900, so it gained about 3,900,000 people since then. Beijing's population is changing very rapidly: in the ten years between 2000 and 2010 censuses, the number of people living in the city grew by 44%—from 13,569,194 in 2000 to 19,612,368 in 2010. Beijing had a population of 4.2 million when the Communists took control in 1949. China puts a whole new perspective on your idea of population growth.

After walking for a short time through the heat, I started looking for a place to sit for a while in the shade. Turning the corner, I came across a thin man in shorts with no shirt selling watermelon by the slice. He had a group of small wooden stools parked under a large shade tree. I bought a big slice of the warm fruit and took a seat on one of his stools. I sat there thinking about all the things I needed to do when I got home to get the project back on track. The sight of me sitting cross-legged on the short stool caused every person that passed by to stare at me.

"Good afternoon," I heard from behind me as I sat thinking about the junk and spitting seeds into the gutter. I turned around and found an older gentleman looking down at me, smiling broadly.

"Good afternoon," I replied, juice dripping from my chin. "*I wonder what this guy wants.*"

"I can tell you American from cowboy boots," he said. Uninvited, he sat down on one of the small stools. Before I could respond, the street vendor started yelling in our direction and making a motion like he was shooing flies. My new friend ignored him. I guessed he was yelling "For customers only!"

"I don't think he wants you sitting on his stool," I said as a small group of people started gathering on the sidewalk to stare and see what the ruckus was about. Two men in the group wore police or army uniforms. The street vendor continued to yell and wave his arms wildly.

"Pay no attention him; he is, what say, 'country pumpkin,' I think." The man took his time and introduced himself as Old Chang. He had just turned sixty and had lived in Beijing since birth.

I looked at him while thinking, "*What should I do?*" Not wanting to create a bigger street scene or have someone lose face, I decided it was time to leave. I stood holding my watermelon, juice dripping from between my fingers, and said, "I'm sorry, you will have to excuse me. I was just leaving." I started walking down the sidewalk, away from him and the hotel as I finished up my treat.

"You wait me," I heard Mr. Chang yell as he ran to catch up. His English was much better than what I had heard earlier from the cab driver.

He walked along beside me without saying anything; maybe he thought I was pissed because he had caused all the commotion with the watermelon man. After a while, he started to talk and said that if I didn't mind he would enjoy the walk, the company, and, of course, a chance to practice his English. By this time, I had decided he was just a friendly, harmless old man.

"My name is Walt. Some people here think that is my surname and call me Mr. Walt, but actually my family name is Hackman." Not bothering to give him all the details, I continued, "I just flew in from Shanghai with two friends; we have a bit of business tomorrow, and then we are going to spend a few days looking around Beijing."

"Pleased meet you, Mister Walt," he said, smiling broadly. I don't know if he was being funny or didn't understand what I had just said. "I retired and live not far here. Park ahead; maybe you me talk there?"

We walked into the park and found a bench in the shade, where we began talking; though mainly he talked and I listened. He told me he had a large family living in Beijing and the surrounding area. He said his way of life would soon change because his whole neighborhood was being torn down to make way for a high-rise development. He did not want to leave but had no choice; he was being moved to a high-rise outside the city. If you have money in China you have a choice, but Mr. Chang, with only a modest retirement income, had no choice but to move. He said he would soon have a long commute to see his children and grandchildren. The area where he had lived was made up of some of the oldest of Beijing's traditional courtyards and alleyways. Some of these areas date back to the thirteenth century when Marco Polo was in China. In his book, Polo wrote about what a grand city Beijing was way back then.

The face of Beijing is changing fast. Back in 2008, when the Olympic Games were in town, the city changed rapidly and now looks very different from the one that existed for centuries. Factories were moved outside the city in an effort to improve the air quality and make room for more people.

After telling me all about his problem that "the common people" could do nothing about, Mr. Chang started talking about his large family. He told me when he was young and Mao was in charge, there was no limit to the number of children a married couple could have. Mao thought more was better; a man was born with one mouth and two hands, after all, so how could there be a problem? When Mao said something was not a problem, it was not a problem—*period.* While Mao reigned over China, Beijing's population grew from 540,000 to 975,500. Mr. Chang had five children who were all grown now and had families in and around Beijing. Since they lived in a major city, each couple was limited to one child (though offspring of one-child families may have two children). If they didn't comply, they would face a cut in pay and have restricted access to housing and medical care. Here again, if you have money in China you have a choice because rich couples can pay the fines. He said if they lived in a rural area they could have two children if the first child was a girl. He also said that members of small ethnic groups are permitted two children, and some have no limits.

"So, see, China have no one-child policy," he said, smiling, as if to imply that there was no population problem, as Mao had preached for decades.

I asked Mr. Chang if we could talk about food since I was interested in learning more about Chinese cooking. There were a few older men sitting on benches not far away from us, so I did not want to ask any questions that might get my new friend in hot water with the authorities. I wasn't sure what constituted state secrets, but I was sure they didn't include food. He said since Peking duck was known all over the world he would share his secrets in preparing this king of duck dishes. He and his family had it only on special occasions. He went on to say that before special occasions he would go to an outdoor stall not far from his house that sold live ducks, live chickens, and other things. I didn't ask what other things. He recommended the purchase of a duck that weighed about four kilos. I'd brushed up on my metric before coming to China and knew that was about nine pounds. He said he took the duck home and put it into a special wire cage that just fit the duck; the duck could not walk around. I got the picture. He lamented that when he moved to his new apartment he would no longer be able to fatten up a duck. He then fed the bird a special grain mixture, and it got fat in a short time. The next step was to kill the duck, scald it, and clean it well. He said I must make sure to leave the head on. He said the intestines were removed carefully through the "bottom small hole." I got the picture. The idea is not to break the skin. Next, you tie a string around the neck and hang up the duck. He said the next step is to pump air—that's right: air—into the small hole, so the skin is puffed up and separates from the carcass. This sounded to me like a good job for a bicycle pump. He said to plug the hole but didn't go into any details—and I didn't ask.

Then the duck is hung by the tail from a hook in a cool and airy place for a day or two to dry the skin. The weather in Beijing may be cool and dry at times, but this sure wasn't the season. At this point, I interrupted him and declared that I wanted to tell him a true duck story.

One day I was eating in a small restaurant in Chinatown in downtown LA when a city health inspector came in. Health inspectors make sure that restaurants follow a book full of detailed procedures governing cleanliness, food handling, and the preparation of food. The inspector found several violations, one of which was a number of ducks hanging by their tails on hooks in the kitchen. An old, portable fan was blowing air at the ducks. The health inspector told the proprietor that he needed to put the ducks in the refrigerator. The owner resisted his suggestion, saying that his Peking duck preparation would be ruined, and his Chinese customers would not come back. Besides, this was the way Peking duck had been prepared by his father, his father's father, and in China for over a thousand years. The inspector became irate and told the business owner he didn't care if this was the way Confucius did it; he couldn't. The ducks must go in the refrigerator—*now*! After the owner reluctantly took the hanging fowl down and put them in the refrigerator, he turned off the fan. The inspector smiled at him as he handed him a list of infractions, turned, and left the small restaurant. After the inspector had left the owner got out the ducks, hung them back up, and turned on the fan while commenting that the inspector knew nothing about the preparation of Peking duck.

Old Chang laughed and said he thought it was a funny duck story; he said he would tell it to his friends the next day when he met them for tea. He returned to his story about how real Peking duck is prepared. After a day or two the bird is ready to cook. He said he takes the duck over to the house of his friend, who has a small oven, and bakes it for an hour or so, then puts it on an electric rotisserie over a low charcoal fire in this stove until it is golden brown. While the duck is cooking, his wife makes Mandarin Pancakes and sauces and chops up scallions. The duck is thinly sliced, placed on a pancake with some sauce, and then rolled up. He held up his hand to show me the proper way to hold the rolled pancake so that the sauce will not drip out the bottom. Now I better understood why he only had Peking duck on special occasions.

The day had passed quickly talking with Mr. Chang, and it was time to get back to the hotel. I shook his hand and thanked him for his stories about kids and Peking duck, and for being so hospitable and friendly. He said he'd had a wonderful afternoon practicing English and that he hoped we would enjoy our visit to his city. I left the park and headed back toward the hotel, backtracking down the narrow street until I saw the watermelon man. I passed several old men who weren't there before sitting in bamboo chairs with their birdcages talking and smoking. When I walked past the peeling, red-painted door I had noticed earlier, I knew I was not far from the hotel.

Don, Mei, and I had dinner at the hotel that night. I ordered a small serving of Peking duck served as an appetizer with a couple of pancakes, sauce, and green onions. I had a bowl of white rice and a gravy dish with vegetables that went well with my duck appetizer. I couldn't tell if the wonderful duck had been hung up to dry for a day or two before cooking, but it sure was good. This delicious culinary specialty, with its crisp skin and juicy meat eaten like a Chinese burrito, shouldn't be missed if you find yourself in Beijing.

The next morning Don, Mei, and I took a cab to Don's business appointment. He had a customer in the States who wanted to purchase a large quantity of baskets direct, and he had brought along a selection of baskets for the large basket company to look at and price.

The meeting was conducted in the basket company's office area in a room that was designed not to look like a meeting room. We all sat in comfortable chairs around a low round table that held a bowl of fruit, large metal containers of hot water, teacups, and, of course, ashtrays. We talked and drank tea, and I wasn't sure when the meeting actually started. Mei translated the conversation. I was just an observer, so I didn't participate in the meeting. I was again amazed at how much conversation it took to answer a question, and how she made such a short English translation out of it. After several hours of talking, drinking tea, and looking at baskets Don had all the information he had come for. As the meeting came to an end, we told them that we were off to visit spots around the city for the rest of the day and part of the next day.

"How are you going to get around the city?" the Communist manager asked.

"By bus and taxi, I guess," Don shrugged.

"Nonsense," the manager said. "Allow me to offer you my car and driver."

We shook hands with everyone, said goodbye, and the manager took us downstairs to where his car was parked. It was a long, black four-door sedan that looked just like a brand new Packard from the 1930s. It was the kind of car that gangsters drove around in old movies. The young driver, all dressed in black, was wiping the dust off the car as we walked up.

"What kind of car is it?" I ask.

"It's a Red Cloud, and we're out of here," Don said as he opened the door and jumped in.

CHAPTER ELEVEN

THE TOUR CONTINUES

China in the Twentieth Century - Communism

The idea of Communism in China didn't begin in China; it originated in Russia. The new Russian government had set up a program to spread Communism worldwide and had sent agents to China with instructions to form a Chinese Communist Party. Russian involvement was to last on and off for over thirty years.

In 1920, Mao Zedong happened, by chance, to get involved with the founders of the Chinese Communist Party (CCP). In 1921, the Party members in Shanghai were instructed by the Russians through their agents to formalize the CCP. Mao was lucky enough to be in the right place at a critical time in history.

WHILE DRIVING FROM the business meeting toward Tiananmen Square, I looked over the inside of the car and was amazed to find that the design appeared old although the car was in remarkably good shape—it was as if we had somehow been transported back in time. Beginning in the early 1960s, the Red Flag car was designed (copied) for use by Chinese officials with ranks higher than vice-minister and visiting heads of state. Who knows, maybe Nixon or Kissinger rode through Beijing in the old beast. Production ceased in the 1980s but began again in 1998, and recent models are available to China's new rich. Looking out the window of the Communist manager's personal car gave me just a hint of what it means to be connected in China. I'm sure it would take a month of a worker's salary to feed this gas-guzzling monster for our trip. This car made me think about the design of the diesel engine I had seen aboard the fishing boat at the boatyard: the design was ancient, but the engine was new.

This car and the fishing boat diesel engine help explain how I could still get a boat built using a design made a thousand years ago. The leaders of China before Deng Xiaoping, like Mao and his followers, pursued a path of deep conservatism and saw no need to build a car better than the Red Cloud or a diesel engine better than the one on their fishing boat. In a way, this is what the Empress Dowager Tzu-His must have thought when she decided in 1888 that the Chinese navy didn't need to be modernized. Instead, she spent the money on the opulent Summer Palace northwest of the city, which included a large marble boat.

Not far from the heart of the city you see a skyline spiked with high cranes and high-rise apartments, just like those in Shanghai. The city seems to have an inhuman feeling of vastness caused by the sprawl and, much like Los Angeles, seems to go on forever. Parts of the city are being ripped up and deliberately destroyed in the rush to modernize and provide more housing for an unending line of new city dwellers. The makeover I saw had been going on since the Communists took over. Back in the 1950s, they ordered the old city wall, with its towering gates, demolished to expand Tiananmen Square to the size I observed as we approached. Our driver stopped at the edge of the square and dropped us off. We had made arrangements to have him come back and pick us up in the same spot later that afternoon.

We walked around Tiananmen Square in the heat, looking at the outside of various Soviet-style buildings. One of the largest was the Great Hall of the People, which was one of ten buildings in that fashion built in 1959 by an army of workers in only ten months, working around the clock. We didn't go in, but at the price the government charges to enter, and considering the wages paid back in 1959, it is probably a money-maker for the government. The area's bloody association with popular dissent down through the years, coupled with all the monumental buildings, surveillance cameras, and railings for crowd control, left me a little cold. As I passed a young boy flying a colorful kite, it was hard to imagine that this vast area had spawned so many violent demonstrations, starting way back in the early 1900s.

We next walked over to the Monument to the People's Heroes. The huge edifice was completed in 1958 and depicts eight major events in China's liberation struggle. The monument goes back to 1840 and moves through history to the crossing of the Yangtze River by the People's Liberation Army (PLA) to "liberate" Nanjing on April 21, 1949. At the base of the monument is an inscription that reads, "The people's heroes are immortal."

I couldn't help but think, as I looked up the white stone monument, that someday the Chinese may affix a new statue onto the front of the existing one. The newly added section would bring the monument up to date by depicting the events in Chinese history since 1949. The first statues on the new section would depict the "liberation" of Tibet. The next section would represent the thousands of soldiers who died in the Korean War, and after that would be a group of statues representing the intellectuals who were persecuted during the Hundred Flowers campaign in 1956. The millions of Chinese, who died during the Great Leap Forward in the late 1950s, would be the focus of the subsequent grouping of statues. The next set of figures would represent all those lost during the Great Cultural Revolution and would be the largest, including statues of real people who were professors, teachers, doctors, writers, artists, Buddhist monks, and others who were lost. The Cultural Revolution was a holocaust for millions of Chinese and needs to be remembered. The new front section of the Monument to the People's Heroes would represent all the protests that have taken place here in Tiananmen Square since 1949. The new front would depict a lone Chinese man standing in front of a tank and would read, "These people were heroes, too."

We weren't interested in Mao's mausoleum, so we skipped it and headed for the Forbidden City. I agree with Deng Xiaoping (he ran China after Mao) when he said that Mao's tomb should never have been built. The Chairman would probably roll over in his casket if he could see what his comrades have done to his utopian visions of Chinese society, which have evolved since they pickled him in 1976.

To get to the Forbidden City, you must pass through Tiananmen's Gate of Heavenly Peace. This gate forms part of the national emblem and is honored as the spot from which Mao announced the founding of the People's Republic of China in October 1949. It was from this location that he viewed the vanguards of the PLA passing in review, driving captured American equipment. From this location, many rallies have been held and speeches given by members of the government. A large portrait of the Chairman hangs over the entrance and looks out over the square.

Once through Tiananmen we had a long walk past stalls selling useless tourist souvenirs like those you can buy in any Chinatown. We walked until we reached the Wumen gate at the entrance of the Forbidden City, where twenty-four emperors of the Ming (1368–1644 AD) and Qing (1644–1911 AD) Dynasties once lived. As we sauntered through the gate, we found ourselves in the vast paved courtyard, where a hundred thousand people could be accommodated. As I discussed in Chapter Eight, "Junks in Chinese History," the Forbidden City was built during the Ming Dynasty (1368–1644 AD). Right after its completion, a fire triggered by lightning burned up sections of the palace, which caused parts of the palace to be rebuilt at a later date. It fell into total disrepair and neglect after the downfall of the empire in 1912. There have been many restorations done on the palace, beginning in the 1950s. We walked around the vast empty space and through the various major ceremonial halls and gardens in the palace. We stopped and looked at the treasures and exhibits, and I learned that when the Nationalists fled to Taiwan a large portion of the palace treasures went with them. I hope the valuables and Taiwan will both be returned to China one day soon without any bloodshed.

We walked back out the way we had come in, through the Gate of Heavenly Peace, under Mao's picture, and out across the vast expanse of Tiananmen Square to meet up with our driver and head back to the hotel.

The next morning the driver met us right on time, and we headed out for another day of sightseeing. That day we were going to visit the Great Wall of China and the Ming Tombs. Our young driver headed northwest of the city to a section of the Great Wall known as Badaling.

Before coming to China and reading about the Great Wall, I had always thought of it as a long continuous structure that snaked across the rolling hills of China, but I found out that this was a myth: most of the ancient sections had been made of packed dirt that had decayed long ago. There never was a continuous Great Wall in ancient times. At the beginning of the Ming Dynasty, (1368 AD) when the Emperor moved the capital to Beijing, there was no wall marking the northern border of China. The Emperor was faced with an open frontier. The Ming began creating a vast system of fortifications, the remnants of which we see and think of as the Great Wall. But just like the Maginot line the French constructed to keep Hitler out of France, the fortifications in northern China did not work. Like Hitler's forces, the Mongols had no trouble finding a way through or around these massive fortifications to take Beijing and set up the Qing Dynasty (1644–1911).

After the arrival of the Manchus from the north there was no longer a need to protect a northern border, so the fortifications built by the Ming (many out of dirt) were no longer maintained and started to decay. Over the following centuries, Mother Nature worked year after year to pull down the walls. It wasn't until the Cultural Revolution that she'd get some help from Mao. During the Cultural Revolution, a vast amount of the brick-and-stone wall and tower materials were destroyed and carried away to build something more useful than old walls (I wonder if the materials were used to build all the government buildings I saw in Tiananmen Square). The wall continued to deteriorate until Mao died and Deng Xiaoping stepped in and said, "Let us love our country and restore our Great Wall." I think Deng saw the money in tourism, and he needed a new symbol for contemporary China besides all the Russian-looking edifices left him by Mao. Deng also needed a symbol of a culturally cohesive society, and the Great Wall provided that symbol. The myth continues.

It was going to be another sweltering day. The section of wall at Badaling that we were getting ready to climb was restored in 1957 before Mao decided that anything old should be trashed. This restoration consisted of building a new wall on the old foundation. The place was crowded with Chinese, hordes of tourists, and stalls selling more useless items. The weather seemed to get hotter as we climbed. The climb was steep, so we stopped along the way to sweat and rest. After making it to a high location on the wall, I decided that for me, the experience didn't seem genuine. After a brief rest, we agreed to head for the Ming Tombs where it might be cooler.

The Red Flag next headed for the Ming Tombs, not far from the Great Wall. The driver found a shady place to park, and we piled out. I think the car also came with parking privileges. The location chosen by the third Ming (1368–1644 AD) emperor is truly a beautiful location surrounded by hills and woods. We headed toward the entrance, down a long walkway lined with colossal fifteenth century stone statues of men and animals; I couldn't figure out the significance of the statues. At the end of the path stands the tomb of the third emperor, Chang Ling. The tomb belowground matched the scale of the statues aboveground and was cool and massive. But unless you are an archeologist or interested in details, the trip turns out to be about chambers that are so many meters square and so many meters underground that are all made of stone. The part I liked best was the chilliness of the eerie vaults.

As I wrote in the chapter on junks, during the Ming Dynasty (1368–1644 AD), the great fleet of large sea-going junks was left to rot away unused while the Emperor concentrated on domestic issues like building the Ming Tombs. Mammoth expenditures of manpower and money went into building this weird graveyard, with bigger-than-life animals and men standing guard, now a tourist attraction.

After coming out of the cool air down in the tombs, we stopped at one of the tourist spots so Mei and Don could get their picture taken. The photographer had a large plywood panel painted up to depict two people dressed in old-style Chinese clothes standing next to each other. Don and Mei leaned over, put their heads in the cutouts, and smiled, sweat dripping down their faces. The photographer took a Polaroid picture of the memorable occasion, collected the money, and went back to hustling new customers. The place had the feeling of a county fair back home. We walked out past the stone officials and animals and back out to the parking lot where we found our driver dusting the shiny black car.

We gave the driver a tip after he dropped us off at the hotel and thanked him for the ride. He said goodbye, headed the big car out into the swarm of Beijing traffic and was gone. The next morning we flew back to Shanghai.

CHAPTER TWELVE

A CHINESE BREAKFAST

China in the Twentieth Century - Nationalism and Communism

In 1923 Dr. Sun, who still headed the struggling Nationalist government, agreed to form a United Front between the Communist Party and the Kuomintang. They agreed to cooperate and put an end to the warlords. The dragon now had two masters, which never works out. Sun Yat-sen died in 1925, and Chiang Kai-shek [Jiang Jieshi] inherited the mantle of the KMT. The United States supported the Chiang Kai-shek regime. The Japanese were angry about this, seeing it as more American meddling in Asian affairs

In 1926, Chiang launched the Northern Expedition from the Canton area to defeat the warlords. By 1927, the Kuomintang-Communist coalition came to an ended and Chiang decided to destroy the Communists. Mao Zedong became their political leader.

FROM THE AIRPORT we took a cab back to the Hengshan Hotel.We would stay the night and get well rested before catching an early flight back to Los Angeles, California. The flight is about twelve hours, so with travel time to the airport and time at the airport on both ends of the trip, it makes for a long travel day.

The next morning, I left the hotel early to find myself a Chinese breakfast. I knew Don and Mei would probably sleep in as our flight was midday. What do the Chinese eat for breakfast? It varies from region to region, but in this part of China, especially if they are country folk, they more than likely eat *congee.* It is a rice gruel with the consistency of porridge. *Congee* was the main dish in my first-ever Chinese breakfast served at the Hengshan Hotel and had become my favorite breakfast.

I didn't have to walk far before I came to a busy little restaurant with a steaming container of *baozi* out front, and I saw people inside with bowls of *congee.* Figuring this place was suitable, I walked in and sat a small table. A young man came over but didn't speak English, so I pulled out my little book and pointed to *congee, baozi,* and green tea. Sometimes with my bowl of *congee* instead of steamed buns I got fried bread, known as yuzakue or "deep-fried devils." These are twelve-inch twisted strips of yeast dough that have been deep-fried in a large wok and are a popular item sold on the streets. The fried bread is dipped into the *congee* just as you would dunk a donut in coffee.

When the waiter came back, he brought me *congee* and a *baozi,* then went back and brought out a porcelain teapot and small teacup. The *congee* was topped with a little chopped green scallion and a bit of dried, shredded pork to contrast with the *congee*'s blandness and give the meal a higher nutritional content. Some type of topping or side dish is normally served as well.

By watching the cooks and street food vendors on this trip, I made notes and picked up enough knowledge to make this simple breakfast myself. I don't mean to imply that there are no other Chinese breakfasts available; this was just my breakfast of choice.

Most Americans don't eat much rice and think that rice is eaten only at dinnertime; in most parts of China, though, rice is eaten three times a day. Like this morning, I ordered *congee* for breakfast, but it is also served for lunch, dinner, or as a snack. There are many different types of *congee.* Some cooks add ingredients at the end of the cooking process, like fresh mushrooms, cooked chicken, shrimp, fish, tofu (bean curd), or a few ingredients I didn't recognize (maybe squid parts). Sometimes dry ingredients, like dried shrimp, are added at the start of the cooking.

Congee

At both the Hengshan Hotel in Shanghai and the Yushan Hotel in Changshu, I saw so much *congee* being served in the morning that I concluded large quantities of it were being made from scratch early each morning, rather than being reheated from the previous day's leftover rice. So I came up with this simple recipe that uses raw rice. You can make *congee* from leftover cooked rice by just adding water, and it can be made thick or thin by varying the amount of water added. The *congee* is done when it reaches the consistency of porridge. The next time you are cooking white rice for another dish, make an extra amount and freeze it for some easily prepared *congee.*

Ingredients:

½ cup raw long-grain or short-grain white rice
6 cups water (or chicken broth)
Pinch of coriander (Chinese parsley) or spring onions for a garnish
Pinch of salt

Start by washing the rice several times in a medium pot with cold water. Put the rice and liquid in another pot and bring it up to a boil. Add a pinch of salt. Bring it back to a boil and then reduce the heat. Cover and let it slow simmer for an hour, or until it thickens. Too much heat will cause it to boil over, and don't forget to stir it occasionally to prevent sticking.

While it is cooking, make several side dishes to accompany the *congee* after it is cooked. For condiments you can use coriander (Chinese parsley), chopped green scallion, fermented tofu, hardboiled eggs, pickled ginger, pickled vegetables, salted peanuts, sesame seeds, or any other side dishes you wish. I usually put a little soy sauce in my *congee.*

Steamed Buns (*Baozi*)

To cook steamed buns, you will need two round Chinese bamboo steamers that stack, about ten inches in diameter, and a lid. Steamed buns can be eaten plain or stuffed. If you wish to stuff the buns, mix the stuffing before making the dough. (The recipe for stuffing follows the recipe for the buns.)

Ingredients:

½ teaspoon dry yeast
½ cup warm water
1½ cups flour
1 teaspoon olive oil
Pinch of salt
1 tablespoon sesame seed oil for rubbing

In a large bowl or bread machine, dissolve the yeast in the warm water and let it stand for ten minutes until frothy. Add the flour, olive oil, and salt to the liquid and stir well. Cover with a cloth and let rise until it doubles in size (about an hour).

Poke the dough down and knead for a few minutes. Form the dough into a log two inches in diameter, and then slice it into about 1½-inch pieces. Flatten each round until it is about three inches in diameter. Rub the round with a thin film of sesame oil. If the buns are going to be stuffed, this is where the mixture is added. Close the circle into small, round buns leaving a little hole at the top.

When you place the buns in the steamer trays, leave enough space between the buns so they can expand without touching. Stack the steamer trays on top of each other and put on the lid. Let the dough rise for about 20 minutes. Place the bamboo steamer trays with the lid in place on top of a pan of boiling water (a wok can be used). Steam the baozi for 20 minutes. Serve hot. If there are any leftover buns, put them in a plastic bag and freeze them. They can be reheated after they thaw out in about 10 minutes.

Baozi Stuffing

Ingredients:

4 ounces ground pork
8 ounces finely chopped Chinese cabbage
3–4 dried Chinese mushrooms, presoaked then finely chopped
½ tablespoon fresh ginger root, peeled then finely chopped
1 spring onion, finely sliced
½ tablespoon light soy sauce
½ teaspoon sesame oil
Pinch of salt
Pinch of pepper

Put all the ingredients in a bowl and mix. Add the stuffing right before shaping into small, round buns. The steam cooks the stuffing.

Tea

First, let me say a few words about tea and food. I like tea with my breakfast, but sometimes tea is served at the end of a family meal. You will find that in southern China (as in American restaurants) tea is served with the food, and is always served during formal dinners or banquets in all parts of China.

So why would anyone need a recipe for making green tea? Don't you just pour boiling water over the tea? Not really: green tea leaves are delicate, and you need to let the water cool slightly before making tea. Boiling water will ruin green tea leaves or green tea in a tea bag.

Coffeehouses created a revolution in American coffee-drinking by using good coffee beans and paying attention to all the details. The same is true of making good tea; you must pay attention to the details.

Ingredients:

Good bulk green tea or green tea bags

16 ounces (4 cups) bottled spring water or other good water

For green tea, use a glass or porcelain teapot and cup. Put the water on to boil. After it has come to a boil, remove the pan from the stove. While you wait for the water to cool slightly, put hot tap water in the teapot and teacup to heat and cleanse them. After about ten minutes, the water should be around 160 degrees Fahrenheit (70 degrees Celsius). Pour out the water in the teapot and cup. Put two teaspoons of bulk tea or two teabags into the teapot. Pour in 16 ounces (two cups) of hot water. Put on the lid, and let it brew for a few minutes. You will need to experiment with this step because all teas are not alike; don't let it brew too long. Once the pot is empty, you can refill the pot with more hot water. If you want to make just one cup, use only half the water and tea. Properly brewed green tea has a great taste and aftertaste *without adding anything*. Please, oh, *please*, take it straight.

After breakfast, I headed back toward the Hengshan Hotel. As I neared it, I noticed a small shop across from the hotel that was just opening for the day. It looked interesting, so I walked in. The shop was dimly lit, so it took my eyes a minute to adjust. It was an art supply store that sold paper, brushes, ink stones, and all sorts of art-related supplies; the aisles were narrow and packed with everything imaginable. As I walked down a crowded aisle, I noticed a small display case. Inside the case were a variety of chops (seals) that are still used in China for some business purposes, and artists still use them as signatures on their artwork. I had seen a collection of chops at the Forbidden City in

Beijing; back in Chinese history emperors and high-level officials used them to authorize important documents.

The old man who ran the shop came over and asked in broken English if he could help me. I pointed at the chops, and he proudly unlatched the display case and showed me his various blank chops, which appeared to be soapstone. He told me more than I needed to know about each one and also showed me various red inks he had for sale. To be truthful, I didn't understand some of the finer points about how the inks were made. After looking at all the choices and discussing prices, I told him I wished to purchase a name chop and some red ink that came in a round, porcelain container with a lid. The chop I chose had a Chinese lion carved on the top. I explained that I needed to pick it up on my next trip to China. He said it was no problem as long as I paid him in full. He assured me that the store had been in business since liberation. When the engraver was finished he would put it safely away for me. He assured me I had nothing to worry about, and I believed him. I lettered my name on a piece of paper, paid him, said thanks, and headed out the door and across the street to the hotel to finish getting my things together for the long flight home.

CHAPTER THIRTEEN

STATESIDE AND HIRING LARRY

China in the Twentieth Century - The First Japanese Invasion and the Long March

In 1931, while Chiang Kai-shek was busy with the Communists, the Japanese took over Manchuria [Manzhou] and parts of northern China. In 1932, the Japanese gave Pu Yi, the last emperor, Manchuria to rule as they continued to nibble away at northern China. The United States' only response was to not recognize Manchuria. Chiang did not oppose the Japanese but instead concentrated on attacking Mao's growing force of guerrillas.

It wasn't until 1934 that Chiang was able to move the Communists out of southeastern China and the Communists began their famous Long March north. Chiang's troops shadowed the Communist peasant army for a year and marched over six thousand miles.

I HAD NO idea when I returned from China in August 1991 that it would be eight months before I would go back again. I had learned from my first trip that building a boat on the other side of the world was not going to be easy, but I underestimated how much time and effort was involved just to get the project started. It must be noted that I was still working, which left me only evenings and weekends.

Not long after I returned home, I received a fax giving me the size of the engines they had calculated. I decided to proceed under the assumption that we would arrive at a price on the junk that I could afford, regardless of who supplied the engines. My first order of business was, therefore, to find a marine engineer and determine the costs associated with the engineering effort.

I began calling marine engineers who had offices along the coast of California. The first thing I found out (which should have been obvious) was that, in addition to design work done on yachts and boats, marine engineers are involved with the design and construction of ships, waterfront cargo facilities, port construction, and the operation of ships and support vessels. So when I called, many were not interested in my project because they were in another field of marine engineering. If they worked on boats and yachts they were too busy, the job was too small, or they just weren't interested. After many telephone calls, I had worked my way down the coast to San Diego.

Rrring . . . rrring . . . rring . . . "*I hope this is the one*," I thought. "Good morning, this is Larry Drake."

"Yes, good morning, Mr. Drake. My name is Walt Hackman, and I am looking for some engineering help on a wooden boat I am going to have built in China."

"Did you say China?"

"Yes, I am getting ready to have a Chinese junk built, and I need help engineering the various systems that will be installed."

"Well, I have worked on every size yacht, boats, and small ships, but I have never worked on a Chinese junk! It doesn't matter though because I have experience engineering systems on a broad spectrum of vessels; so if I can fit it in, I might just be able to help you."

"I think this might be the man," I thought. By this time, I was down to the few entries in the San Diego telephone book. My next step after San Diego was to start calling Northern California. Before he could change his mind, I said, "I would like to come down to San Diego and discuss my project with you." We made an appointment to meet early the next week at his office on Shelter Island. *"Yahoo!"*

The day of the meeting I left early for the long drive down to San Diego, locating his office on Shelter Island without any hitch. He had an upstairs office right next to a boatyard. As I walked up the wooden steps, I could hear the noise from the boatyard and see a fleet of sailboats and power boats up on blocks being worked on. His office had a big glass window, and there was a small gold-leafed sign over the door that said "Larry Drake and Associates."

When I opened the door, he was on the telephone. He waved me to come in; the associates were nowhere to be seen. His office was one large room with pictures of boats that I presumed he had worked on. Against one wall were a stool and an old drafting table covered with drawings and blueprints. Against the other were several metal filing cabinets that had obviously been around for a long time. Larry's big wood desk was beside the front window, and he had a view of the industrial boatyard next door.

He hung up the phone and turned to me. "You must be Walt."

"Yeah," I said, walking over and shaking hands. He was a large man in his sixties, with a complexion and a firm grip that confirmed a lifetime spent working on boats.

"The pictures you see around the office are of projects I have worked on over the years. On most of the new vessels I worked with a naval architect during design and construction; on others I did major refitting."

We walked down the line while he gave me a verbal snapshot of what he had done on some of the vessels; there was every type of boat and yacht imaginable, including several ships, just as he had said. He stopped and pointed to a fishing boat. "See that boat? I designed her systems about thirty years ago and she is still in service right down here." As we continued walking around the room, he would stop at certain pictures as if he were introducing me to members of his family. A tenth of what he showed me would have more than qualified him to work on my project.

"Sit over here by my desk and tell me a little about this project of yours," he said as he slid back into his old, worn chair.

I told him that I had just returned from China and had no doubt the Chinese could build the junk, but thought they needed help with the details related to installing the engines and the other systems involved as the engines and systems are quite different from the ones on their boats. I told him what I had seen aboard one of their fishing boats. He reminded me that we also needed to include all US Coast Guard requirements for a fifty-four-foot boat.

He said he did not do electrical systems but that any other systems work would be no problem. When he said, "No problem," I believed him. I told him I could get assistance with the electrical system design from whoever did the power panel I was planning to supply for the junk.

At this point, it was too early to talk about specifics, but I took the opportunity to tell him I was thinking about using Yanmar marine diesel engines on the junk.

"Yanmar makes great engines," he responded without a pause. "For the money I think they build one of the best marine diesels on the market, and you can get parts and service worldwide. I did a job in Hong Kong some years ago and found that you can get almost anything in Hong Kong. You could probably order the engines in Hong Kong and have them shipped to mainland China from Japan where they are manufactured. I'm sure Yanmar sells engines to all those limeys [Britons] in Hong Kong for their yachts."

I told him I had a preliminary specification I had taken to China, but that I planned to update the material into a detailed book of requirements for the Chinese to use. I said I would send what I had as well as all the updates. We agreed that as soon as he could start, I would make another trip to San Diego to discuss where to begin the design work. He assured me his rates were reasonable, and most of the work was in his head, waiting to be written or drawn on paper. After looking at the pictures and talking to him for a short time, I did not doubt him for one minute.

We shook hands, and I went out of his office a lot happier than when I came in—I had found the help I'd been searching for. I found that over time he did what he said he would do for a reasonable price, and without his help and guidance I could not have done the project. That's how I met Larry Drake, the man who was to help me turn my dream into reality.

CHAPTER FOURTEEN

BACK TO THE BOATYARD—SECOND TRIP

China in the Twentieth Century - The United Front

In 1935, the Western powers controlled large parts of China through unequal treaties and concessions imposed on the Chinese. Japan also controlled vast areas in northern China.

In 1936, the Communist Party under the leadership of Mao and the Kuomintang under Chiang decided to stop fighting each other again, combine forces, and go after the Japanese in northeastern China. Chinese disunity and civil strife had favored the Japanese for many years. It was an uneasy alliance, however, and neither side trusted the other.

LIKE PAGES TURNING in a book, the weeks slipped by while I worked on the project at the gallery a little during the day and in my small apartment in the evenings and on weekends. By this time my divorce was final, the house had been sold, and my half was in the bank. All that remained was to sell the businesses. The best thing about staying so busy was that it kept my mind occupied, and I had little time to think about my son's death. I continued going to the Zen Center in the heart of the city to just sit and meditate.

When I had more work done on the detailed requirements, I made another appointment and drove back down to San Diego to get Larry started working on the project. The day I left in my truck was a bright, sunny day, and the time went by fast as I listened to oldies. Larry was working at his drafting board when I walked in. "Pull up a stool and take a look at this," he said. I grabbed a stool near the drafting board and sat down. He was working on a drawing depicting the freshwater system design for a boat. "I suggest we provide them with isometric drawings like this one, keyed to a bill of materials, since I don't know all the hull design details."

With an isometric drawing, Larry could present a design in three dimensions without knowing the exact design details of the junk, because the drawing didn't show any measurements.

"You've told me most of the people at the boatyard don't speak English. How are we going to work this since I don't know any Chinese?" Larry asked, a puzzled expression on his face.

"The boatyard has arranged for the services of an engineer named Mr. Ru, who speaks and writes English. Not that it matters, but he also speaks and writes Russian. When I wrote my first list of requirements, he translated every page so they could discuss the project before and during my first trip to China. We will send your work to him a month or so before our next trip as part of the junk requirements document, and he will translate all the English into Chinese characters. When we get there, everyone will be able to understand the new design requirements and maybe this time there will be more discussion."

We talked for a while about the project, and I agreed to use isometric drawings to convey his designs to the Chinese. I told him his drawings (with Mr. Ru's additions) would not only communicate the plan to everyone on the project but could also be used by t he workers who had to execute them. We talked about money and agreed on a price (time and material), and then I left to make the long haul up Interstate 5 to LA. In December 1991, Larry started designing the various systems for the *Mei Wen Ti.*

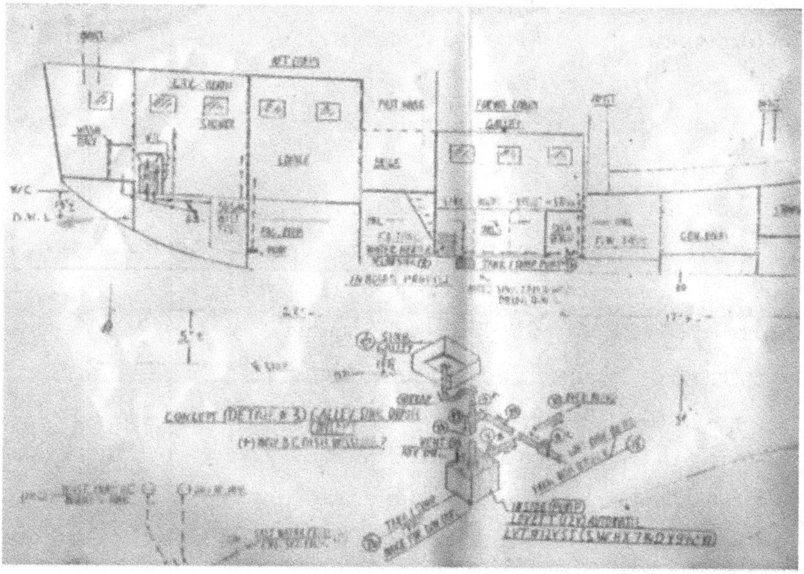

Once Larry had started on the work, I decided it was time to talk to my bank before the upcoming trip in April. There, I arranged for a Commercial Letter of Credit, allowing me to transfer funds to the boatyard's bank in China (if all went well on the next trip). After I signed all the required documents, the loan officer asked if there was anything else that the bank could help me with.

"Sure. After the surprises in the first trip, I need some way to protect myself in the event things don't turn out the way they are planned. Is there a way to protect me just in case the Chinese don't deliver the junk? I plan to send the boatyard a down payment, two engines from Hong Kong, several pallets of parts from the States, and then pay the balance when the junk is delivered," I said.

"Absolutely. What you want them to provide you is a Standby

Letter of Credit. If anything goes wrong you are covered," the loan officer said with confidence.

"How does it work?" I asked.

"You have the boat builder set up a Standby Letter of Credit with their bank in China. It provides you assurances of their ability to perform under the terms of your contract. Every time you send money or parts to them, they increase the amount of their Standby Letter," he explained, then added, "You and the seller do not expect that the Letter of Credit will ever be drawn upon."

After the trip to the bank, I finished working on the contract, and I added the requirement for a Standby Letter as my banker had suggested. I sent the contract off to China, believing if anything went wrong I was covered. (As it turned out, the Standby Letter of Credit was worthless—but that story is in another chapter.)

While Larry was working on his part, I would periodically drive down to San Diego to go over minor questions, like where things would be located, and to review the work in process. I would take his drawings back and add them to the design document and write text to go with each drawing. The document grew and grew as Larry got one system after another designed. The last drawings he made showed all the important details related to installing the engines.

I sent a price request for the engines and accessories off to China-Japan Marine Services Limited, the Yanmar marine diesel distributor in Hong Kong. Once all the junk's systems were devised, Larry began developing a series of parts lists detailing all the parts depicted in his drawings; there was a series of parts lists for each system he had designed. This phase of his work took months because of the vast number of parts in all the systems on the junk. In February of 1992, I sent the completed design requirements document that included all of Larry's design drawings to Mr. Ru.

I worked with Larry on the parts documentation, and before I knew it, it was April and time for another trip to China. It had now been about twenty months since I first wrote my basic requirements down so Don could talk to the Chinese about building the junk.

Sitting on the flight, I stared at a monitor above my seat that showed a symbol tracking the flight path of the plane. When one flies to China from the States, the plane goes close to the top of the world, so as you approach China you are heading in a southwest arc down across the island chain of Japan. We passed Hokkaido, the northernmost island, then Honshu, past Shikoku, and then past Kyushu.

The map showed the familiar names of cities like Tokyo, Yokohama, Nagasaki, Hiroshima, Kobe, and Sasebo. I had visited these cities, and a lot of others I don't remember the names of, back in the mid-1950s when I was a kid in the Navy. At that time, my ship was stationed in Sasebo, on the island of Kyushu. The small symbol on the monitor moved at the speed of a snail, but we were probably doing a ground speed of over six hundred miles an hour as we moved out into the East China Sea headed for Shanghai.

The Yangtze River deposits enormous amounts of silt out into the East China Sea, and as we approached Shanghai, I could see a huge silt plume that extended far out into the ocean. I am sure the plume is caused by human activities, such as farming, deforestation, and large amounts of manufacturing waste. The river provides critical irrigation for the agriculture in Jiangsu Province, which straddles the Yangtze next to the Shanghai municipality. There is extensive agriculture in Jiangsu Province, in addition to all the other provinces the river passes through on its way east to the ocean. On my first trip, I saw the deforestation that has been going on for centuries and the waste in the canals connected to the Yangtze River.

The small symbol on the monitor moved over Shanghai, and we made an uneventful landing on a cool, rainy April day. Don, Mei, and I grabbed a Mei-picked cab to the Hengshan Hotel. Driving from the airport to the hotel, we could easily observe more changes from the massive program of market reforms Deng Xiaoping had fathered; I saw differences in the skyline and the infrastructure, which had changed in the eight months since we were last here.

"Welcome, Mister Don and Doctor Mei, good see you," the old clerk said as he handed them registration cards to fill out. "Have message, Mister Don." I recognized the clerk from our last trip. The message was from the boatyard and said that they would pick us up the next morning at seven. It was going to be another long day.

"And remember, Mister Walt, too, you build *chuan*—no?" he asked, handing me a registration card.

"*Chuan* is boat," Mei said without being asked.

"That's right, you have a good memory," I told the clerk as I started filling out the registration card. When I got to the date, I had to stop to think. The International Date Line roughly follows the meridian of 180° longitude, down the middle of the Pacific Ocean, which I just had crossed coming to China. "*Let's see ... traveling east to west I need to add a day.*"

"Welcome all—glad stay here," he said. He gathered up the registration cards and handed out the old-style door keys.

"Let's meet at six for breakfast," Don suggested as we headed toward the elevator. "If all goes well we should be back here in three or four days. Mei's parents want us to come over and see their new apartment. They don't live too far from here. I have a little business to do, and you and I have an appointment with Mister Ru to tour his facility at the University."

Before calling it a day, I decided to walk across the street and retrieve the chop I had ordered from the little store on my last trip to Shanghai. The old man who ran the shop was about ready to close when I walked in.

"Glad back, USA," he said. He walked over to the display case, unlatched it, removed a small cloth-covered box held closed by a sliver of bamboo, and handed it to me. While I was looking at it, he got out another closed box, and it set it on the counter.

"I show," he declared, as he got out a small piece of clean white paper. I handed him the chop. "Pick up—lion face face," he said as he opened the box on the counter, took the porcelain lid off the ink, and touched the chop lightly onto the top of the thick, red ink. "You rock easy, easy—that all."

Indeed, that's all there is to using a chop. The only part I didn't understand was the "lion face face," until he lifted the chop and I saw that the characters on the paper were right side up and straight for reading, as they were on the back of the chop. When the lion was facing you, the chop was in the proper position. I realized that "lion face face" is a good way to remember how to hold a chop without looking underneath to see if you have it in the right orientation.

He had guaranteed me I had nothing to worry about, and he was right—I loved my new chop. I put it and the ink back into their respective boxes, thanking him then heading out the door and across the street to the hotel to get some sleep before an early start the following morning.

The first day of the second meeting went very well, much better than our first trip. Mr. Ru had gotten everything translated, and everyone participated by asking questions and making comments throughout the day. Larry's drawings seemed to be working, and I thought they must be the reason for the increased interest and participation.

During a break in the meeting, I looked over at Don and nodded my head toward the back of the building. We got up and walked down the stairs and outside where the outdoor latrine was located. I stopped and said, "I don't have to take a piss, I just wanted to talk to you."

"Is something wrong?" he asked, looking a little worried.

"No, not at all, I just wanted to tell you that it seems like all of a sudden they get it. Why do you think there are so many more questions and comments?"

"Well, they have had about eight months to look at it and think about it. I think the new requirements document is great, and Larry did a fine job on the drawings, but I also think they just don't want to lose this work and are trying harder. They have put a lot of effort into this project also, and our last trip here wasn't exactly a winner—and they know it."

"Well, if this keeps up we should get through the new document, the contract, and other matters in a couple days and then get back to Shanghai like we planned," I said, as we headed up the stairs to the meeting.

Everyone was standing around the table covered with Larry's drawings, talking and drinking tea when Don and I returned. As the meeting continued through the rest of the afternoon, I had a good feeling that everyone understood what was required and would be able to do it. As we wrapped it up for the day they informed us that the van had a problem and had to be worked on the next morning.

"Well, I have some work I can do at the hotel tomorrow. Why don't you and Mister Wen grab the bus in the morning? The bus station is an easy walk from the hotel. They can come get us after the van is repaired," Don said.

"I would love to do that," I exclaimed. I wanted a chance to look around on the way to the bus station. Mei told Mr. Wen about the plan, and he smiled and gave me a finger sign for seven, showing

that he understood we were to meet at seven o'clock the following morning. He held up his hand with the thumb and index fingers, making an "L" with his little finger raised also. I got the message even though I don't speak Chinese. "*He probably learned that to communicate with other dialects, not with someone like me. I sure wish I could speak Chinese.*"

I smiled back at Mr. Wen and gave him the same sign. "Seven o'clock at the bus station."

CHAPTER FIFTEEN

GREEN TEA AND TSINGTAO

China in the Twentieth Century - Japan's Second Invasion

In 1937, the Japanese decided to strike before national unity was a reality. Near the Marco Polo Bridge outside Beijing, the Japanese provoked the Chinese, and all hell broke loose. World War II had started for the Chinese. When the dust settled, the Japanese controlled Beijing and Tientsin; next, they smashed the defenses in Shanghai, Suzhou, Changshu, and many other cities. By the end of the year, they had reached Nanking, where the Japanese soldiers committed atrocities against civilians and prisoners of war on an unimaginable scale.

The Chinese were to fight against the Japanese for four years and five months before Pearl Harbor, which Americans think of as the beginning of World War II.

AS I WALKED down the street on my way to meet Mr. Wen at the bus station, I passed a small teahouse not far from the hotel. It was built of wood and bamboo and had a timeworn look. I saw men of the old order sitting around outside on bamboo chairs, talking and drinking tea. Some had brought their songbirds in small cages. They stopped talking and reading their newspapers to gawk at me as I walked by. I nodded and smiled, and they nodded and smiled back. "*I have plenty of time, and it's only about a ten-minute walk to the bus station, so why not stop and have a cup of tea?*" I thought as I turned around and headed back toward the teahouse.

The customers continued to stare as I walked inside and sat down at a small table by the door. I noticed a boy wandering around the tables carrying an old copper kettle with a long spout, refilling teapots with hot water. Before he came over, I got out my notebook and found the page that listed various types of tea. When he arrived at my table, I pointed to the characters written next to green tea. He went over to an elderly man sitting at a small table covered with teapots and containers of tea, giving him my order, and I watched the man select an old teapot, wash it out with hot water, and put in loose tea. (The Chinese do not use teabags.) The teapot the old man selected was made of porcelain, which, like glassware, is ideal for brewing green teas. The boy brought the pot over and unceremoniously set it down. He went to the rear and returned with a teacup with a porcelain lid. I said "Thank you" in Chinese before he could walk away. He smiled, probably thinking that was the extent of my Chinese. By this time, the customers had gone back to smoking, chatting, and reading; they had already forgotten me.

I knew that the brewing time was only a few minutes, so as the tea brewed I looked at the pot and began thinking about the water inside. Even though it needs to be boiled, they do not use boiling water to make green tea as that ruins green tea leaves. The boiled water is put into large metal thermos bottles to keep it hot, and has cooled slightly by the time it is poured over the leaves. I felt the pot and hoped it had boiled long enough to kill any bacteria or viruses. Dirty water is one of China's most pressing environmental problems; the water problem in China is what made green tea and Tsingtao beer my only drinks, so if you go to China this is a good rule to follow. I didn't trust drinking bottled water in a country that counterfeits almost everything.

After the tea had brewed for a few minutes, I filled my cup with the light greenish-yellow tea. I started drinking my tea while observing—without staring—the men in the teahouse as they smoked, drank, and talked. The tea had a fresh flavor and a delightful aroma. Ah, China in a teacup! There were tables of men talking, one table of older gentlemen playing cards, and a man in the back snoozing. There was not a woman to be seen. As I sat drinking my tea, I noticed a statue of Kuan Yin (I will tell you more about Kuan Yin in Chapter Twenty-Five) on a shelf near the table. The statue made me think of a Chinese story about tea and Kuan Yin.

There are many stories about the origins of tea in China, but the one involving Kuan Yin is my favorite. As I recall the story, there was a Buddhist monk from India by the name of Bodhidharma, who came to China around 500 AD to teach the Chinese how to meditate. After his arrival, he sat facing a wall in a monastery day after day for nine years. One time, he allowed his eyes to close only briefly; as penance he arose and cut off his eyelids to make sure it would not happen again. Where his eyelids fell, Kuan Yin caused China's first tea plants to grow to help Buddhists stay wide awake while meditating. So, I guess she is the one responsible for "all the tea in China."

While I drank my tea, I watched the boy move through the teahouse filling teapots. He seemed to know when a customer needed more hot water. As I watched him, I noticed he would stop at a table when he saw the lid was balanced on the handle. He would fill the pot and replace the lid, then move on, and from time to time go into the back for more hot water. After drinking several cups of tea, I took the lid off the pot and put it on the handle. In a few minutes, he came over and filled my teapot with hot water. I wondered how long this method had been used to ask for more hot water.

Paying the bill required that I get out my notebook to show the boy "Please bring bill" in Chinese. I paid the bill and walked out of the teahouse and headed toward the bus station to meet Mr. Wen.

We spent all morning going over more of the design requirements document, and then it was time for lunch. Don and Mei hadn't arrived yet, so I left the boatyard with Mr. Wen and a couple of boatyard employees and headed down the dirt alley toward the restaurant. Along the way, we passed a small group of boatyard workers making hemp rope. Hemp has been grown in China for thousands of years, and the hemp they use is the fiber and oilseed form. They were using a mechanical contraption that looked ancient, which slowly twisted long strands of hemp into a line with two tight braids about an inch in diameter that stretched down the alley like a snake.

After a short walk, we came to the two-story building where we'd had lunch on the last trip. We went up the creaky wooden steps to the second floor and sat at the same large round wooden table. I began to feel that dining elbow-to-elbow at this round table was producing an all-togetherness and unity that is an important part of Chinese meals. I sat next to the window to avoid the cigarette smoke and get a little fresh air. Indoor air pollution is a serious problem all over China because of smoking and the use of charcoal for cooking inside. No one spoke English, but because I was becoming a regular, it wasn't long before someone brought me a bottle of Tsingtao beer. I poured myself a bright golden glass of room-temperature beer and took a long sip. Ah, China in a bottle.

When you think of beer, China doesn't come to mind, but beer has become a national drink in China, added to Chinese culture back at the dawn of the twentieth century when Germany came to China to establish a naval base. The British had Hong Kong, and the Portuguese were in Macau, so the Germans choose Tsingtao, a city on the south coast of Shantung Peninsula, about fifty miles southeast of Beijing. Little by little, China was being carved up like a Peking duck. The Germans forced themselves into occupation and compelled the Chinese to sign a ninety-nine-year lease on the area, so all the area around Tsingtao was under German protection. German society couldn't exist without beer, so in 1903 they built a brewery to serve the fleet and the area. Within a few years, the area was industrialized, and another European-looking city was built on Chinese soil. At the beginning of the Great War, Japan declared war on Germany and occupied the province until 1922, when it was once again made part of China. The Germans are gone now, but the beer survives as Tsingtao, China's largest brewing concern, with about fifty breweries all across China.

The US Navy used the naval base in Tsingtao after WWII in support of the Chinese Nationalist forces. In fact, the ship I served on in the 1950s spent time in Tsingtao during the late '40s.

Eating lunch and drinking my beer, I heard many conversations in the background, like a radio turned up a bit too loud. As each course was brought up from the kitchen downstairs, it was put on a large lazy Susan in the center of the table. When the food came around to me, I would pick up a small amount with my chopsticks and put it on my plate. This routine continued until all the dishes were served, all the food had been eaten, and my Tsingtao bottle was empty. All that remained on the lazy Susan were empty serving plates except for one containing a fish head, all the bones, and a tail. Lunch had taken a little over an hour; it was time to get up and go back to work. I almost tripped over a spittoon as I headed for the stairs.

CHAPTER SIXTEEN

SUZHOU AND THE JUNK TEST DOCUMENT

China in the Twentieth Century - Civil War and WWII

Beaten badly in battles for Shanghai and Nanking, the Kuomintang government relocated to a wartime capital of Chungking, in southwest China. The Communist resistance, led by Mao Zedong, was still in Shensi. China was now in a civil war and at war with Japan.

In 1941, the U.S. was forced into the fight when the Japanese attacked Pearl Harbor. The Japanese may have destroyed our ships, but they brought a unity that would last for the entire war.

While we hopped from island to island toward Japan, the Communists grew stronger in the countryside. President Roosevelt died, and the war ended in 1945 when we dropped atomic bombs on Nagasaki and Hiroshima in Japan.

HEADING BACK DOWN the alley toward the boatyard, I saw the men still cranking the mechanical contraption, twisting hemp, which the Chinese still use in the caulking of their wooden boats, into a longer rope. On the last trip, I saw a fishing boat having several planks replaced, with a group of caulkers squatting underneath, pounding hemp covered with a white caulking compound into the spaces between the planks. I can only assume they have been making hemp line as long as they have been caulking boats, which goes back to the Shang Dynasty (1766–1122 BC). If so, what I was witnessing walking down the alley was a skill that has been passed down through the ages. The contraption they were using looked like it might be an early 1900s design.

Don and Mei had arrived just before we returned from lunch. We started back where we left off, and it wasn't long until it was time to call it a day.

"I can't tell you how pleased I am that things have gone so well the past two days," I said as I gathered up my paperwork. "I expect we may finish up with the new spec tomorrow. We then need to talk about the contract, and that about finishes us up for now."

"Mr. Chao should be here tomorrow," Don said. Mr. Chao worked for the import-export company, and his job on the project was to handle the contractual matters and manage the receiving of the parts and engines and the shipment of the junk.

Mr. Ru made an indication that he would like to speak. "If you have an extra day I would like to ask if we can go over to Suzhou. There is a government office that must test the junk before it can be shipped and their office is in Suzhou. While you are here, I think it would be a good idea to go there and talk about testing the junk. I'm sure I can set up a meeting for day after tomorrow."

"It's fine with me," I replied. "Where is Suzhou?"

"The city is about fifty miles west of Shanghai. Maybe we could stop there on the way back to Shanghai. Suzhou is one of the most beautiful cities in all of China; maybe you guys can take a look?" Mr. Ru suggested.

We all agreed that if we got finished with our discussions about the junk and got the contract agreed upon, we would all go to Suzhou the following day.

The next day we got hung up. The design required two anchors forward with a twelve-volt electric windlass for raising the anchors. Their plan was to fabricate the anchors and build an anchor windlass powered by a drive motor. The Chinese said, "In all of China there no twelve-volt drive motors." They wanted to use an AC motor that would run off the junk's generator. I had never heard of an AC motor used in this application and knew that in the States DC motors were used. I did not want to power the winch with an AC motor. "There are no DC motors in all of China." So that we could move on, I finally had to settle the matter by saying that I would investigate the issue when I got home. As the day progressed, there were several other minor changes required before we finished with all the necessities.

In discussing the design requirements with the Chinese over the past few days, I learned something I had not fully realized before: in the States, if a boat builder needs something like an anchor, the anchor is purchased. Like the anchors, many things I thought they would purchase were going to be fabricated instead. On my first trip, I had noticed that when a boat was to be repaired or constructed trees were ordered instead of finished lumber. Instead of ordering large wood beams, teams of men transformed trees into perfectly square, large beams. I saw two men hand-sawing giant trees into perfect planking; I even saw a man making a bucket out of scrap wood. It was clear that everything I didn't supply would be fabricated by the boatyard—including the anchors. I believe that the grapnel anchor with four flukes that they were going to use on the junk was another very old design that had survived down through the ages. Like the hemp lines they made—and the way they caulked their boats—it was just the way it was done: nothing special.

The contract I had written to build the junk was only five pages long, but it took the rest of the day to get the main issues worded in a manner that was acceptable. The final price couldn't be determined yet because of the anchor windlass and drive motor issue and several other factors. After these matters were resolved and a new price had been established I would need to draft another contract and send it over for their signature. We were finished with the paperwork and were going to Suzhou the next day.

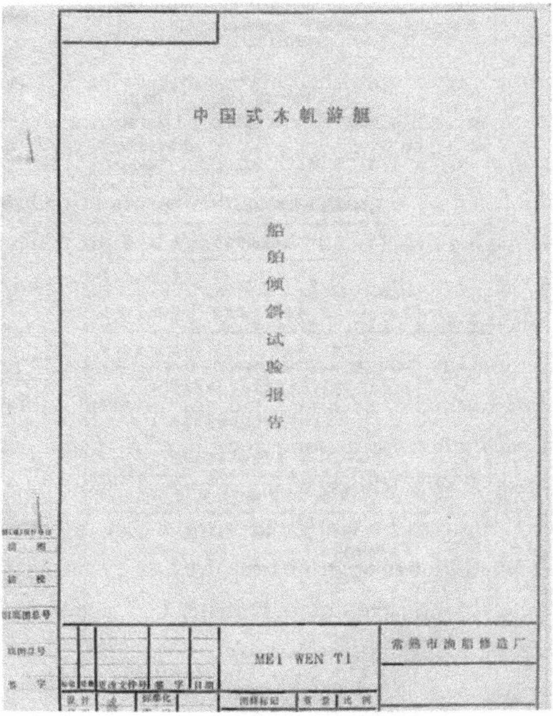

中国式木帆游艇

船舶倾斜试验报告

MEI WEN TI

常熟市渔船修造厂

The next morning the van arrived at the hotel early. Mr. Ru, Mr. Chao, and Mr. Wen were all going with us. After the meeting in Suzhou, the van would drop us off in Shanghai.

Our route took us through the Yangtze Delta area. The area is crisscrossed with canals, irrigation ditches, and fields of crops everywhere. It wasn't long before someone was pointing out the pagodas of Suzhou. In Suzhou, the streets were narrow enough for the trees to form an almost continuous leafy bower. We made our way into the old part of the city along cobblestone streets. Many of the houses were traditional in style, single-story (and sometimes two-story), largely whitewashed or with a wooden fascia. There are houses and fantastic old bridges along the many canals in Suzhou but, as in the older sections of Shanghai and Beijing, there were signs that the old cobblestone streets and old houses were going in favor of the steady march of progress. We pulled up in front of a plain old two-story building with no outward indication of any importance. Inside it was quite dark and cool. The wood paneling and all the furniture looked as if they had been in service for generations. I saw a small round emblem with Chinese characters around the top and an anchor in the middle; across the bottom it said "Register of Shipping of Jiangsu." "*This must be the place,*" I thought as we walked up a wooden staircase to the second floor where we met a small group of men who were obviously waiting for us. We moved into a large room with a wooden table big enough for a peace conference and sat grouped around one end. The purpose of the meeting was to discuss the testing of the junk. This government office served Jiangsu Province and had the mandate to pass inspection on all boats and ships before they were put in service, or in the case of the *Mei Wen Ti,* shipped to the States.

I asked what I could do or how I could be of service, and I think something got lost in Mei's translation. After listening for a while, I thought to myself, "*I don't think there is anything quite like this in the States.*" The government agency as an independent third party was going to subject the finished junk to a series of tests and record the results. I concluded that what they wanted to know was what tests I wanted them to add to their test document. This sounds like a simple statement, but it took me a while to arrive at that conclusion.

"Mei, please ask them if they want me to provide them with tests or checks that will be performed in addition to their normal testing program," I said.

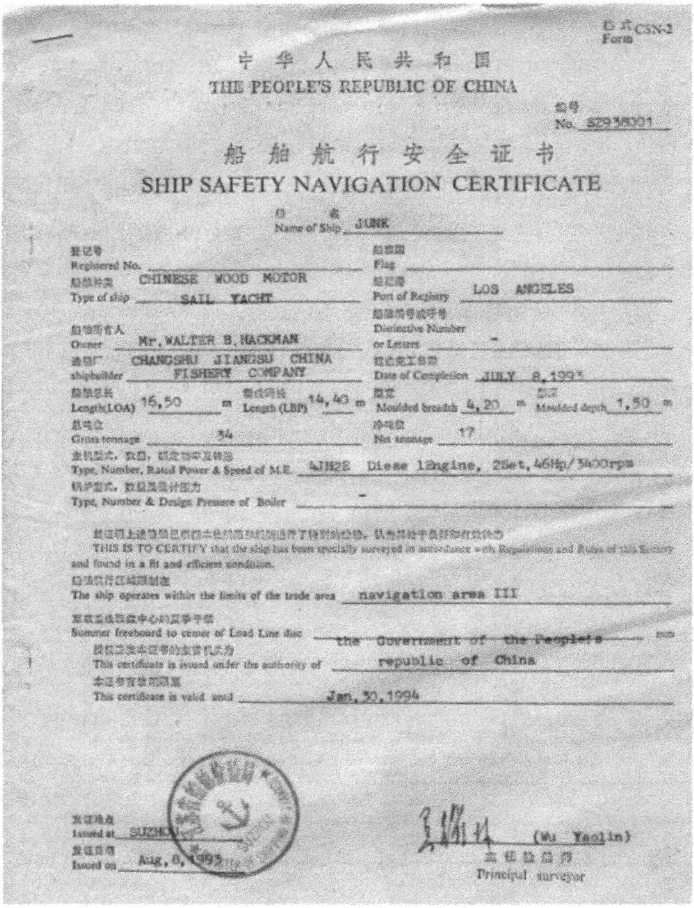

Form CSN-2

中华人民共和国

THE PEOPLE'S REPUBLIC OF CHINA

No. 5Z938001

船舶航行安全证书

SHIP SAFETY NAVIGATION CERTIFICATE

Name of Ship JUNK

Registered No.

Flag

Type of ship CHINESE WOOD MOTOR SAIL YACHT

Port of Registry LOS ANGELES

Distinctive Number or Letters -

Owner Mr. WALTER B. HACKMAN

Shipbuilder CHANGSHU JIANGSU CHINA FISHERY COMPANY

Date of Completion JULY 8, 1993

Length(LOA) 16,50 m Length (LBP) 14,40 m Moulded breadth 4,20 m Moulded depth 1,50 m

Gross tonnage 34

Net tonnage 17

Type, Number, Rated Power & Speed of M.E. 4JH2E Diese 1Engine, 2Set, 46Hp/3400rpm

Type, Number & Design Pressure of Boiler -

THIS IS TO CERTIFY that the ship has been specially surveyed in accordance with Regulations and Rules of this Society and found in a fit and efficient condition.

The ship operates within the limits of the trade area navigation area III

Summer freeboard to center of Load Line disc mm

This certificate is issued under the authority of the Government of the People's republic of China

This certificate is valid until Jan, 30, 1994

Issued at SUZHOU

Issued on Aug, 8, 1993

(Wu Yaolin)

Principal surveyor

She translated my question into what sounded to me like a much longer question, and when I listened to their reply, it sounded like a long reply. Mei looked at me and confirmed, "Yes, that is what they like you do."

I knew there would be things about the *Mei Wen Ti* that were different from any boat they may have tested in the past. I mentioned everything I knew that would be different and asked that these areas be added to the test document—like all the US Coast Guard requirements. After we got through talking, I offered to make a list of the items I had just suggested and send it to them. Everyone smiled, and we were finished.

We spent the afternoon walking around visiting several of the gardens that are the main attraction of the city. Among Chinese, Suzhou is their favorite tourist destination, which made it difficult to enjoy the serenity for which the gardens were designed. The gardens were originally built around lavish houses by rich merchants, landlords, and retired court officials, starting back in the Song Dynasty (960–1280 AD), who went there looking for a quiet place to retire. The Ming style gardens you see today have been rebuilt many times and are only representative of the hundreds of gardens that once flourished in bygone days.

They told me Suzhou was famous for its silk, classical gardens, and beautiful women, and that there was a famous old saying: "Above is Heaven, below is Suzhou and Hangzhou." The Grand Canal with its hectic canal traffic I wrote about in Chapter Nine was what really put Suzhou on the map. I learned that the city had suffered much destruction down through the years, in incidents such as the Taiping Rebellion in the late 1800s and the fall of Shanghai in 1937, when Japanese forces passed through on their way to lay siege to Nanjing.

After acting like tourists all afternoon, we drove back into the Yangtze Delta area, past the canals, irrigation ditches, and crops, and headed toward Shanghai.

CHAPTER SEVENTEEN

MEI'S PARENTS' NEW SHANGHAI APARTMENT

China in the Twentieth Century - Another Civil War

In 1945, peace returned all over the world when the war ended—except in China. The uneasy alliance between the Communists and Chiang failed, and the inevitable civil war started. America intervened for a short period, trying to prop up the Nationalists, then attempted to mediate the situation, but the talks did not succeed.

In 1949, Chiang Kai-shek and what was left of his army retreated to Taiwan (Formosa), aboard US Navy ships. Mao stood before the masses in Tiananmen Square and proclaimed the establishment of the People's Republic of China. Mao took up the Mandate of Heaven as a modern-day emperor. The dragon had a new master.

THE DAY AFTER returning from Suzhou, we went to dinner at Mei's family's new apartment, which was located in one of the tall new concrete, bunker-looking buildings not far from the

Hengshan Hotel. This type of building can be seen all over Shanghai, and there are always more under construction.

Before moving to the new apartment, Mei's family had lived for many years, like a very large percentage of Shanghai's poor residents, in a *lilong* neighborhood. These areas were typically in the poorer part of the city and consisted of row upon row of low-rise buildings set within a grid of alleyways and narrow streets. In some areas, families would live in plots where the average living space was fewer than fifty square feet per person, often much fewer. Their old place had been torn down since our last trip to Shanghai to make way for more apartment buildings. I learned while I was in Shanghai that the city (the largest in China) has experienced decades of industrial development and a fast-growing urban population from the steady movement of people from the country into the city. Shanghai's current population is around twenty-four million, but because of the temporary workers, estimates vary (like trying to estimate the number of illegal workers in the States). Many of the newcomers who arrive in the city are on the bottom rung of the economic ladder and are forced to live in shacks, attics, or subdivided rooms. Sometimes four generations live together in the substandard housing.

In addition to the massive government-sponsored resettlement program of lower-income families, the government has also made better housing available to the middle- and higher-income groups. It seemed like everyone was moving. The higher-income families can buy their apartments on the property market. Middle- and low-income families can buy nonprofit housing from either their employers or the government. They also have the option to rent public housing. As in the States, the government can subsidize families with financial difficulties. Since the government can't build housing in the suburbs connected to Shanghai with six-lane freeways as we do in California, they are doing about the only thing possible, and that is to tear down old neighborhoods and build up. In order to cope with the flood of people moving into cities like Shanghai, the government is planning to build hundreds of new cities in the near future.

In addition to the extraordinary influx of people from the country, another factor fueling this rapid transition has been the death of state-run companies that owned massive housing projects. These companies can no longer support such housing without the heavy subsidy they once received from the government before Deng set China on a new economic heading. As a result, they've had to sell off housing assets to raise cash and reduce their overhead. Soon the new homeowners were better credit risks than the companies they worked for. The right to own property is another element of their old socialist economy that is slowly changing. How much of it must disappear before it is no longer socialism?

When I saw the improvements in Mei's parents' housing situation and the colossal job the government has undertaken in Shanghai to provide decent housing, I was impressed. China is changing things in a big way, and I think America needs to quit harping about how the Chinese are running their country. I must say from my personal observations that the housing settlement project the government has implemented has improved the living conditions and environment of tens of thousands of households in Shanghai.

I was in the bar enjoying a room-temperature beer when Don and Mei showed up to leave for dinner. We walked out of the hotel and down the tree-lined street toward the area where Mei's parents now lived. The street soon gave way to one with no trees. We were soon in a new Shanghai neighborhood of tall apartment buildings. There were many more apartment buildings under construction with tall cranes and tall bamboo scaffolding everywhere. We stopped in a little stand and bought some Tsingtao beer to take to dinner (remember, you can't drink water in China).

Their building looked like it had been done on a tight budget and had opened in a hurry; it had a raw, unfinished look. There was no landscaping yet, but the large bicycle rack crammed full of bicycles told me that there were plenty of people living there. When we walked into the building, I saw smoke and stopped in my tracks; there was a fire somewhere inside.

"You never mind—come on," Mei said. "That only cooking smoke."

"Why is there cooking smoke in a brand new building?" I pondered, and then it dawned on me. "*Everyone in here is cooking dinner using charcoal just like they did in the old neighborhood.*" As I looked down the hazy hallway toward the open window at the other end of the building, I saw small charcoal stoves outside each door, belching smoke into the hall, where it vented out the window like a smoke stack. Everyone had a new building but old stoves.

I recalled the last time I was in Shanghai, and we went to Mei's parents' small place for dinner. As we approached their house, the streets were narrow and crowded with whole families trying to escape the heat. I remembered the people sitting on short stools and chairs that were set up everywhere along the narrow sidewalks and the sides of the street. But most of all I remember the haze in the air caused by women cooking on small charcoal stoves.

With eyes watering, we made it to the elevator. I said a prayer that it was working as I stood there waiting for it to arrive; their apartment was on the sixteenth floor. When the door opened, a young elevator operator welcomed us in Chinese into her rather plain elevator. As she pushed the button to take us up to their floor, I thought to myself, "*This is probably about as safe as getting under way on a Chinese submarine.*"

When the elevator door opened, I noticed that the air looked a little thicker as we walked down the hall toward their apartment.

"She say elevator not too reliable," Mei said as we stood in the hall and knocked on the door of the apartment.

"I think going down I will take the stairs," I said to her as we walked into the small apartment and closed the door to keep the smoke out.

Like last time, the family was happy to see Mei and the loud, nonstop conversation started immediately. The apartment was small, maybe four hundred square feet. There was a little front room with the couch from their old place that could be made into a bed, a small cooking area, a tiny bedroom. There was a petite bathroom with no bath. I recognized the old piece of screen-covered furniture against one wall for holding food. The Goddess of Mercy had made the trip along with the small pot containing sand for burning joss sticks. One large window was open and next to it was their small bamboo birdcage with a tiny songbird inside. We had an elevated view of the massive neighborhood construction project. The small succulent plant in a ceramic pot I'd given them as a gift sat on a small bookcase next to the window. I looked around and saw the children's dictionary I'd brought over on the last trip, about eight months before, and I was silently happy to see that it looked used. A picture frame on the wall held photos of the family but no old pictures. I wondered if those were more casualties of the Cultural Revolution. This trip I had brought over some school stuff, coffee, a small coffee pot (don't know exactly why), and some Marlboro cigarettes.

This time, my head didn't touch the ceiling when I walked into the kitchen to watch the women preparing the evening meal. Mei's parents had gone shopping earlier and bought all the necessary ingredients. They shopped every day, so everything was fresh, and I'm sure the menu begins with what they find at the market. By this time, most of the preparation was done, and they were just starting to prepare the rice. Most Shanghai families serve rice as we serve bread, and it is a part of almost every meal. I was about to learn something over half (the female half) of the population learns at an early age: how to cook rice.

First you take a flat-bottom pan ("Velly important have straight side") and put in about two cups of rice (more or less depending on how many people you are feeding). You then add fresh water and wash the rice as much as necessary to get clean, rubbing it vigorously between your hands. Pour out the water after the last washing, leaving the rice in the bottom of the pan. Next is the thousand-year-old trick. Smooth the rice flat in the bottom of the pan, using the back of your fingers. Now, holding your index finger straight ("Velly important") with the thumb pressed next to the index finger (like the old Uncle Sam on the "I Want You" poster), point your index finger down over the rice pot and move down until your finger hits the bottom of the pot. Now the most important part: move your thumb until it just touches the top of the washed rice. Keep your index finger in straight and don't under any condition move your thumb. Move your index finger out of the rice and rest it on top of the rice gently in another location. Since you probably used your right hand and can't pick up the water container, have someone pour in the water stopping when it reaches the tip of your thumb. For those of you who are not engineers, the volume of the rice is equal to the volume of the water. If you are cooking short-grain rice, reduce the water a "rittle." If you like soft rice, you can put in water until it is part way up your thumbnail. Not too far.

The rice is then put on a heating device. Wait until the water is almost absorbed and then put on a tight lid and let it simmer another twenty or thirty minutes. You can stir and peek at the water level. Once the water has been absorbed the heat must be very low.

While they waited for the rice to cook, the final food preparation was finished up. I opened the beer I had brought and poured glasses for everyone. I grabbed a chicken wing from a plate that had been prepared earlier and walked out into the hall to see how the stove was doing. This piece was made with a round opening on the top, where a large, round hockey puck-shaped piece of charcoal full of holes was warming up. Once the charcoal was red hot, they were ready to cook. The wok with its curved bottom fit into the hole in the top and rested close to the red-hot piece of charcoal. Superior stir-frying requires high heat and a short cooking time. However, a wok can also be used for steaming, frying, and other type of cooking; it is the basic utensil in Chinese cooking. In Chapter Twelve I presented a few recipes I learned on my trips to China.

After the soup was heated up and the wok out in the hall got good and hot, the rest of the cooking began. All the dishes were stir-fried quickly, one at a time, and put in a serving dish, and one of the cooks would disappear briefly into the hall to stir-fry another dish. The meal began with a bowl of soup and then all the dishes were shared. Rice is not shared; we each received a bowl, and good manners dictate that you eat every grain. All the dishes served were considered an accompaniment to the rice. Using chopsticks, you take a small quantity of food from the serving dish and either eat it or transfer it to the rice bowl. En Route, you might dip it in a sauce. Almost unnoticed, the cook finished cooking and joined in the hearty meal. After all the food was eaten and the beer I brought was gone, we gave out presents, and then sat around and visited for several hours.

When it was time to leave we headed toward the elevator and then I remembered. "I'll see you guys at the bottom; I'm walking down," I said as I headed for the stairwell. I found out that Chinese stairs are made to different dimensions. The steps are closer together and not as wide, so I wound up taking them two at a time—almost beating the elevator.

CHAPTER EIGHTEEN

SHANGHAI JIAOTONG UNIVERSITY

China in the Twentieth Century - The People's Republic of China

Russia, acting like the Western imperialists and the Japanese of bygone days, retained parts of northern China and became China's new big brother. The US took a "hands off" policy toward China, as it shifted to postwar interests. China began to fade into the background.

Before long, fighting Communism became America's new national obsession; in 1950 we found ourselves involved in the Korean War. When General MacArthur headed toward the Chinese border the Chinese, fearing invasion, entered the war. As a result, we imposed a strict trade embargo on China.

In 1951, Tibet was "liberated" by the People's Liberation Army. In 1953, the Korean "police action" ended at the 38th Parallel. The Chinese marched out of Korea as quietly as they had marched in.

WHILE WAITING FOR Don in the lobby of the hotel, I looked out the window at the park across the street. I could see the park from the window in my room upstairs, and it was always full of people walking, doing exercises, or just sitting on benches talking. Today, as on other days, there were several games of mah-jongg in process and people dancing to music I couldn't hear.

When Don showed up, I suggested we go across the street for a few minutes and walk in the park, which looked more like an outdoor gym than a park, full of beautiful old trees and bushes. There was an organized group on the other side of the park doing *tai chi* with a leader, but, for the most part, it was full of people separated from each other doing their morning slow-motion exercise. Don and I stopped to look at a couple ahead of us on the sidewalk dancing with no music. When we stopped to watch, I noticed that the man was wearing earphones probably connected to a tape player in his pocket.

"Excuse me," I heard from behind me. We turned around, and a middle-aged woman dressed in a colorful spring dress stood behind us. "I'm sorry to interrupt your stroll in our wonderful park on such a splendid morning," she said in perfect English. She handed each of us a calling card, and I wondered what the pitch was going to be, but I would never have guessed what she wanted. Her card read:

Faye Wong
Deputy Division Chief
State Bureau of Foreign Experts PRC
Department of Economic and Technical Experts
Friendship Hotel 71644
Beijing 100873, China

"My name is Faye Wong, and I work for the government. I wonder if I might talk with you for just a minute."

I glanced at Don and said, "Sure, what can we do for you?" I was a bit apprehensive when I heard "I work for the government." "*What the hell is the Department of Foreign Experts?"* I thought as I turned her card over, only to discover her card in Chinese with her name reversed.

"Are you Americans?" she inquired.

"Yes, we're here on business," Don said. "I'm Don McClure, and this gentleman is Walt Hackman."

"I'm pleased to meet you. My job is to search out economic and technical experts who would like to work in China. You could be an expert in making beer or running a bank; we need all kinds of experienced businesspeople. The government doesn't pay much compared to America, but it would be a good way to see China and be of service to the country."

"I have a job that allows me to see China," Don said. "I don't think I'm looking for a career change for a lot less money."

"I love China, and I wish I could get involved, but Don and I are engaged in a project that will keep me busy for a while," I said.

"I understand. Please keep my card and if either of you change your mind, please contact me in Beijing. Goodbye and thank you for your time, and do enjoy our park," she said as she walked away past the dancing couple.

"That was different; I can't believe that the party that was built on Mao's revolutionary theories is out recruiting capitalists to help with the industrialization and modernization of the country. It wasn't that long ago when 'Rightists' were classified as nonpersons and were persecuted by this same government. How did the despised capitalist system become a partner in the people's working dictatorship?" I said

"Money," Don replied as we turned and walked back toward the hotel past an old man playing a well-used accordion to catch a cab.

Before parting ways the day before with Mr. Ru, Don and I had made arrangements to meet him for a tour of his facilities at Shanghai's Jiaotong University, where he was a professor in the Naval Architecture department. I assumed that since the university and most of the shipbuilding in China is controlled by the government, Mr. Ru was just assigned the job of providing engineering services to the boatyard. Sometimes in this people's working dictatorship it was hard to figure out how things are done and who pays for what.

We met Mr. Ru on schedule and walked around the campus, looking at classrooms and labs in the section where he worked. When the school was founded back in 1896, it was known as Nan Yang Public School. Down through the unstable years of the twentieth century it had thirteen different names as it mirrored a changing Chinese society until the present name stuck back in 1959. The Xuhui Campus of Shanghai Jiao Tong University Ship Design and Research Institute offers undergraduate, graduate, and postgraduate degrees in naval architecture and marine engineering. His department's prize possession was a huge model ship basin. The large indoor basin is used in conjunction with scale wooden ship models to provide hydrodynamic tests and numerical calculations to support the design and development of ships. He explained how it was used to investigate the effects of waves on ship's models. China is now firmly the world's largest shipbuilder and its quality and technology have much improved since I started writing this book in the summer of 2008.

Earlier in the story I wrote that the Ming Dynasty (1368–1644 AD) by the early 1400s had amassed a fleet of thousands of junks, many of them used for world exploration, coastal defense, and protection against pirates. China had the most powerful navy and the best shipbuilding technology in the world, but the Ming let the great fleet of large sea-going junks rot away unused and let their shipbuilding technology slip through their fingers as they concentrated on domestic issues like the Ming Tombs near Beijing, unaware of what was happening in the rest of the world. The Qing Dynasty (1644–1911 AD) followed the Ming in not keeping up with the development of a modern navy. The Qing Dynasty engaged in a long series of wars that changed Chinese history for the next 150 years because they did not have either a powerful navy or the technology to fight a modern war.

As I sat in the cab headed back to the hotel, I reflected on what I had seen and decided that China learned a hard history lesson they haven't forgotten, that China must have a strong shipbuilding capability and must also have power at sea. I think China's declared goal to become the world's largest shipbuilding nation is part of a long-term plan that includes Chinese-flagged domestic vessels to carry oil and other strategic materials coupled with a strong navy. I think these long-range plans are what put the foreign-built ship model basin in Shanghai's Jiaotong University.

CHAPTER NINETEEN

TRAVELING CHINESE STYLE

China in the Twentieth Century - Hundred Flowers

After the Korean War, Mao, with the help of Soviet aid, began slowly moving China forward after a half-century of war, starvation, unrest, and disasters. He decided to launch the Hundred Flowers campaign in 1956, in which China's intellectuals were encouraged to speak out freely about the government, and a tidal wave of criticism followed from all segments of society. Mao didn't like the results, so under Deng Xiaoping's leadership, the government reacted by sending hundreds of thousands of intellectuals and other "disloyal Chinese" to reform in far-off places for a long time. Mao would never forget the government leaders who had opposed him over this campaign.

DON, MEI, AND I left the hotel early the next morning so we could check in early and get front-row or exit door seats on the China Eastern Airlines flight to Los Angeles. I didn't particularly like the airline; we flew it only because they had the lowest fare from Los Angeles to Shanghai. This trip would be my sixth flight on China Eastern Airlines, and I knew the seats were hard and narrow, and legroom was lacking. Getting front-row seats on the long flight was important.

We got in line at the check-in counter and were slowly making our way to the head of the line when we encountered a problem that is widespread in China: queue-barging, where a person behind you in line pushes, shoves, or skips line.

"Excuse me!" Don said to the man that had just slipped in front of him. The man paid no attention to Don and acted as if he had just got in line behind the last person in line.

I had noticed that many Chinese people have bad public behaviors, including spitting and littering in the streets, smoking in public, and, of course, queue-barging. In both Shanghai and Beijing, I had seen them push each other, harshly and aggressively, when trying to get on crowded buses, so much so that existing passengers had to force their way against the boarding crowds to get off.

"Am I so small that you didn't see me?" Don screamed in the man's ear. There was still no response from him, just like the old man I'd met in Beijing who was being yelled at by the watermelon man—nothing.

"Don, maybe you should just let the guy go," I said. "It's not worth getting into a brawl over."

"I don't like to be pushed and shoved around like that," Don growled. He then took the man by the back of his coat and shoved him out of the line. Mei said something to the man as he walked past on the way to the end.

When we eventually got to the head of the line, we laid down our tickets together and asked the check-in person for front-row seats. She looked at her monitor and then quietly started talking with the staff person next to her.

"Sorry, that not possible," was the reply.

"How about getting seats near an exit door?" Don asks.

"Not possible, plane left three days ago," the counter person said as calmly as if she were informing us that we had missed the plane not three minutes ago.

"See the date and time on those tickets?" Don said in a loud voice. "There must be some mistake."

"No mistake, not lie, flight three days past," she assured Don.

"But, we have to be in Los Angeles tomorrow!" Don responded. "When is the next flight?"

They punched their computer and talked the situation over amongst themselves. She said, "Next flight not full five days."

"That's impossible!" Don replied.

We were holding up the line, and I could see we were spinning our wheels. "I suggest we grab or bags and sit down and try and come up with a solution."

We first checked other airlines, but everything was full for days just like China Eastern Airline. What to do? "*Maybe we can find a way through the back door*," I thought to myself.

"As I understand it there are two ways to do things in China," I said. "You can do business 'through the front door,' like we are trying to do. Or you can go 'through the back door.' You guys have been here way more than me. Can we solve this by going through the back door?"

"Sure," Don said. "We just find an airline employee to bribe."

It didn't take Mei long to find an airport employee who was sure he could help us get a flight out the next day, but he didn't want to talk to us at the airport. The plan was to go back to the Hengshan Hotel and wait until he got off work. Later that day he came to the hotel and said he had a "connection" who worked for Japan Airlines, and for twenty-five dollars he could guarantee to put in touch with a person who could sell us tickets on a flight out the next day. When we purchased the tickets, we were to give his friend twenty-five dollars cash in a sealed envelope. We agreed to the "backdoor" solution, but it cost us $3,000 for three one-way tickets to Los Angeles; the legitimate one-way fare on Japan Airlines. The one-way fare was the same price as a round trip ticket on China Eastern.

And what do you do with airplane tickets for a flight you missed by three days? It turned out that it was our fault, and the airline told us, "Sorry, if you miss a flight by three days you no get money back." Oh, well, that's just traveling Chinese style.

CHAPTER TWENTY

GOING HOME: THE LA RIOTS

China in the Twentieth Century - Hundred Flowers and the Great Leap

Mao's next great venture was the Great Leap Forward, launched in 1958. He wanted to fast-track China's economy by introducing a communal land system, massive public works projects, and more kids.

Mao ordered the peasants to labor also at ramshackle, jerry-built smelters set up in each commune. Millions of these smelters were built, and farmers melted their tools and took up steel production. After the available coal was gone, all the trees in the area were felled for fuel. Meanwhile, the snails, sparrows, mosquitoes, mice, and fleas were hunted down and killed in a nation-wide campaign that turned into an ecological nightmare. Remarkable results were reported to Mao, but in reality the country was headed for another man-made disaster—or, should I say, "Mao-made" disaster.

WHILE I WAS in China, riots in Los Angeles convulsed America's second largest city. I had no idea that the massive violence, arson, and property damage had occurred while I was away.

What lit the fuse that exploded into three days of hell in Los Angeles? It was when a jury of one Filipino juror and eleven white jurors found four white Los Angeles police officers not guilty in the videotaped beating of Rodney King, a black man. The cops' defense attorney had said King was under the influence of PCP, and that excessive force was necessary.

The mayor and thousands of people in South Central Los Angeles and elsewhere in Los Angeles County didn't agree. What happened next might better be looked at as the sudden climax of a year of racial strife over the whole matter surrounding the beating, the justice system, and the Los Angeles Police Department.

The wave of destruction started in South Central Los Angeles and quickly spread to the downtown area, Hollywood, Korea Town, and Pasadena. It wasn't long before the LA insurrection surpassed the Watts Riots of 1965 in destruction, death, and mayhem.

I missed the news, or maybe it just wasn't news in China. On May 5, 1992, when we landed in Los Angeles, we did not know about the event or that thirty-eight people had died, and more than twelve hundred had been injured. We didn't know fire units had been called in from all over California to fight thousands of fires throughout the city.

We got off the plane at LAX and picked up a shuttle headed toward Hollywood. As usual, I had parked my pickup truck way back in Don's driveway. I was anxious to get home; it had been a long day. Looking out the window as the airport van approached Hollywood I couldn't believe my eyes: I was amazed and shocked at the devastation. It looked like a civil war had taken place while we were gone.

"What happened here?" I shouted to the driver.

He turned around, looked at me and said, "Where the hell you been, man, in China?"

"Yeah."

I went back to work at the gallery during the day. In the evenings and on weekends I worked on my project. This routine would continue for the next five months until our next trip to China. The first thing I did was to call Larry and talk to him about the meeting and how well it had gone; I told him everyone's understanding was enhanced by his drawings. He was glad to hear his isometric drawing suggestion had worked out. We talked about the anchor windlass problem that needed to be resolved. I told him I had gone through an assessment of my funds and needed to cut the parts cost. Since the current design included a three-kilowatt inverter, I said I would like to remove the generator. This change would also eliminate the need for a generator cooling system, exhaust system, generator room ventilation, and remote start, further reducing the parts cost. He didn't see any problem in removing the generator, but we decided to increase the size of the alternators on the main engines from the standard fifty-five amperes to eighty amperes to provide sufficient power to charge all the batteries. Larry agreed that the Chinese needed to locate a twelve-volt motor to power the anchor windlass.

A few days after returning, I sent Mr. Ru a fax message saying I wanted to leave the requirement in the junk design for a twelve-volt DC motor to drive the anchor windlass. I also informed him of my decision to remove the generator and all the associated equipment. Next, I faxed the revised design document and contract, and the electrical system design. As the weeks passed the first message to Mr. Ru slowly disappeared into a pile, as one fax after another was sent or received.

One day, at home working on the project, I accidentally ran across my birth certificate while looking for my passport. On it I noticed that in 1935 when I was born, my mother, father, and older brother lived at 3669 ½ South Vermont in Los Angeles. I remembered seeing images of the area around South Vermont during the televised reruns of the riots, showing the fires, looting, and craziness that had gone on. I had not been in the neighborhood since the family moved away right after I was born, and I wondered if there was any chance the old place was still there.

About a month later, I happened to be in a little local coffee house in Los Angeles. The joint had lots of bad art and chairs that didn't match, but the coffee was the best in town. As I sipped, it occurred to me that I wasn't far from South Vermont. After a refill and another Bukowski poem from a book in their free library, I decided to see if I could find the old place.

Driving along, I couldn't help thinking about all the generations of people who'd lived in this area. It's not the nicest part of Los Angeles now, and I suspect it wasn't back in 1935 either, but my mom once told me they liked the area, knew their neighbors, and were acquainted with some of the local merchants. My dad worked hard as a soda jerk, and everyone believed in the American dream. But then, like many of their neighbors, my parents moved on.

As I turned onto Vermont, I was saddened to see the effects of the rioting. I felt down about what had happened to the area and concluded that things don't always change for the better. I watched the numbers get larger as I drove block after block toward 3669 ½. What would the old place look like? Would it still be there? Could it have been one of those buildings I saw go up in flames in the endless reruns of the riots on television? Finally, I got to where the old place would—or should—have been. There I found a large, old, run-down '60s-style apartment building. My first house, at 3669 1/2 South Vermont, like the aspirations and mores of my parent's generation, was now gone, along with other reminders of that era.

My quick trip down South Vermont let me understand a little better what Old Chang in Beijing and lots of other people in China must have felt when they lost part of their roots.

The months passed as one fax after another filled the metal tray on my small desk. There were questions about the navigation lights, the engines, and the main power panel, Letters of Credit, questions from Larry about parts, and many more. The pile of faxes grew and grew.

In time, the contract was signed, and I opened my Letter of Credit in June 1992. The Chinese responded by opening their Standby Letter of Credit; so far, so good. I opened another letter of credit to purchase the engines in Hong Kong. One day, the mailman delivered a builder's risk insurance policy from The People's Insurance Company of China, along with a schedule showing the junk would be delivered to Shanghai by the end of the year. Using the information Larry had developed, I started ordering parts for my boat. There was no turning back.

Through the summer, I worked on the details associated with ordering all the parts identified on Larry's drawings. By late September, I had managed to get together about ninety-five percent of all the parts and made arrangements to ship them to Shanghai.

Before leaving for China, I sent Mr. Chao a message indicating I had shipped the parts on the *President Jackson*, Voyage #43, from Los Angeles to Hong Kong. I gave him the total amount of the parts shipment and asked him to please amend their Standby Letter of Credit. I remembered the bank loan officer who set it up saying, "If anything goes wrong, you are covered." I hoped he was right.

CHAPTER TWENTY-ONE

SHANGHAI, CRICKETS, AND PU YI—THIRD TRIP

China in the Twentieth Century - Mao's Revolution Stalls

Because of the failure of the Great Leap Forward Campaign, food shortages caused mass starvation in the countryside. Mao's Long March friend Peng Dehuai observed that the Great Leap Forward had caused the starvation. He was stripped of his title of Defense Minister.

Over the next few years, Liu Shaochi, Deng Xiaoping, and others imported food, broke up the communes, dumped the homemade smelters, returned property, and put the peasants back to farming. Under the new rules, the peasants were allowed to produce income on the side. It is estimated that thirty million people died in the aftermath of the Great Leap Forward.

In 1965, Mao was about to begin his most bizarre plan yet—the Great Proletarian Cultural Revolution.

ON THE THIRD plane ride from Los Angeles to Shanghai in October of 1992, I saw for the second time the Academy Award-winning movie *The Last Emperor.* Parts of it were filmed in the Forbidden City, which I had visited, and so I now enjoyed the film more than I had when it first came out. It is a fascinating story based in the life of Pu Yi, the last emperor of China. The movie was made in 1987 and starred Peter O'Toole as Pu Yi's teacher and mentor. It was in this movie that I first learned about the unique role of crickets in Chinese culture.

At the beginning of the movie, the three-year-old Emperor Pu Yi is sitting on an enormous throne in the Hall of Supreme Harmony inside the Forbidden City in Beijing. During his coronation ceremony, he gets down and runs outside, to the consternation of his father. He walks down the stairs from the Hall of Supreme Harmony onto a large parade ground, where a throng of soldiers, eunuchs, Buddhist priests, and other faithful are kowtowing to him. As he is walking around, he hears a cricket and searches out a soldier who has a round container under his arm. "It is my cricket, your majesty; now it can be the emperor's cricket," the soldier says, giving the tiny insect to the boy emperor.

Toward the end of the movie, taking place around 1959, the elderly Pu Yi returns to the Forbidden City not as emperor, but as a brainwashed Communist citizen. He has been in prison since the end of World War II, and has undergone ten years of "re-education." The aging Pu Yi walks slowly up the long stairs into the Hall of Supreme Harmony. There doesn't seem to be anyone around, so he steps over the cord roping off the throne and starts up the stairs.

"Stop, you are not allowed here!" he hears from behind, as a small boy guard runs up and stops at the bottom of the stairs.

"I was the emperor of China, and I use to live here," Pu Yi states.

"Prove it!" the small guard retorts. So Pu Yi continues up the stairs to the throne, reaches down behind it, and pulls out the cricket cage from long ago. He dusts off the cage much like an old Chinese merchant would while trying to make a sale. The last emperor presents the cricket cage to the boy. After a few moments, the boy guard looks up, and Pu Yi is gone.

We had planned to spend a few days in Shanghai before heading to Changshu and the junk project. The day after we arrived I was out for a walk; it was a cold day, and I had forgotten all about the movie, crickets, and Pu Yi. As I was walking along going nowhere in particular, I looked down an alley and saw what appeared to be a market, and decided to investigate. What I found were small stalls selling a variety of goods. As I walked around, I came upon an old man and a young boy selling crickets and a huge selection of cricket paraphernalia. Looking about, I saw small pots used to hold the singing insects, large cages built of bamboo and wood, and small ones that resembled miniature birdcages. There were tubes constructed for keeping a cricket in your pocket and gourds that looked similar to the cage I had seen in *The Last Emperor.*

The young man dressed in a faded brown cotton padded jacket walked up to me and said in Chinese-sounding English, "You American?" He looked like he might be the grandson of the owner.

"Yes," I said, continuing to look at all the cricket cages.

"You know crickets kept purely for enjoyment of song since Tang Dynasty?" I knew that was a long time ago, but in spite of all the reading I had done on China, I didn't remember the span of years of the Tang Dynasty. As it turns out, it was 618–906 AD.

"No," I said, "I don't know much about Chinese crickets, except what I saw in a movie recently, and what I've have read in some Chinese poetry books about singing cricket chirps. It would be delightful to hear more about them."

The young man's face lit up, and he went on to tell me that the cricket culture in China goes back over 1,000 years, and includes both singing and fighting crickets. "Fighting crickets?" I exclaimed. He assured me that, indeed, cricket fighting was widespread in Shanghai and other parts of China. He thought that gambling was what made the sport so popular and certain types of fighting crickets so expensive.

He went on and on about various aspects of the Chinese cricket culture as I looked at all their wares for sale. Moving around the table, I noticed a large, round, plastic container with a lightbulb inside. As I got closer, I could see hundreds of small crickets inside. It was then I decided to buy one. The young boy had done his job; I was hooked.

First I picked out a small cage I could carry in my shirt pocket under my coat so the cricket wouldn't freeze. I selected a carved wooden one that was about the size of a package of cigarettes and was much like a Chinese puzzle. A piece across the base slid out, allowing a portion of the top to slide open. Under the sliding door was a piece of glass that also came out, allowing the cricket to be put inside. Once the piece across the back was installed, the box was tightly closed. The wooden lid could be left off to allow light into the cage. There was a small, honeycombed opening in the top of the box to allow air in and singing out.

Once I had picked out a cage, I walked over to the large container with the light inside. The bottom was strewn with toilet paper rolls and pieces of paper towel rolls. The old man reached inside and swiftly grabbed a small piece of the scrap, shaking several crickets into his palm. He looked at them, and like someone who was serious and knowledgeable about his job, lifted one of the throng and dropped it into the cage I had just selected. What a way to choose a new pet!

After paying the equivalent of less than three US dollars, I thanked the boy for taking the time to explain about cricket culture to me. I told him he had done well with his English. He seemed pleased at my comment and told me he had been studying English since age six. Every young person I met in China was learning English. How long will it be before there are more people in China that speak English than in any other country, including the United States?

I thanked him in Chinese and thought as I turned to leave, "*What do crickets eat?*" As if anticipating my question, the boy said, "Feed fresh fruit vegetable." Not a surprise, considering that's what almost everyone in China eats.

As I walked back out of the alley, I decided that the reason crickets are so popular in China was because they don't cost a lot, have no special food requirements, don't take up much space, and provide entertainment. In a land where pet cats and dogs are rare, the keeping of singing crickets is still regarded as an elegant hobby.

Wandering the streets is the best way to see Shanghai. I think a good traveler is one who does not know exactly where they're going. Many travelers to Shanghai travel on heated or air-conditioned buses that stop at the Shanghai Museum, Shanghai Opera House, or Longhua Temple, the biggest and oldest temple in Shanghai. They eat their meals with their fellow travelers at the favorite rendezvous of American travelers, consuming white bread and butter or donuts, just like back home. I skipped all that and instead just set out walking in a different direction from the Hengshang Hotel each time I was in Shanghai, and I always ate the local food. I think food ought to be tasted in its place of origin. What better place to find good Chinese food? The Chinese food in the United States was developed to fit American tastes, just as the French make their champagne sweeter for export to America.

Back on the main street, I walked past blocks of homes that were once occupied by the upper and middle classes before the Great Proletarian Cultural Revolution (1966–1976). One of the best books written about this period in Shanghai's history is by Nien Cheng. She lived in this part of Shanghai and survived the Cultural Revolution to write *Life and Death in Shanghai.* Back when this part of Shanghai was originally built, it was China's largest metropolis, and it provided a study in contradictions as the home of American, European, Russian, and Japanese imperialism in China before the Communists came to power. It was here in 1966 that Mao called on his Red Guard to begin the long nightmare of the Cultural Revolution, and that thousands of Red Guard youth translated into violent action the words of one of Mao's earlier writings from *Quotations from Chairman Mao Zedong.*

A revolution is not a dinner party, or writing an essay, or painting a picture, or doing embroidery; it cannot be so refined, so leisurely and gentle, so temperate, kind, courteous, restrained and magnanimous. A revolution is an insurrection, an act of violence by which one class overthrows another.[4]

As I walked down this serene old street in Shanghai, it was hard to believe that the terrible, violent periods of the Cultural Revolution ever happened.

Since the Communists came into power, there has always been a housing shortage in Shanghai. Many of the early agricultural reforms the Communists tried to implement didn't work out exactly as planned, and many peasants fled to China's larger cities. The migration has persisted for many different reasons, and thousands continue to find their way to Shanghai. The city is growing by leaps and bounds. So these once upper- and middle-class abodes I walked past now house many families. Many of the older sections of Shanghai are being demolished, with giant apartment buildings built all over the city. If the trend continues, one day Shanghai will be nothing but a city of ugly, tall cement-colored apartment houses and tourist hotels that surround areas waiting to be torn down.

After walking for several hours, I decided to return to the Hengshan Hotel. As I started back, I began thinking about what to name my new pet. *The Last Emperor* started playing in my head again, and I could see the little emperor at the time of his ascension to the Dragon Throne running around, saying, "Cricket, cricket, where's the cricket?" I decided to name my new buddy Pu Yi. The cricket would remain with me until I turned him loose in Hong Kong near the end of the trip. My second cricket is probably the only one of its kind to log about forty-eight thousand miles flying.

CHAPTER TWENTY-TWO

A SMALL, PLAIN HOUSE AND OTHER PLACES

China in the Twentieth Century - The Cultural Revolution

By 1966, Mao was ready to launch his largest campaign ever. With the army firmly in place behind him, he launched the Great Proletarian Cultural Revolution against the hacks he saw in the Communist Party: intellectuals, all things bourgeois, and everything old. The students, peasants, workers, and soldiers were the backbone of his revolution, but soon some became victims. The Cultural Revolution affected the whole country, and the number of those who committed suicide or were displaced or killed would be in the millions before it ended over ten years later. No one was safe, as you will see.

THE NEXT MORNING I got up early. Don and Mei had something to do so I was on my own for the day. I normally don't visit museums and such, but in reading about Shanghai I had noted several places I wanted to visit. Shanghai is a museum of the old and the new and that was what I wanted to see. As I was dressing, I glanced out of my window to take in what was happening in the park across the street. I saw a strange sight: there in the park was a long, straight line of Shanghai police officers with their pistols drawn and held at arm's length. An officer walked slowly down the line, looking at each man and checking to see if their arms were straight out and the pistols steady. The officer walked back and forth as everyone held the pose. It seemed like a bizarre form of *tai chi*, or part of a large dress rehearsal for a monster police raid. As I watched them, I wondered what possession of a firearm would get you. "*I must not ever forget that I am in China,*" I concluded as I locked my door and headed for the elevator.

When I got down to the lobby, I stopped to ask the old clerk a question. "I wish to go to the house where the Communist Party of China held their First National Congress," I said. In one of the books I was reading, I learned that the Communist Party was officially formed in Shanghai in 1921 somewhere in the old French Concession. I knew that the Hengshan Hotel was originally located in the old French Concession also.

"You want visit?"

"Yes, could you please write address in my book?"

"I no write English."

"No, no, I want you to write First National Congress house in Chinese right here." I pointed to a page in my little book where I had written a few keywords.

"All cab know where is."

"Yes, but sometimes it is difficult to talk to cab drivers because their English isn't very good and they don't know where I want to go."

"Okay, I write."

When I arrived, the building was swarming with Chinese tourists; it must be one of the sites that all Chinese visit when they come to Shanghai. The small, plain house where the First National Congress of the Communist Party of China (CPC) was held had been rebuilt and didn't look like the picture I had seen. Like so much of China's past, it had a new, shiny look. The area around the building was also under development, which made the rebuilt house seem even more out of place.

The large rebuilt facility is located where the 1920s house of one of the members of the Shanghai Communist Group once stood. In those days, it was located on Rue Wantz in the old French Concession. As I walked in with the crowd of Chinese tourists, the feeling of the old house, the one that was once there, had gotten lost. The present structure was just another tourist stop, but I decided to take a look anyway.

I saw the reconstructed meeting room of the First National Congress of the CPC. There was a wooden table with stools all around and, as for every meeting in China, tea things. There doesn't seem to be agreement on what month in 1921 the first Congress was held. Mao recounts May, but other accounts say it was held in July, but there is no doubt that in a building like this one, a group of urban intellectuals representing the various Marxist study groups met. Two of the founding members of the CPC were not present. There was one foreigner present, a left-wing socialist named Maring, who represented the Comintern. It was the Russians, not Mao, who were the driving force behind forming the CCP. There is a story of intrigue associated with the meeting. A suspicious person appeared on the evening of the fourth day. The meeting was promptly adjourned for fear they'd be arrested by the French police. On the following day, they resumed the meeting aboard a pleasure junk on a local lake, and I'll bet they had a tea service. One of the outcomes of the Congress was an agreement on cooperation between the fifty-three-member CCP and the Kuomintang under Sun Yat-sen. A disaster was in the making, but Moscow was behind Sun's

Nationalist movement, which the Western powers shunned like the plague.

The building housed documents and pictures of China's long revolutionary struggle. As I walked through, I saw pictures of Sun Yat-sen presiding over one of the dozens of cabinets that tried to form a new government. After reading about his efforts, I just don't think China can ever be a Western-style democracy though Sun Yat-sen and a score of others tried hard to make it happen. There were pictures taken on May 4, 1919, of the "patriotic" students demonstrating in Tiananmen Square against the Treaty of Versailles. The picture made me think about the students who demonstrated in Tiananmen Square in 1989. Why was the May 4th demonstration so different? I have concluded that the people were behind the students in 1919 and not fully behind the students in 1989. The government gets to say which is a "patriotic student demonstration" and which a "counter-revolutionary rebellion."

As I made my way through the facility, I came across a crowd looking at a map displayed for the purpose of showing "how China was carved up by the imperialist powers." When I walked up and viewed the map I got an uneasy feeling; there was a large bald eagle with the Philippines in its talons. I had the same feeling once, long ago, when I visited Hiroshima in Japan and had people just stare at me as they walked past. On the map, there was a bear standing astride of northern China and a frog (representing France) sitting on Vietnam, and a lion (England) stood near Hong Kong. There was a hot, rising sun over the islands of Japan. I couldn't read the Chinese characters on the map, but I got the message. The Americans, Russians, French, British, and Japanese were all responsible for what happened in China before 1949.

"You American?" an older man in the group asked.

I nodded.

"What do you think of map?" he asked.

"It is historically accurate," I said as I smiled and walked away. I didn't think talking to anyone in China about anything political was a good idea.

In this emporium depicting China under the rule of imperialism, feudalism, and capitalism, America doesn't get top billing. I guess a few Chinese still see America as it was before 1950 when we were always at China's side with talk of democracy, Christianity, dollars, military bases, guns, and advice. I'm sure many Chinese still think we don't have a nickel's worth of history and that many of the things Mao said about us are true. I understood not everyone's *Quotations from Chairman Mao Tse-Tung* had been trashed. The incident with the crowd around the map convinced me that it was time to see some other sights around Shanghai.

Shanghai is not a city of first-rate monuments and historical sites, but there were several other places I wanted to visit, so I got out my Shanghai map and headed for Sun Yat-sen's one-time residence.

The walk to Sun's residence took me past a park that looked inviting. I looked on my map and found out that it was Fuxing Park. The very clean parks in China are wonderful places to visit. Walking past Marx and Engels etched in stone I passed a couple dancing. As in the park across the street from my hotel, I saw people stretching, walking, dancing, eating lunch, or practicing martial arts.

Further into the park I spotted a person doing calligraphy, using a large mop-type paintbrush to write characters on the old concrete walkway. His "ink" was water, so his work slowly disappeared in the sunshine. In Chinese culture, good writing is an art form, and you don't need to know Chinese to appreciate it. From where I stood, it looked like disappearing abstract art. As I stood watching him make a long series of bold fluid strokes, he looked up, smiled, and said, "Happiness."

I stopped to watch two old men play chess for a while and concluded that the rules of the game are the same in China. After they had finished their long game, one of the men motioned to me as if to ask me if I would like to play. I accepted and took his friend's place on the wooden bench. I hadn't played for a while but remembered an opening move that some chess players fall for. Luck was with me; he didn't counter my opening. The move was basic, and he didn't think it would be a short game. He was in checkmate in nothing flat. His friend laughed heartily, and I felt bad knowing he would rib him for some time for not seeing such an amateur opening. I bowed, shook hands and thanked them both and headed for Sun Yat-sen's residence before I got asked to play again.

Sun Yat-sen is famous for helping overthrow the Qing (Manchu) Dynasty (1644–1911 AD). His house was purchased by a group of Chinese in Canada and was Sun's residence from 1919 until 1924. I had always thought that Sun had admired and studied America's style of government as a model for his country and wondered why China celebrated him now as the father of China's revolution. During the period, he lived in the house he "reformed" the Kuomintang and entered into an agreement with the Communist Party of China. Maring, the foreigner present at the First National Congress, brokered the deal. The West had refused to help Sun, and he began to see that Great Britain and America were no better than Japan when it came to exploiting China. Sun accepted Russian help—their foot was in the door. Sun dispatched Chiang Kai-shek to Russia for training, which didn't make the CPC happy and the snowball that was to grow into a civil war started its long roll downhill. Sun died in 1925, and Chiang could never get Sun's Three Principals of the People and his National Revolution off the ground. The farsighted father of China's Republic was to go down in history praised by the Communists and forgotten in the West.

The next place on my list was the People's Park. The Communists constructed it out of the northern half of Shanghai's old racetrack, and they built the People's Square out of the southern half. The racetrack was in an area known as the International Settlement, quite a distance from where I was, so I decided to head for the hotel and visit the People's Park and Square on my next outing.

As I said earlier, I'm not much for museums but had come to think of Shanghai itself as a museum of the old and new. In a museum you can't see bizarre *tai chi* (holding pistols), a frog sitting on Vietnam,

Marx and Engels watching a couple dancing, disappearing calligraphy, or Sun Yat-sen's house.

CHAPTER TWENTY-THREE

HAVING NOODLES WITH MR. WEN

China in the Twentieth Century - Lao She

Like many Chinese citizens abroad, Lao She returned to China in 1949 to participate in the new society that promised freedom and equality to all.

Lao She was a great contemporary writer and the author of many books and plays, including the novel Rickshaw Boy and the play Teahouse. Lao was sixty-seven in the summer of 1966. That summer he had to attend a gathering in the Great Hall of the People where a mass meeting was being held to denounce China's two top leaders, Liu Shaochi, and Deng Xiaoping.

Little did Lao She know that before long he also would be labeled an arch-reactionary by Mao's Red Guards, beaten, and tortured. He chose suicide or was "suicided" like so many of his countrymen.

AS ON MY past trips, the boatyard sent a vehicle to Shanghai to pick Don, Mei, and me up at the Hengshan Hotel. Mr. Wen and a driver arrived right on time in a small work van that looked as if it had not been washed since the last time I saw it. We piled in with our bags. One of my bags contained the junk's main power panel and battery selector panel, which I had brought over on the plane as carry-on luggage. The small van eased into the cold morning traffic of Shanghai and headed for Changshu.

Mei, Mr. Wen, and the driver immediately broke into a long, animated conversation. I said to Don, "I wonder what all the discussion is about."

He said, "Christ, the previous day we got in a cab, and she talked to the driver for ten minutes about the fare and the route he would take before she would let him leave." Their conversation continued almost unending as we slowly moved through Shanghai's clogged streets.

It is hard to imagine the early morning traffic in Shanghai unless you have experienced it. This is a city of almost twenty-four million people. That morning it seemed as if they were all out walking or riding on bicycles, mopeds, motorcycles, or in cars, buses and trucks, forming a tumultuous mass of slow-moving humanity.

Don continued, "After we finally left, we hadn't gone far when the cab pulled over to the curb, and the driver shouted something to Mei and then jumped out and ran back towards an intersection we had just gone through. I asked Mei what the hell was wrong, and she said the driver had made a 'driving slipup.' He had evidently entered the intersection late, and the policeman directing traffic waved him over as he passed the center of the intersection. The police made him stand there and wait about five minutes before they talked to him. They then looked at his license, gave him a stern lecture, and sent him on his way. When he returned to the cab, he was visibly shaken. He said, 'They almost took my license! Without it can't drive for a living.'"

I said, "It seems Chinese justice is swift. Remember our first trip over? They caught a bunch of guys trafficking drugs in Shanghai. They had the trial a few days after they were captured, found them guilty, and shot all of them on the day the trial ended. The government even sent the families a bill for the bullets."

As we rolled along headed toward Changshu, it was obvious that the streets and highways in and around Shanghai were undergoing a massive upgrade. I saw many large-scale road construction projects using vast numbers of workers, with few if any pieces of road-building equipment. It appeared similar to what I visualized if they built a flat Great Wall of China because their construction methods haven't changed much since then. When the infrastructure around Shanghai including the port is finally finished, I predict this area will one day eclipse Hong Kong as the business and financial center of China. Hong Kong will slowly fade in importance to become just another tourist destination along the coast.

In Changshu, as in past trips, we stayed at the Yushan Hotel. Upon arriving, Don said he and Mei would meet me at the boatyard in the late morning, so I was on my own to get there. I asked Mei to ask Mr. Wen if he would meet me at the bus station the next morning at seven o'clock. Mr. Wen smiled broadly at me and held up a hand signal to show that he understood the message.

The next morning, early, I went upstairs to the restaurant in the hotel to have breakfast. The dining room was almost empty when I arrived; all the servers were standing in a group talking to each other. They paid me no attention as I walked across the dining room and chose a table next to a window that looked out over the front of the hotel. As I sat down, I thought to myself, "*It looks chilly outside; I'll have a Chinese breakfast. Service must still be thought of as bourgeois idea,*" I thought as a young waitress finally showed up to take my order. "*Yingwen?*" I said in bad Chinese, to see if she spoke English. She shook her head no. I reached in my coat pocket and got out my book of short Chinese sentences and thumbed through it until I found, "Please bring *congee* breakfast." I set the book down so she could read it and pointed at the statement in Chinese characters. She scribbled something down, and before she could dart away to the kitchen, I said, "Thank you" in Chinese. I waited some more until she arrived with my standard Chinese breakfast, consisting of a bowl of *congee*, fermented tofu, cooked greens, a *baozi*, and green tea. Since first having a Chinese breakfast at the Hengshan Hotel in Shanghai, I had developed a taste for it. Let me warn you, this breakfast takes getting used to.

I peered down and noticed a group of pedicab drivers standing in front of the hotel. They formed a tight circle of worn padded jackets, talking and smoking cigarettes while they waited for customers. "*That might be a fun way to get to the bus station on a cold morning,*" I contemplated as I ate my breakfast.

After breakfast, I stopped at the front desk to speak with Mr. Li, who I knew could speak some English, to inquire about a pedicab.

As I walked up to the counter, I said, "Mr. Li, could you find out for me what the fare is for a pedicab ride to the bus station?" I knew it was unlikely that any of the drivers spoke English.

"Mr. Walt, you stay here, I find for you." He rushed around the counter and out the front door.

I pondered as I watched him through the front window of the hotel talking to the pedicab drivers, "*Why are they having such a long, heated conversation about the fare to the bus station?*"

Sometime later he came back in and said, "I don't know how you say, but fare not same for me-you."

"You mean because I am bigger and heavier the fare is more?" I replied.

"No, it's you foreigner and me Chinese," he said.

"That's not right!," I said to myself. I got the fare, said thanks to Mr. Li, and walked out the front door of the hotel on my way to the bus station. I don't want to know what the pedicab drivers said to each other as I walked past them that morning, but I'll bet it was some nasty Chinese. After this incident, I never rode a pedicab.

One of the pleasures of visiting China is walking along the streets early in the morning with the masses. As I headed toward the bus station, the city was bustling with activity and the thoroughfares were full of people. The girls in front of me held hands on their way to school—I noticed all over China that women and girls walk hand in hand, or with one arm around the other's shoulder. Many older women were out buying vegetables from the vendors along the street: the family unit includes retired family members, and they stay home and watch the kids and do the shopping. Healthy, active seniors, are something you will see wherever you go. I passed a small teahouse just past a curved, stone bridge that was built long, long ago. Outside were older men talking and drinking tea. Each had brought his small birdcage, and all the birds were singing. They all stopped talking and gawked at me as I walked past. The Chinese seem to enjoy staring at foreigners. I tried not to be offended by the practice but never got used to it. However, I did learn that offering a smile will get you the same in return. The smells of cooking seemed to follow me down the street.

From time to time on the way to the bus station, I would stop and buy a snack from a street vendor. Sometimes it was the "deep-fried devils." Sometimes it was *baozi.* The street vendors would have round bamboo containers filled with *baozi* stacked tall, forming a chimney with steam pouring out the top. The buns in the stack gave off a slightly yeasty smell.

When I arrived at the bus station, it was bustling with people going to work; buses were coming and going and parked everywhere, but our bus was always in the same spot. I headed in that direction, looking around for Mr. Wen. He would ride his bicycle from home and leave it at the old gray bus station with hundreds of other black bicycles that all looked alike. How he managed to find his, I do not know. I met Mr. Wen as he was parking his bicycle. We walked over to where the bus was parked, got on, and took our seats. The bus, about the size of a small school bus, had a well-used look and apparently didn't get washed except when it rained, but never on the inside. Chinese buses are built for Chinese-size passengers, period: my head always touched the ceiling if I was standing, and the bench seats made me feel as if I were sitting at a child's school desk.

This morning, like almost every other morning, the passengers on the bus were talking loud and fast and smoking cigarette after cigarette. As I ate my share of the snacks and waited to leave I thought, "*Mr. Wen must explain the same story over and over about what I am doing with him sitting on this bus.*" Every few minutes, the bus driver would stand outside screeching the destination, and we would wait until he had enough passengers to leave.

The bus ride was a rush. I loved to sit behind the driver and look down the road as we raced along, honking and dodging bicyclists, other vehicles, and pedestrians. He drove as recklessly as Mr. Kamikaze had on my first trip to China. When he got to a little downhill grade, he would kick the transmission out of gear and let the bus coast to save gas.

I looked at all the other passengers, and they looked at me. As we sped down the narrow road, the ancient scenery rushed past my window. It was winter and awfully cold on the bus, but no one seemed to notice but me. A young woman got sick and vomited out the window, but no one paid the slightest attention and everyone just kept right on talking and smoking. "*Is it all right to stare at foreigners, but not sick fellow passengers?*" The constant din of the engine didn't seem to bother anyone, and I soon got used to it. After roughly a half hour, we reached our destination. In getting off, the other passengers waved good-bye to us before they rushed off to work. We started walking toward the boatyard.

Mr. Wen and I would sometimes grab a bowl of noodles and pork at a small noodle shop on our way to the boatyard. He would motion with his head toward the noodle shop, asking in a silent way, "Want to stop for noodles?" I would respond by nodding my head, "Yes." Going into the small restaurant, I would hand him some *renminbi* (people's currency) to pay for the noodles.

While he went to the counter to order, I would grab an empty table. I noticed that all the other customers were looking at me. I sat there quietly doing nothing, looking back at the other customers. I started thinking, "*This is* wei wu wei." I had learned the idea of *wei wu wei*, an ancient Taoist concept, on an earlier trip to China from a young man who spoke a bit of English. *Wei wu wei* means "to do without doing," or "to act without action." Could just sitting quietly and doing nothing in a Chinese noodle shop be *wei wu wei*?

The silence was broken when Mr. Wen returned with two large bowls of noodles and chopsticks. I picked up the chopsticks and dove into the bowl of noodles like the Chinese do. "*I'm going to beat him this morning,*" I thought as I held the bowl up near my mouth and attacked the contents. The other customers watched to see how I did. Everyone's breath was visible as they ate because it was so damn cold. I almost beat Mr. Wen in annihilating the huge bowl of noodles, but he could spit out the unwanted parts (pork bones) onto the tabletop faster than I could. In just a few minutes we finished, stood up, and left everything on the table. After we got up to leave, a young girl in an apron that needed changing a week ago rushed over. She picked up the bowls and chopsticks, and with broad strokes with a soiled rag brushed all the excess pork parts onto the floor. The table was ready for the next customer—truly fast food.

Ahead of me, Mr. Wen strode down the street toward the boatyard, and tugging on my gloves, I walked fast to catch up. On the way, we saw others walking on both sides of the road. "*It seems like, in China, everyone goes to work,*" I mused. We walked and walked, and the town street turned to a dirt road in the countryside. Only a short distance from town we were hiking along the sides of fields that looked as if nothing had changed in hundreds of years. Since we couldn't talk to each other, I had time to look and think.

All along the road were fields planted with grass-like Chinese greens. I had eaten these many times and assumed it was one of the few crops that could grow in such cold weather.

I thought to myself as we walked along together, "*Spring comes, and things grow (*wei wu wei*).*" As we arrived at the boatyard a thought came to mind about the trip that morning: miraculous power and wonderful activity–riding a bus, eating noodles, and walking down a road in China.

CHAPTER TWENTY-FOUR

SEEING THE JUNK FOR THE FIRST TIME

China in the Twentieth Century - Deng Xiaoping is Persecuted

Mao's colleagues, who had needed to implement policies to correct the disaster and suffering caused by his Great Leap Forward, fell on hard times. In 1966, Deng was purged as a "capitalist roader." In 1969, he was sent away to work in a tractor factory. For years, he waited and walked along a curved dirt path to get to work. His son, Deng Pufang, was taken prisoner and beaten badly by young Red Guard students trying to get him to tell lies about his father. He did not die but has spent his life in a wheelchair from the injuries received during the Cultural Revolution.

AS MR. WEN and I approached the front gate of the boatyard, it looked as if nothing had changed in the past two hundred years, much less since my last trip five months ago. When we went through the ancient front gate, I noticed a faded red star over the top of the gate. Walking in I said *"Ni hao"* (it's "hello" and sounds like "knee-how") to the old man in the wooden guard shack. He smiled broadly and responded with a drawn-out reply I didn't understand. I gave him a big smile and just kept walking.

As we had always done in the past, we stopped at the two-story office building to say hello and have a cup of tea. We climbed the outside stairs to the second story where the offices were. I looked around and did not see the junk. As we walked in, Mr. Tao and a few of the boatyard people were talking and sipping tea. After greeting those in the room, I made myself a cup and walked out on the landing to see if I could locate the junk. Mr. Tao saw me looking and pointing across the boatyard said, "It over behind big building."

I looked but couldn't see anything but the sunshade behind the building. I wanted to run right down and look at the boat, but decided not to appear rushed, so I slowed down by having another cup of tea and talking with Mr. Tao about several matters related to the project. After what seemed like an eternity, he finally suggested we go down and take a look at the junk.

We walked across the boatyard where a variety of wooden fishing boats were being repaired. The work going on was the same type of work that had been done here for generations using the same old tools. I saw large trees that may have come from America being hand-sawed into lumber. China doesn't have many trees left after building things out of wood for thousands of years, and Mao's insane plan to make steel in backyard smelters consumed thousands of trees for fuel.

Clear across the yard, behind a big, unpainted metal building, the junk sat under an enormous makeshift canopy. The roof of the cover was supported by long bamboo poles about four inches in diameter lashed together with rope; the roof frame was also made out of lashed bamboo poles. The covering was an assortment of different-width boards and pieces of canvas. The edge of the roof stuck out unevenly all around and was, without doubt, constructed to keep the junk out of the sun, not the rain. The partially completed vessel looked beautiful sitting there atop a wide variety of old, bent, fifty-gallon drums and wooden support structures. On top of each metal drum was a small pile of wooden pieces stacked up to fit the contour of the hull. I was amazed that such a large vessel could be held up on what appeared to be junkyard leftovers. *Wow, it's big and solid,* I thought. I noticed several workers aboard working on the aft deck as I walked around and around the junk. Scaffolding was attached to the large bamboo poles that supported the roof and went around the sides of the junk. Leaning against one side was an old, rough, handmade wooden ladder. I stood there looking up at enormous vessel. "*How fantastic the junk looks; it's so solid and massive.*"

Following Mr. Tao, I scurried up the rickety wooden ladder to the main deck forward. We ambled around looking over the completed work. At this stage of construction, they had finishing planking the outer hull and had installed the forward part of the main deck. I carefully walked around and looked down into the holds and at the partially completed pilothouse. The holds were originally intended to carry ice and fish, way back when the junk was designed to be a fishing boat. From the minute I stepped on board, I had a good feeling about how the junk was coming together. To my relief and satisfaction, the *Mei Wen Ti* was becoming enough of a reality that I could walk around on it. My examination of the partially completed pilothouse was interrupted when Mr. Tao announced, "Time for meeting."

In addition to seeing the junk, the main purpose of the trip was to discuss any problems, all the documentation, and the parts situation. When Mr. Tao and I arrived back at the main offices of the boatyard, small crowds were standing around having tea and chatting.

Don was eating a banana and chatting with Mei. Professor Ru, Mr. Wen, Mr. Chao, Mr. Li, and several others from the boatyard were in a group talking. I got a cup of tea and then walked around greeting everyone.

As I approached Professor Ru, he said, "What you think of junk?"

"It looked great. I'm pleased with the workmanship and plan to spend more time looking it over." He translated what I said, and everybody smiled. The Chinese sometimes give you the answer they think will please you, not the one in their heart. My brief answer was from the heart, for they had earned my praise. In this game of face, it is given, taken away, earned, or lost.

After more tea, the meeting got started. They had the latest copies of everything that Mr. Ru had translated into Chinese. Also, all of Larry Drake's drawings were on the table, as well as a Yanmar marine diesel manual I had sent over. Alongside all the English on Larry's drawings and in several sections of the Yanmar manual, Mr. Ru had written thousands of Chinese characters. So, now we had Chinese drawings and parts lists of all the main systems on the junk as well as some sections of the Yanmar engine manual in Chinese. I worked with them almost all morning resolving problems and answering questions. I felt more comfortable now that questions are being asked. We were building a relationship of trust.

Since the construction of the junk was moving right along, there was a lot of curiosity about the status of the parts I was supplying.

"The first shipment of about ninety-five percent of the parts will arrive in Shanghai soon from Hong Kong," I said, as I handed Mr. Ru a list of all the parts that were in the shipment. As part of preparing the parts for shipment, I had the parts supplier mark and package them according to the system on the junk where they would be used. In other words, all the parts for the freshwater system would be in boxes marked with 'Freshwater.' I did this so the parts would not arrive in boxes all mixed up.

"I am going down to Hong Kong for several days after our meetings to take care of some business associated with the Yanmar engines, see a bit of Hong Kong, and go to the Canton Trade Fair. I will get a delivery schedule and a set of Yanmar engine manuals printed in Chinese."

We went over several questions related to the engine cooling system. I was having difficulty getting them to understand how the engine cooling system worked, so I was glad when it was time to break for lunch. We had the meal at the restaurant where we normally ate, not far from the boatyard.

After lunch, we finished with the engine cooling system and began a discussion of the China Classification Society's Test Document. This document would be used to test the junk once construction was completed. The test document is a requirement of the Chinese government and is written in Chinese, so I didn't have much to say about it. We talked specifically about the tests that I had requested be added when I was in Suzhou on my second trip to China. I was satisfied that the junk would be suitably tested before it was shipped, as they had added all the tests I had requested.

Through the rest of the afternoon, we discussed various matters related to the project. I said I wanted to break early to spend some more time looking at the junk, and I told them I had noticed something while looking earlier that I needed to investigate. We adjourned the meeting, and all walked down to the junk.

When we arrived, we found a small group of kindergarten-age children gathered around the bow with their teacher. I asked Mr. Tao what the teacher was telling the children, and he said, "She telling them China used many thousands of boats similar to this one for coastal trade and fishing a thousand years ago."

We went aboard and examined the pilothouse. Having looked it over earlier, I was already aware there were several problems. "*This is going to have to be modified,*" I thought as I walked around the area. "*I*

need to ask them to raise part of the floor and then raise the roof to improve visibility from the helm. This reminds me of the Chinese bus where my head hit the ceiling." The ladder into the pilothouse from the main deck was already built. "*The stairs are too close together and too narrow for my long legs and big feet.*" I didn't want to ask them to build the ladder over, but I did ask them to add an extension to the back of each step to make them wider. This was agreed to, and we decided to meet the next day at eight o'clock.

When I got back to the Yushan Hotel that evening, I began drafting a trip report to capture all the things we had discussed and the decisions we had made, such as improving visibility from the pilothouse. The main elements of the report would be incorporated into the latest revision of the design requirements.

When I got there the next morning, the table was covered with drawings and parts lists Larry Drake had prepared. We spent the morning with Mr. Ru and various personnel from the boatyard going over issues they had regarding the drawings and matching the drawings to the parts list. During the construction, I often saw these dog-eared drawings down on the boat being used by the workmen; they eventually became charred with cigarette burns and stained with a variety of food droppings, tea splatters, and dirt.

These conversations continued for days until we had covered all the parts lists and every drawing in detail. We identified some new parts they wanted me to supply. Most of the discussion was to educate those who would direct the installation of the parts. I looked at this as building a relationship of trust.

Every day I tried to spend at least an hour on the junk. It was fun to see the daily progress on the hull. We spent a whole day going over the planned physical location of such things as the two water heaters, the sinks, a nd the toilet. In the process, we revised th e planned location of a few things for easier installation or maintenance.

As the week progressed, we decided to spend one whole day going over the entire electrical system. The boatyard electrician was a young man who came to the meeting well prepared. I had sent the boatyard detailed electrical requirements, including sketches of the two power panels. Mr. Ru had translated the document into Chinese, and from these electrical requirements, the Chinese prepared electrical drawings. He proudly laid the drawings out for us to look at. They were covered with Chinese characters, but there was no problem understanding them because direct current (DC) and alternating current (AC) work the same way all over the world.

The main power panel and battery selector panel I had brought to the meeting were now set up on a table for all to see. The design and construction of the two pieces had cost nearly four thousand dollars, and God only knows how many hours of my time. The excellent design and workmanship showed, and I was proud of the end product.

We proceeded page by page through the documentation and drawings, making sure the Chinese translations of the English front panel engravings were correct for each circuit. The main power panel was constructed with a large terminal board section in the rear, so all the Chinese electricians had to do was wire each independent circuit to the right terminals. The young electrician had no trouble understanding the design, and it turned out they also had no trouble with any of the electrical system. I think this was because he was an excellent electrician, and because so much work had gone into the design and fabrication of the panels. The first parts shipment would contain all the various sizes of wire, wire lugs, crimping tools, etc. for the entire electrical system on the junk.

We went down to the junk and talked about the physical location for the two power panels and all the batteries. The forward part of the main deck was planked but going aft; it was necessary to walk on planks. The main deck planking on the junk was pine. They called the wood *sha-mu,* and they used large amounts of it in the boatyard. After our discussion, I stayed on the junk for a while, watching the workmen going about their duties.

From the main deck, I could look down and see an older man planing wood. His plane was a long, old, wooden-style with the blade inserted on an angle into the body. He had been there every day working on a large pile of teak planks that would eventually be used to cover the pine planking on the main deck.

Down inside the junk, two men were caulking one of the transverse bulkheads that separated the junk into six watertight compartments below the main deck. Large heavy timbers had been used to construct the partition; I believe the light-colored wood was laurel. Their job was to fill the cracks between the planks with caulking. With their hands, they pressed the soft white caulking compound onto long strands of hemp. I had visited the small shop on the boatyard where a man made the caulking compound out of a combination of lime and *tung* oil, using a homemade mechanical device that did the mixing. The strands of caulk-covered hemp were then pounded into the cracks. The caulkers used the head on the back of a small ax and a metal caulking tool to pound the hemp in.

Notice the Chinese carpenter's hammer in his hand. When I look at this picture, I wonder if it doesn't represent what Marco Polo saw in his travels to China during the reign of the Yuan Dynasty (1280–1368 AD), otherwise known as the Mongol.

CHAPTER TWENTY-FIVE

THE EIGHT IMMORTALS AND OTHER GODS

China in the Twentieth Century - No One Was Safe

Mao's chosen replacement, Liu Shaochi, was thrown in prison where, without medical treatment, he died. Lin Biao, the Defense Minister, took over as Mao's successor. Peng Dehuai, who had said that the Great Leap Forward had brought starvation, was put in prison and began a long death—he lasted until 1974. Even old Emperor Pu Yi was persecuted as he lay in a hospital bed in Beijing dying of cancer.

In all of China, no one was safe. Every school in China saw atrocities. After the schools were smashed, the Red Guards fanned out against certain people in the Communist Party, intellectuals, and all things bourgeois, and they destroyed everything old. Looting, killing, and torture were commonplace in every city and town. Even the army was not exempt from Mao's purge.

THE NEXT MORNING was our last day before going back to Shanghai. I spent some time in the office going over some questions. When we finished, I ask Mr. Tao if we could go over and look at the furniture in the old building near the junk where they were constructing all the furniture for the project. The design requirements did not detail the furniture, but only outlined the type. For example: "A four-foot-by-seven-foot berth is built-in with large storage drawers below." It was up to the Chinese to design the piece to fit in each location mentioned in the requirements.

When we walked into the building, which I was sure was over a hundred years old, it was apparent this is where they did all their lofting work. "Lofting" means taking the drawings of a boat and reproducing them full-size on a loft floor, in this case, the building floor. The shapes for making the wood patterns for the keel, frames and anything else can be taken off from the lofted lines.

There was a lone cabinet and furniture maker working in a small area of the large building creating the furniture for the junk. Sunlight made little spots here and there on the floor. The worker was busy building a drawer for the small desk-and-bookcase unit when we walked in.

All his tools were well-used, old-style hand tools. The craftsmanship was a bit crude, but the work I saw looked well-designed and strong. All the furniture designs were plain. The drawers opened by reaching under the front of the drawer; there were no knobs.

As we walked around, we came across a pile of wooden panels that had been cut out in an intricate Chinese pattern. The cutout panels would be used in the construction of the lights to be installed inside the junk.

The idea for the light covers came from my trip to Beijing: during the trip to the Forbidden City, I took a picture of a wonderful old Chinese cutout window panel. When I was putting the detailed requirements together, I remembered the beautiful window pattern and decided to incorporate it in the design of the inside lights. The panel design in the specifications was much simpler than the fine-looking one in the photograph.

Not far away, stacked next to a wall, were sixteen carved wooden panels about two-foot square. The top panel had a sword carved on it. I looked at the next panel, and it was a basket of flowers. But there was nothing in the design that called for sixteen carved panels.

"What are these carved panels for?" I ask Mr. Tao.

He talked to the man making the furniture for a while and then said, "They are for decoration. They are not for something."

"Where on the boat are they going to be installed?"

After more discussion with the furniture worker, Mr. Tao explained that eight of the panels would be installed along each side of the junk for decoration beneath the hand railing, which would run around the aft portion of the junk on the main deck.

"What do they depict?"

"Depict?"

"Yes, what do they portray, or better, what do they show?"

After a long discussion Mr. Tao said, "It like old fairy story about the Eight Immortals which I not know or never hear. He from Shanghai and I have hard time understanding. I ask him write down for you. He say story about old Eight Immortals."

The man working on the furniture wrote out rows and rows of Chinese characters and then handed me the small slip of paper. I thanked him and put the "fairy story" in my journal with the intention of learning what it all meant later.

The wooden panels would be added to the junk for decoration, but also because there is a long tradition of beliefs and superstitions associated with Chinese culture, and specifically with fishing boats and junks. They had already installed a wood panel with a carved dragon, a benevolent spirit associated with rain and water, and clouds on each side of the bow. I found out the dragon has always been of immense importance to fisherman and seamen. In addition to the panels on the junk, I saw many statues and small altars in homes and businesses I visited. The Communists have attempted to stamp out all religion, old gods, beliefs, and superstitions, but I think they have, for the most part, failed.

The deity I saw most in China was Kuan Yin, the Goddess of Mercy. When I first went to visit Mei's parents, before they moved into their new apartment, I saw a statue of her on top of an old piece of screen-covered furniture used for holding fresh food. Like one of the family, she got moved to the new apartment. She is maybe one of the most revered supernatural beings in China and has many recognized functions and supporters. I learned she is mainly associated with compassion, love, and mercy, and is thought to protect women and children, so is therefore also thought of as a fertility goddess. I'll bet through the centuries she has heard millions of "Please bring us a boy" prayers. (Maybe it is Kuan Yin and not abortions that has caused there to be more men than women in China. Looking at past population growth figures, she has been doing a superb job since "liberation"). She is also seen as the champion of the poor, sick, and unfortunate. I saw her statue in the restaurant near the boatyard, so she must also protect fishermen and those who make a living on boats.

Earlier in the story, I told you about seeing Kuan Yin in a teahouse where I had stopped to have a cup of tea one day, as I was on my way to meet Mr. Wen at the bus station. I think among businesspeople, she is looked upon as a goddess of luck and fortune. I told you the story about how she is given credit for having caused China's first tea plants to grow to help Buddhists stay awake while meditating, and concluded that she is the one responsible for "all the tea in China." So now maybe you can understand why there are so many statues of Kuan Yin and why she is one of the most revered supernatural beings in China, with many recognized functions, and millions of supporters.

The next deity who was well-represented everywhere I went (mainly in kitchens) was the kitchen god Zao Jun. They say he is stationed in the house all year to observe the conduct of the family and then report to Heaven. Once a year, on the twenty-third day of the twelfth lunar month, right before the beginning of the Chinese New Year, he returns to Heaven to give his report on the family to the head god, Yu Huang. This god is not well known in the Western world, but in Chinese Heaven he is the "head honcho"; the kitchen god is only a member of his celestial administration.

That is why, in any Chinatown at the New Year, you find paper pictures of the kitchen god, paper money, and other offerings that are burnt by the family to give him a royal send-off and ensure a favorable report on the family. Firecrackers blast away the negativity from the area to help his celestial ascent. After the magnificent send-off, a new copy is put up; if there is a statue the family will clean it. You will learn what follows later on when you read about the Chinese New Year celebration in Chapter Twenty-Nine.

The last deity I will tell you about is Lu Pan, the carpenter god. I didn't see pictures or statues of him but read he is the favorite of those involved in carpentry and boatbuilding. Since I was soon to own a wooden Chinese boat that might be surrounded by a multitude of spirits (both good and bad), I figured it wouldn't do any harm to make friends with the god of woodworking and shipbuilding.

When the missionaries arrived in China, the enormous pantheon of gods must have seemed totally preposterous and beyond blasphemous. The long menu of deities were aided by a vast array of supernatural creatures, such as dragons, fairies, and natural creatures, such as the tiger and crane; this must surely have convinced the Westerners everyone was going to be blasted by firecrackers straight to Hell. But the Chinese people's lively superstitions remain in spite of all the work of the missionaries and the Communist campaigns against old beliefs and superstitions. A system where the gods can be bribed, flattered, or even cheated seems to fit well in a country where capitalism and Communism are good buddies.

After finishing our inspection of the furniture, we headed back to the office. Walking across the boatyard, I looked over toward the junk and witnessed a man standing at the bow, on top of a drum, waving his arm as if conducting an orchestra. We were too far away to see exactly what he was doing, but as we approached, I realized he was painting a picture on the bow—the head of a large South China tiger.

When we got back to the office, I picked up my notebook, said goodbye to everyone, and headed back to Shanghai. With part of the day off, I decided to take my cricket Pu Yi and do a little shopping before leaving for Guangzhou and the Canton Trade Fair: I wanted to buy myself something as a reminder of Shanghai. I left the hotel with the intention of catching a cab to the downtown area when I remembered seeing a shelf of old teapots and other things in the little shop across the street from the hotel where I had purchased my chop. So I changed plans.

I ambled into the small shop and found the shopkeeper sitting in the back. He recognized me as soon as I walked in. He set down his teacup, got up from his chair, and came toward the front of the store with a broad smile on his face.

"Welcome back my humble store. Please, you come have tea," he said as he motioned toward the back. I followed him through the narrow aisles to his small office area, which contained a small wooden desk and two chairs; a small cast-iron stove with a crooked chimney sat in the corner. An old dented pot with a spout sat on the stove.

"Please, you sit," he gestured with a big smile, pointing to an old-fashioned Chinese chair. It was a little short for me, the bottom was flat, and the back was straight. I found it most uncomfortable.

"I stopped in to look at your old teapots."

"First have tea," he said. He dropped a small amount into a cup and filled it with hot water from a tall, well-worn metal thermos. When he returned, he said it was better to relax and have a cup of tea and then talk business. It reminded me of the time I was in the Chinese Embassy in Los Angeles before my first trip to China. One of the business attachés invited me into the back to have a cup of tea.

"Americans are always in a hurry," the attaché had said. "It is better to have a cup of tea and visit first. When you go to China, try to slow down and remember this." Little did I know this piece of advice was to have a profound effect later on the project.

So I sat in the hard chair and had some fine-tasting green tea. Before long, we were talking about his shelf full of old teapots; he said he had a supplier who only purchased them in excellent condition. The teapots were certified old by the government, and he showed me one with a small band around the handle, linked with an official government seal. In a land that counterfeits everything, I could only hope he had an honest supplier.

The teapot I picked out was shaped like a small pumpkin. The lid had a curved handle that looked like the lid for a jack-o'-lantern, and the inside looked like several generations had brewed thousands of cups of tea in this pot.

"Good choice," he said, taking the pot and removing the lid. He looked inside and smelled the pot. After a long explanation, I deduced that the hand-molded stoneware teapot was originally used to brew black or oolong tea.

He pointed at an old map of the Shanghai area on his office wall and said the classic teapot design was from Yixing [Yicheng] in Jiangsu Province. I looked at the map and the city he was pointing to; it was west of Shanghai, out past Suzhou, on the other side of Lake Tai Hu. He said teapots had been made in Yixing for thousands of years. Then, again before I knew it, we were back to just drinking tea. He knew the sale had been made, so we talked about tea for a while. I paid for the wonderful little teapot and thanked him for inviting me to drink with him.

As I was leaving, he said, "Make sure only use black or oolong tea in pot. Pot so old it could make tea with just water."

"I'll bet that is why you got such a good price. See you next time I'm in Shanghai," I said, gently closing the door.

CHAPTER TWENTY-SIX

CANTON TRADE FAIR AND HONG KONG

China in the Twentieth Century - Before Nixon's Visit

"One night late in October (1971), the guards once again called the prisoners to sit quietly and listen to a special broadcast. The loudspeaker was switched on, and a man's voice lectured the prisoners on 'the excellent situation created by the Cultural Revolution.' The central theme of his speech was the announcement that President Nixon was to visit China in February of the following year. He told us that the great GPCR had so raised China's importance in the world that the United States of America, which had hitherto adopted a policy of hostility towards the People's Republic, was now on the point of realizing the futility of that policy."[5]

Nien Cheng spent six and a half years in prison during the Cultural Revolution and later wrote a book about her experiences, titled Life and Death in Shanghai. Her daughter, Meiping, died as a direct result of persecution during the Cultural Revolution. What were their crimes? The mother had worked for Shell Oil in old China, and the daughter just had the wrong class origin.

The Cultural Revolution officially ended in 1969, but China remained in chaos for years afterward. Deng was out in the country planting a garden and raising chickens. Mao's chosen successor, Liu Shaochi, was dead, and Peng Dehuai was in prison being tortured because he told Mao the truth about the Great Leap Forward. When it was all over three million people had died and 100 million people had suffered greatly.

IT TOOK ABOUT two and a half hours to fly from Shanghai to Canton [Guangzhou], about sixty miles from Hong Kong. During the flight, I finished reading a book I had started in Shanghai, titled *The Opium Wars in China* by Edgar Holt. I will begin this chapter with a little about what I learned from the book and other reading about the area.

Canton was where a Ming emperor permitted the Portuguese to establish a trading colony in 1514; it was here that Western trade with China began. In the early 1700s, the British showed up and were allowed to establish trade. For most of the eighteenth century, Canton was the major outlet for Chinese goods. All foreigners were required by the Qing Dynasty (1644–1911 AD) to conduct business only under strict supervision and only during the summer. At the end of summer, they were required to spend the rest of the year in Portuguese Macao, which is about forty miles from Hong Kong. Early in the nineteenth century the US, French, and Dutch had joined the club of the unwanted. To settle the trade imbalance (more silver in than silver out), the British decided to make Indian opium available to speculators, who then shipped the drug to Canton and exchanged it for Chinese goods. The emperor decided to stop the opium sales by closing Canton to all foreign trade. The first Anglo-Chinese war (1840–42) followed because of trade issues first, opium second, and last but not least: English face. The war led to the founding of Hong Kong, brought the Chinese into much more contact with the Western world, and resulted in more face, equality, status, and trade for the "foreign devils." China got more opium and foreigners. The treaty ports of Shanghai, Canton, and others were now open for business; after all, trade was a God-given right. Treaty after treaty followed and it wasn't long before the barbarian guests started to take on the role of the master. Warships began to anchor in the treaty ports, and privileged zones began to appear in cities like Shanghai; in these zones Chinese were now second-class citizens. The expansion continued and resulted in the second Opium War and the Treaties of 1858 and 1860. Eleven more ports were opened, and the importing of opium was guaranteed. In 1898, an area known as the New Territories, near Hong Kong, was leased for ninety-nine years, where much of the "Made in Hong Kong" items came from down through the years. The British now controlled a land area of over four hundred square miles, and Hong Kong Island covered about thirty-five square miles.

The British agreed to return borrowed Hong Kong in 1984, and the leased New Territories to China in 1997. What could they do with Hong Kong if all the leased territory was returned to China? Hong Kong is dependent on the import of virtually everything, including water. The days of forcing China were over; Deng Xiaoping knew he was in the driver's seat when he negotiated for the return of Hong Kong. The Chinese, in turn, agreed to allow Hong Kong to continue the "economic freedom" allowed under British rule. To do this, a "two systems, one China" agreement was worked out, whereby Hong Kong would be made a special administrative region within China and allowed to operate under the agreement for fifty years. However, Britain made it sound as if after they left the people would run their own government. Sounded simple—but it wasn't.

When we arrived in Canton, in October 1992, there was a battle going on: a battle between the twenty-eighth governor, David Wilson, and the Chinese government in Beijing. Wilson wanted to expand democratic representation in Hong Kong. After all these years of autocratic rule governing Hong Kong, the British had decided it was high time to introduce more democracy into the political structure prior to the return to the Chinese government on July 1, 1997. After all, they had promised democracy to the citizens of Hong Kong. Needless to say, Beijing wasn't happy, and there was much name-calling. I will update you on how it all turned out at the end of this chapter.

When we arrived in Canton from Shanghai, the plan was to attend the Canton Fair for two days. After the fair, we'd go down to Hong Kong for two days to talk to several parts suppliers, and the Yanmar marine diesel distributor, then fly back to Shanghai for a few days before heading home.

First a little about the Canton Fair—or to be exact—the Chinese Import and Export Commodities Fair. It has been held twice a year, in the spring and autumn, since 1957.

I'm sure it is the biggest one in China, if not the world, with the most products, highest attendance, and best of everything a trade show can have. I had been to trade shows in the States but nothing of the magnitude of the Canton Fair. It was like taking a large consumer goods show, adding an electronics one, then adding a machinery and equipment one, and on and on until there were no more shows left to represent. This was the Canton Fair, and if you like kicking tires on a tractor, this is the place to go.

Don had business to do for several customers, so I tagged along. Over two days, we saw endless rows of machinery and equipment, small vehicles of every kind, electronics, appliances, hardware, tools, building materials, consumer goods, and strange food products. We saw more than I had seen in all the trade shows I ever attended or would attend in the future. Before going to the fair, I thought most everything made in China was shipped to the United States. No way. At this trade fair were people speaking every language in the world. It was truly an international event. I had my fill and more.

Needless to say, I was ready to depart when we left Canton and headed for Hong Kong. We wound up in an overpriced hotel in the Central District (business district) of Hong Kong, which is on the northwest coast of the island, the center of all economic and administrative activities. "Economic" is the key word because Hong Kong is all about work and making money—everyone there, from peddlers to executives, is a capitalist or striving to be one. This did not change when the British left and Beijing started calling the shots in 1997. Money is still king, not the bureaucrats in Beijing.

They said you could drink the water in Hong Kong, but I didn't want to take a chance. I saw bad environmental problems when we were in the New Territories, so I stuck to green tea and Tsingtao beer as I had on the mainland.

I left early the first morning to visit several suppliers I thought might be able to provide parts for the junk. Traveling around the back streets of the business district looking at various commodities, I found they didn't look much different from Shanghai. The quality of the products I saw wasn't anywhere near the quality I could get in the States, so I scrapped the idea of trying to buy parts (except the engines) in Hong Kong.

The next day we went to visit China-Japan Marine Services, Limited, the Yanmar marine diesel distributor in Hong Kong. They informed me the engines were in Kobe, Japan, and they were getting ready to ship them to Shanghai along with all the accessories. When I ordered the engines, there was a long list of optional accessories I had gone over with Larry and Mr. Ru to make sure the proper accessories got ordered for delivery—things like instrument panels, wire harness extensions, and an onboard spare parts kit. We spent several hours going over the drawing Larry had made depicting the installation and the Yanmar manual for the 37-horsepower 4JH2 (B) E engines. Their engineer made several suggestions concerning the installation drawing and made a few suggestions for installing the engines.

As our meeting drew to a close, I asked, "Can I buy a copy of this manual in Chinese?" The manager looked at me and said with a laugh, "You have to be kidding; we don't have one written in Chinese." I guess if I had asked for one in French or German he might have smiled and said, "No problem." He probably doesn't sell engines to the thousands of Chinese people living aboard junks or to their brethren living in shantytowns or high-density high-rise apartments on the Kowloon side.

Like tourists, we spent the rest of the day walking around the business district, sightseeing and shopping. I said goodbye to my pet cricket, Pu Yi, when I dropped him off in a beautiful garden. We had dim sum, and I bought a black T-shirt with "Hong Kong" printed on the back. (It lost its shape the first time it was washed). The Central District, with its dramatic skyscrapers, old colonial buildings, and nonstop shopping places was worth seeing, but I was glad to leave when we headed for the airport. Hong Kong had seemed neither British nor purely Chinese. I think it is the prototype for all Chinese cities, with big crowds, bad traffic jams, environmental problems, towering skyscrapers, and endless rows of concrete apartment buildings. Hong Kong is a place where there are lots of jobs and money, and the latter is the new emperor.

As I write this chapter, it has been seventeen years since the British hauled down the Union Jack and China took back its borrowed and leased territory. Before the turnover, half a million people had left not wanting to see how the "two systems, one China" experiment was going to work out. Willing, Mandarin-speaking Chinese professionals seeking a better life flocked in from the mainland, and the Chinese government decided to allow a committee of mostly pro-Beijing business people to select the top leader. The government knew that these businessmen, like their counterparts on the mainland, would be more interested in commerce and money than in democracy; the territory's mini-constitution was thrown out the window. Beijing brought in a large number of army troops and made it clear Hong Kong's administrative autonomy would be controlled by the central government—period.

Britain's promise that there would be local control after they left and that Hong Kong's inhabitants would run their own government was only an empty dream. The British should not have waited until signs started appearing with a big red star and the words "Coming Soon."

China hasn't changed Hong Kong much, but emulating Hong Kong on the mainland is all the rage. That's the biggest reason Beijing couldn't allow it to become democratic; "free" was acceptable, but not democratic. All along the eastern coast new cities are emerging, looking remarkably like Hong Kong—driven by business and controlled by Beijing. China remains a gigantic, money-driven dictatorship with socialist overtones.

On the plane somewhere over the Pacific, I got out my empty cricket cage and thought about buying the pet cricket from the small boy in Shanghai. I remembered the serious old man who had lifted Pu Yi from a throng of crickets and dropped him into the cage, wondering if they sold crickets in pet stores in the States. I was sure they did, but I would never find anyone who was as knowledgeable as that old Shanghai cricket man.

CHAPTER TWENTY-SEVEN

DINNER AT DON'S—THEN TROUBLE

China in the Twentieth Century - Lin Biao Crashes

In 1959, Mao made Lin Biao Defense Minister and later, his successor. Mao and Lin worked together all through the Cultural Revolution. Their partnership worked well until 1971 when Mao sensed that Lin had become too powerful. Lin sensed that his political future was ruined and decided China needed a change of leadership by assignation. The plan failed, and Lin and his family decided to run, scrambling aboard a partially fueled airplane and leaving Beijing in the middle of the night. The plane ran out of fuel and crashed in Mongolia, killing all aboard (or so the story goes). There was now no one in line to succeed Mao.

THE RADIO IN my old pickup was blasting a country song as I headed down Santa Monica Boulevard in Hollywood, past all the fast food joints and other mom-and-pop stores along the busy avenue. As I got closer to Don's place, I started looking for the neon sign on the liquor store that had become my lighthouse in the night, my signal that it was time to turn. I was once again going to Don's house for dinner, only this time there would be guests. Don had invited the business attaché I had met at the Chinese embassy, and his wife to join us for dinner. I tried to remember his name but couldn't, though it was a common name, like Lee. He was the one who had advised me not to be in a hurry but to try and slow down when doing business in China.

When I was in China, I had made that effort. This was facilitated by the need to have what I said translated. I began to talk slower, in short bursts and allowed time for the translator to speak before I continued. When being spoken to it was the same process in reverse, so things slowed down automatically. I used shorter sentences and wrote brief faxes, so the messages didn't get lost in translation. Many times I failed, but slower seemed to work better.

As usual I pulled back into their driveway and locked the truck. "*Can't be too careful around here,*" I thought. When Don opened the door, the television set was booming out gunfire, and another actor fell "dead." I still find it strange that murder has come to be regarded as a regular, innocuous part of American life. I don't think such depictions will ever seem harmless or become a part of my life. Since Wally got shot, movies containing murder and violence have ceased to be entertainment for me.

"Welcome. Stick the beer in the fridge and grab a cold one," he said. I slapped him on the back and headed for the kitchen.

Mei was prepping all the vegetables and cooking the dinner. I had brought two six-packs of Tsingtao, instead of the tall bottles I had brought to dinner at her parents' apartment in China, for the occasion.

"Good evening, Mei, what's for dinner?"

"We have special dishes tonight because of guests. In China, we fix special dishes when have guests. You wait see."

I walked back into the front room.

"What you watching?"

"I don't know, just the usual Hollywood crap. You know—tits, ass, crashing cars, and lots of dead bodies."

I was looking at a magazine, and Don was watching a screeching car chase when the doorbell rang. He hit the "off" button on the remote, and the picture faded just as a car crash was about to happen.

"Sounds like the guests are here," Don said, jumping up to answer the door.

After handshakes, a cold beer for the guests, and a little small talk the women disappeared back into the kitchen so Mei could finish putting dinner together while they continued their conversation. A Chinese dinner for five meant a lot of kitchen work.

I learned the business attaché and his wife had been in Los Angeles about a year on a short tour of duty. His English was very good. They liked America; LA was great, but the food wasn't. He seemed conservative, distant, and careful with his choice of words. He reminded me of the Communist plant manager who had loaned us his car in Beijing. It was like they saw themselves operating in a higher level of the social hierarchy; to both of them social classifications were as Chinese as chopsticks.

It wasn't long before we heard, "You sit now."

We gathered around the table, and Mei served the cold dishes first, just like in China. I had learned by now that sharing the pleasures of a good spread was part of the Chinese social tradition, and I always looked forward to eating at their house. Before anyone started there was a toast by Don and the meal seemed to pause for a short while for the familiar "*kan pei*" ceremony. As we consumed the cold dishes and drank our beer, the conversation slowed, and we just enjoyed the food. Mei disappeared periodically into the kitchen. She next returned with a large tureen of soup, which she dished up. The meat, seafood, and vegetable dishes kept appearing as if Mei had a staff of cooks working behind the scenes though she had surely cooked much of the dinner in advance. As is customary in China, she put a small container of toothpicks on the table for the guests to use during the meal. As before, there was no main dish. Toward the end of the meal, she set before us a stir-fried vegetable dish, rice, and tea. No dessert was served. The whole meal had taken less than an hour to eat but had probably taken Mei many hours to prepare.

After dinner, we drank tea and talked about many things, but the thing I will never forget was the Chinese couple's discussion about leaving their daughter in China. How could they come to America and leave their only child behind? They said the education of children is far more important in China than it is in the United States. They decided to leave their daughter in China because they thought it would result in a better education for her, especially considering our school system. They looked into the Los Angeles Unified School District and found out what is common knowledge in California: the school system has a horrible rating and can be unsafe. Unfortunately, they could not afford a private school on their modest government salary.

They explained that when they returned to China their daughter would have no time to catch up on her schoolwork or make up for lost time. The number of people competing on standardized tests throughout China is great compared with the number of people accepted. Unlike America, how students perform on standardized tests early on determines their future in school and, therefore, affects the rest of their lives. Their daughter had to perform well early to have any chance of going to a university later. If they could afford it, they would love to send their daughter to college in America, but not to public school in Los Angeles.

I was born in Los Angeles and went through numerous schools in the system before I graduated and joined the Navy. I knew what the Chinese couple said was true about the present Los Angeles school system. I didn't try to defend one of the worst school systems in America. It was probably also true their daughter was safer in China, but I didn't say that either. I did say I hoped their daughter passed all the standardized tests and went to college—the dream of every Chinese family I met.

As I backed out of Don and Mei's driveway and headed toward the gaily lit boulevard, I reached over and turned on the radio. The country/western station I'd had on earlier came back on, playing an old, familiar tune. It had been a great dinner, and Mei had received many compliments. Their guests stated it was the best homestyle meal they had eaten since reaching our shores. As for me, I had great food and the chance to hear a simple story about how important parents are to education. I now realize why Chinese students do so well—it's their parents.

The next day I received notice that while I was in China, the engines had been shipped from Kobe, Japan, to Shanghai. A few weeks later, I was notified the engines had been picked up in Shanghai. We were off and running . . . well, almost.

The three pallets and five cartons of parts I had shipped to Shanghai in October before the last trip could not be located. I spent hours and hours trying to help trace down the parts with no luck. There were delays getting the last few parts together, necessitating a *third* parts shipments. Well, there went the schedule!

After several weeks, they finally located the first parts shipment in Shanghai and gave me no explanation as to why it had taken so long to locate.

My biggest concern at this point was that the Chinese had not amended their Standby Letter of Credit. The contract required it and in our last meeting they had agreed to amend the dollar amount to cover the engines, accessories, and the first parts shipment. I began to worry.

CHAPTER TWENTY-EIGHT

BY MYSELF—FOURTH TRIP

China in the Twentieth Century - Deng Returns

In 1972, Zhou Enlai, Mao's loyal follower, and longtime premier, was diagnosed with cancer. Both he and Mao now knew that help was needed, and in 1973, with Lin Biao gone, Deng showed up in Beijing like magic and resumed his official duties. The economy was at a standstill because of years of the Cultural Revolution, and there was much to be done. Despite Zhou's illness, he and Deng worked together to recover from the effects of the Cultural Revolution.

In 1974, Mao complained that he was having trouble reading. He was going blind and was also having speech problems. With death chasing both Zhou and Mao, Deng ran even faster with restructuring the economy. As Deng accelerated, Mao became alarmed. The Gang of Four (Mao's wife and associates) and the Red Guards were still in action at this time.

THE 1993 NEW YEAR rolled around, and I didn't know what to do. The construction insurance policy on the junk had expired in November, and they had not renewed it. We were in a dispute over the delivery schedule because there was a penalty clause in the contract. They had agreed to deliver the junk three months after receipt of the engines, and they were now saying they needed more time because of the "lost" parts shipment. At this point, I had delivered two engines and associated parts, three pallets, and seven boxes of parts. They still had not amended their Standby Letter of Credit—so much for safeguards. It seemed the satire in naming the junk *Mei Wen Ti* had pissed off Lu Pan, the junk builders' patron, or some other deity in their enormous pantheon of gods in China. My project was in trouble.

I drove over to Don's one afternoon to discuss the project and see if we could come up with a plan.

"Well, if you want my advice, I say let's go to arbitration and demand they do what the contract says," Don suggested.

"I have thought about that and did a little looking into what is required. The arbitration proceedings will be conducted in Chinese in China, so we'd have to fly over and get an arbitrator who can speak English. We'd need to work with him until he knows enough to present our case. I'm just not sure we can win; they just don't look at contracts the way we do. The truth is I really can't afford the added expenses."

"Well, it's your nickel; I'll go along with whatever you decide," Don said.

"Not exactly a nickel," I thought. "Why don't I go over by myself and see where things are, and see firsthand how far they are from completion. Maybe I can resolve some of the issues if I meet with them face-to-face. Since Mei won't be available, I'll get someone to do the translating."

"If you think that's the best thing to do—give it a go. Now let's have a beer."

After a cold swallow, I said, "I have to tell you what happened to me today. I went into a pet store to get a new cricket for the cage I bought in Shanghai. The clerk asked how many I needed, and when I responded, 'Only one,' the clerk looked puzzled. 'Won't your pet eat more than that?' she asked, not knowing I wasn't looking for pet food. I told her it *was* the pet."

"That's funny, and it says a bit about our two cultures. The Chinese use them mainly as symbols of auspicious virtue and luck, and write poems about them, and all we use them for is pet food and fish bait," Don said. I grinned and finished off my bottle.

The next day I sent a message to Mr. Chao telling him I was in the process of setting up a trip to China by myself. I said the last parts shipment would arrive in Hong Kong in a few days, and closed by asking him to amend the dollar amount of their Letter of Credit for the umpteenth time.

A few days later I received a fax stating they looked forward to seeing me and suggested the first part of February, but there was no mention of the amendment to their Letter of Credit. Thinking back to when I talked with the bank loan officer about their Standby Letter of Credit I remembered that he had said, "It provides you assurances of their ability to perform under the terms of your contract, but you and the seller do not expect that the Standby Letter of Credit will ever be drawn upon." *"Maybe they have decided not to update theirs because they have a problem that they know will force me to draw against it. What could it be? It would have to be something serious like not delivering the junk. I'll just have to figure it out."*

About a week later I received another fax saying they would like to take the Chinese New Year off. The next paragraph was the surprise of my life: it said they would for sure have the junk ready for sea trials by March 15th. I couldn't believe it. *"So if the junk is going to be ready for sea trials on March 15th why won't they amend their Letter of Credit?"*

I contacted Don to tell him what they had said. We decided to proceed with our present plan. If they were going to be ready for sea trials by March 15th, I would notify Don and he would join me. I went down to the Chinese embassy in Los Angeles and asked them if I could be in China for an extended period on my next trip and they said yes. I was good to go.

One of the last things I did was go to a store in Los Angeles that specialized in nautical maps and pick up several I had ordered. The maps showed the area the junk would be taken on sea trials.

"In all my days selling maps this is my first sale of these. Not many people go to China," he declared.

"Actually, I'm not going to China on a boat," I said. I told him about the sea trials, and he wished me luck.

Before leaving, I made arrangements to have Mr. Li, who worked as a desk clerk at the Yushan Hotel in Changshu, to be my interpreter on a part-time basis. Remember, he was the one who talked to the pedicab drivers for me on the last trip. His English was fair, and I was sure he could do the job. He might have problems with the equipment and technical terms, but I could get by. I told him I would be arriving the first week in February for a long stay.

The last thing I did was get Mr. Wen a pair of white Nike tennis shoes and several packages of the Gillette razor blades he had asked me to bring him.

Pu Yi II and I made a safe entry. I felt like an old China hand traveling by myself. I picked up a cab at the airport, checked the meter, and showed him my book with the characters for the Hengshan Hotel. The cab had a nasty stench, there was no Mao or Li Feng on the sun visor, and the driver smoked foul-smelling cigarettes. He didn't spit out the window—he used a can for a spittoon. He took the right turns as we headed toward the old French section. The traffic was thick, but we somehow made it safely to the Hengshan Hotel with no problem.

"Welcome, Mister Walt, good see you," the old clerk said as he handed me the familiar registration card to fill out. When I wrote the date, I added a day without even thinking about the International Date Line.

"You travel alone?"

"Yes."

"How your *chuan?*"

"Fine." I handed him a few photographs showing the hull, taken on the last trip.

He studied the pictures. "Before liberation long ago, family have *chuan.* Much small. Make many trips Shanghai—much money—carry everything." He handed back the photographs along with an old door key.

"Welcome, you need anything—you say."

"I wanted to buy my daughter, Lynn, a present. Where is a good spot near here to go shopping?"

"Easy. Go street to Nanking Road head Huangpu River." He pointed toward a street outside the hotel.

Nanking Road was a good walk from the hotel. When I hit the street, I turned right and headed toward the famous Bund that ran along the Huangpu River. Like the old man at the desk had promised, Nanking Road was a great place to find a gift: it was a long boulevard lined with shops and stores of every variety. The number of people milling about made it seem like Christmas back in the States. I spent several hours wandering in and out of every variety of store and small shop until I landed in a small antique store up a side street that specialized in old Taoist charms and talismans, another sign that old religion, beliefs, and superstitions were still alive in China. They sold amulets and talismans made of wood, metal, and paper.

First, let me tell you a little about Taoism. After Confucius, one of the most influential philosophers in early China was Lao Tzu (770–476 BC). He is credited with writing the famous book *Tao Te Ching.* Lao Tzu formed the Taoist group that taught "Tao" (the way of nature) as a way of life. It teaches its followers to live a selfless, simple life in harmony with nature. The key to the teaching seems to be the concept of *wei wu wei,* which is to do without doing, or to act without action.

On the amulets and talismans, there were spiritual messages to various spirits or gods adjuring them not to harm the bearer, or they might include a message asking of something like good fortune.

I asked to see a bronze, coin-like amulet about the size of a silver dollar. It pictured two Chinese junks on one side and Chinese characters on the other.

"What does it say?" I asked.

"'Calm wind, good fortune, and return fully loaded,'" the proprietor said in perfect English. "Sometimes those who go to sea feel the need for supernatural assistance."

Considering the current status of my project, I agreed. I bought the old amulet thinking, "*It could do no harm and who couldn't use a little calm wind and good fortune?*"

My next purchase was a small statue of Kuan Yin, the goddess of mercy, for Lynn. The statue was hand-carved out of some type of bone (not ivory). I purchased it in another small antique shop full of old statues. Or at least they said they were old.

After finishing my shopping, I headed to the People's Park, which wasn't far away. I had missed it on my last trip to Shanghai. The Communists constructed the People's Park out of colonial Shanghai's old racetrack. I walked through the park and watched people flying kites, kids feeding pigeons, and men playing chess. The view made me think I was standing in Central Park looking out at New York City. It was hard for me to imagine a cheering grandstand full of Shanghai's elite had ever existed. The People's Park was just another Chinese metamorphosis. I grabbed a cab and showed the driver my little book—he headed for the hotel in the right direction.

The next morning I was up early, so I decided to skip breakfast and get some snacks to share on the ride to Changshu. I knew of a small shop not far from the hotel that sold deep-fried devils. Sitting down at a small table, I ordered a cup of tea and three of the deep-fried breads. I had trouble getting the waitress to understand I wanted them for take-out. She finally got it and wrapped them in yesterday's newspaper.

When I got back to the hotel, I didn't have to wait long for the van from the boatyard to pick me up. I put my bag in the back of the van and hopped in. I said, "*Ni hao*" to Mr. Wen and the driver took a devil and handed over the rest, and we headed out into the busy streets of Shanghai. During the ride I ate my deep-fried bread and listened to a long conversation I couldn't understand—there would be long periods during the trip when I didn't speak to anyone. The traffic in Shanghai and on the highway to Changshu seemed to be heavier on each succeeding trip.

When we stopped at the Yushan Hotel in Changshu, I turned to Mr. Wen, pointed in the direction of the bus station, pointed at myself, and then held up my hand with the thumb and index fingers making an "L" with my little finger raised also. He smiled, made the sign, and I knew he had gotten the message. "Seven o'clock at the bus station."

I got checked in, put my bag in the room, and returned to the front desk. Mr. Li was just getting off duty. He had made arrangements to work nights for a while.

"Do you mind we take walk?" he asked.

"Not at all." We headed out the front door, past the pedicab drivers. *"I'm sure they remember me,"* I thought, recollecting the last trip when Mr. Li had inquired about the fare to the bus station.

"I prefer not discuss things at hotel," he said. "Many nosy people."

We headed down the street in the direction of the bus station. *"I must remember I am in a country where a Chinese citizen can be imprisoned for what he says."*

"I very glad this opportunity. Back during Cultural Revolution, all school shut down and education lost. I went work peasant pig farm. No good time. If my English better I go Shanghai work."

This was the first person I ever spoke to who said one word about the Cultural Revolution and its effects.

I shifted our discussion over to the project. We agreed on a schedule of three days a week. After we had finished talking business, he said he would like to have me help him with his English. I agreed to spend some time with him and thought it might be a good way to spend some of my spare time.

"There many words don't know how say. Maybe you help?"

"Sure," I promised.

We turned and headed toward the hotel. Walking back I started asking him the word for certain things I saw: We went through several words, and then he got stumped.

"What is that on the top of the building over there?"

"Not know how say English?"

I told him since we were speaking English, a better response might be, "I don't know."

"I don't know."

"Good. It is a cross."

"Don't know this cross?" he said.

I thought for a while then said, "The large star on your flag is a symbol that represents the Communist Party. Right?"

"Right."

"Well, the cross is a symbol that represents the Christian religion. Like the Chinese star is also put on buildings and flags." I didn't think it was a good idea to be walking down the street in Changshu discussing religion, so I let it go at that. I didn't meet any Christians in China and think there are a lot of people like Mr. Li, who know little to nothing about any religion.

The next morning we walked to the bus station together and met Mr. Wen, practicing his English on the way. He was getting better with just words. When we got to the station we met Mr. Wen, and all sat on the bus until there were enough customers to leave. On the way to the boatyard, I looked out the window, and they talked all the way to the end of the line like two long-lost friends.

When we got to the boatyard, we went up to the office and had tea and talked a while. Since my last visit the boat had been launched, and I could see it sitting in the canal not far from the office.

Before going down to the boat, they took me to a small building where they had stored all the parts I had sent. A young woman oversaw and issued the parts. I noticed immediately that when the parts arrived they had put all like ones together. From the look of all the shelves stacked full not many had been installed yet. Before my last trip and during the last meeting I told them I had the parts supplier mark

and package the parts according to the system on the junk where they would be used. All the parts for the freshwater system would be in boxes marked with "Freshwater" and so on. I did this so that all the parts would not arrive in boxes all mixed up like they now were. "*Oh, well, no sense getting mad, the message didn't get to the person who unpacked.*" As a consequence, they were having trouble finding items, and I was concerned about mistakes.

After leaving the parts building, we went down to the canal and boarded the *Mei Wen Ti* across a narrow wooden gangway. Walking across, I looked down into the coffee-colored water of the canal. The boat looked great, but there was still much work to be done. The engines were not yet installed, and there were more parts in the parts building than on the boat. I spent several hours looking the junk over from bow to stern, paying special attention to the work in progress and saw a well-used copy of one of Larry's drawings with Mr. Ru's notations being used. The drawing was dirty, creased, and folded, so the many trips to San Diego had paid off.

After my tour, I got everyone together and had Mr. Li explain what had happened when the parts arrived and were unpackaged. I suggested that instead of storing like parts together, we store them according to the system they would be used in. They agreed and the next morning Mr. Li and I started out by making groups for the parts based on Larry's drawings. They were getting ready to work on the freshwater system, so we started by putting everything for that system on one shelf. I noticed again that almost every part I had shipped was still in stock, waiting to be used. "*How could they possibly finish the junk by March 15th*?" After finishing the freshwater system, we put all the parts for the fuel system on another shelf and so on until after a week or so we had unscrambled the puzzle. During this time, I stopped and answered questions, helped find parts, crawled around the junk, and, in general, did anything I could to help.

After I had been there a while I sent Don a message telling him I didn't think there was any way they were going to be ready for sea trials on March 15th; I assured him my trip had been a good idea, and I had been able to help make the work go a little smoother.

One morning while I was up in the office having a cup of tea I heard a loud explosion that sounded like a cannon being fired. I rushed out on the landing and looked toward the junk but didn't see anything abnormal. I learned later in the day, however, that a welder working on a steel workboat tied up not far from the junk had been killed in the explosion caused by some kind of gas in the bilge that ignited with his torch. Employee safety seemed to be of little concern. After the explosion, I asked that all the fire extinguishers I shipped over, which were on a shelf in the parts building, be taken down to the junk and installed. *Mei wen ti.*

Every day I walked around the junk, looking at the progress and trying to assess how much more work needed to be done. By this time, I was absolutely sure they couldn't finish by the fifteenth of March, but since there were still problems to be solved I decided to stay.

One morning I was walking around the junk and came across two employees working in the head (marine toilet). I looked in to see what they were doing and started laughing. They stopped work, puzzled, wondering what I was laughing about. They were installing the hot- and cold-water valve assembly in the back wall of the shower, but not knowing any better, they had installed the showerhead right above the valves, making the showerhead only four feet from the floor. I motioned them out of the shower and marked a spot on the back wall, about six feet above the floor. I pointed at the showerhead and then at the mark on the wall, and they both started laughing. Fortunately, the stainless steel had not been installed in the shower yet.

As days passed, parts moved slowly from the parts building to the junk, and Mr. Li's English got better. "I don't know," came easy, but less often. Therefore, I decided he should start working on sentences, having him tell me about China. We chose the Chinese New Year for our first topic since it had just passed. Walking to work day after day, his English got better, the corrections fewer, and I learned about the biggest celebration in the world—the Chinese New Year.

CHAPTER TWENTY-NINE

CHINESE NEW YEAR

China in the Twentieth Century - The Year of the Dragon

As Mao and Zhou lay dying, Mao's wife, Jiang Quin, began to build a group intent on succeeding Mao. Deng and Jiang were in a power struggle. People told Mao that Deng and Zhou were in a conspiracy to undo all he'd accomplished. Mao appointed a relatively unknown Hua Guofeng to lead the country as acting Premier.

Zhou died in 1976, the year of the dragon. There were mass demonstrations in Tiananmen Square for Zhou and against the Gang of Four, and hundreds were arrested. Deng was blamed for the demonstrations and dismissed once again. Maybe this is why he took such a hard line when there were demonstrations in Tiananmen in 1989: he didn't want to make the same mistake twice. Hua Guofeng, the acting premier, took over running the government.

BEFORE COMING TO China, on this trip, I received a request from Mr. Chao regarding the upcoming New Year or Spring Festival. He had requested slipping the schedule another two weeks to allow everyone working on the project time to celebrate the Chinese New Year. I knew the Chinese New Year celebration was a long tradition and responded saying it was fine to give everyone time to celebrate with their families. For many of the workers, I was sure their families were not near the boatyard. I told him the time would not be held against the builder in any future discussions about the schedule. I didn't want to be the Grinch that stole New Year's.

When I planned the trip, I didn't arrive until after the celebration had ended and everyone had gone back to work. Travel during Spring Festival pushes to the limit their already overloaded planes, trains, and buses.

So every day Mr. Li and I would discuss aspects of the Spring Festival on the way to work. Some parts of the story we went over and over until the sentences were better—but not perfect. So this chapter is a compilation of what I learned walking down the street on the way to the bus station and what I already knew about the Chinese New Year's celebration.

The first thing you learn that is different from the New Year celebration in the West is that the Spring Festival starts on a different day each year. For example, in 2008, the Chinese New Year started with the New Moon on the first day of the new year (February 7th) and lasted until the full moon on February 21st. This is because they use the lunisolar calendar.

Mr. Li told me there was much to be done before the start of the New Year. He said in most homes the celebration starts sometime in the twelfth lunar month of the old year. During this period, everyone gets a haircut, buys gifts for friends and relatives, and goes shopping for new clothes, shoes for the children, and special food items. The home is cleaned outdoors and indoors, down to the pots and pans. He said it is the custom to pay off all debts before the end of the old year. If we tried this in the States, we would find there is nowhere near enough cash in the banks. It might even cause a run on the banks because of the enormous debt we have in America. The kitchen god, who has been stationed in the house all year to observe the conduct of the family, is sent off to report to Heaven. Once a year on the twenty-third day of the twelfth lunar month, right before the beginning of the Chinese New Year, he returns to Heaven to give his report on the family to the main god. His family has burnt paper money and pictures of the kitchen god to ensure a good report on the family. He returns the last day of the old year and takes up his station once again in the home.

Cooking for New Year's Eve begins several days in advance because it is the most important feast of the year. People who are mystically minded don't want to use scissors or knives during the first day of the New Year because they might "cut off" the family's good luck.

We went into a shop on the way to the bus station, and he showed me a vast array of paper products sold for celebrating the New Year. There were many Spring Festival poetic couplets written in calligraphy on red paper strips. A favorite is *fu*, meaning "happiness." He showed me paper pictures of the kitchen god, the god of doors, the god of wealth, and many more. There were red lanterns. These products are used to decorate the just-cleaned house for the upcoming holiday. Walking down the street we saw Spring Festival couplets and red lanterns still hanging on front doors and in windows.

He said the most important part is the eve of the Spring Festival. This is when family members get together, much like Christmas in the West, and is why the transportation system goes into overload starting about two weeks before the Spring Festival. Since it is a time for family reunions, all family members will normally be present for a meal together and stay up to see in the New Year. He said after paying respects to his parents and elders they shoot off firecrackers with everyone in the neighborhood. I've been down to Chinatown in Los Angeles right after New Year's Eve, and the gutters run red with debris from millions of firecrackers.

On New Year's he said everyone had on new clothes; children, relatives, and unmarried friends were given *lai see*, little red envelopes that contain good luck money. The lively celebration spreads out into the streets, lanes, and alleys. There are a series of activities that last for days, with a dragon dance and many local temple fair celebrations. The last activity is the Lantern Festival on the fifteenth night.

One morning on the way to the bus station Mr. Li told me he had to stop at the doctor's office on the way to work to pick up some herbs for his mother. We took a narrow side street and after a short walk we stopped in front of an old, two-story building. We walked up some inside stairs to a small room at the head of the stairs. Mr. Li opened the door without knocking. I knew it was a Chinese doctor's office, not just a Chinese pharmacy because there was almost everything around the room I had seen in Mei's small home office. On the walls were similar-looking Chinese medical posters. One depicted the channels carrying the "vital force" and another showed the acupuncture points. Next to the posters were official-looking certificates. The biggest difference was the large number of cabinets containing small drawers. Each drawer had ingredients for making Chinese prescriptions: half his office was a pharmacy. The room smelled like all the Chinese shops that sold food and herbs I had ever visited—strange.

After introductions, we were invited to have a cup of tea. We sat around a small, round table and drank tea while the doctor talked to Mr. Li about his mother's herbs. There was a small bowl of tangerines on the table. As they talked, I examined all the strange things in his office. When the doctor concluded, Mr. Li got a brown bag containing the prescription with Chinese writing on the outside and we headed back down the stairs and out onto the narrow street. We turned the corner and joined the crowd going toward the bus station.

"He would like to have you come back and visit."

"I would like to visit again. We can stop again someday on the way to work."

"I think he wish more often."

"More often?"

"Yes. You see, he would like to practice English."

So the next day we started leaving an hour earlier three days a week to allow time for tea and English lessons at the doctor's office. The next chapter is a compilation of what I learned at the doctor's office and what I already knew about several elements of traditional Chinese medicine.

CHAPTER THIRTY

NATURAL CURES

China in the Twentieth Century - The Dragon Screams

In the year of the dragon, 1976, China experienced the world's greatest earthquake in modern times. Hundreds of thousands lost their lives. The Cultural Revolution finally ended with the death of Mao and the arrest of his wife, Jiang Quin, and her gang. With the nation stalled, the Communist Party brought Deng back to climb back on the dragon once again.

A struggle for political power began between Deng and Mao's appointed heir, Hua Guofeng. The military and many party seniors backed Deng, and he took over from Hua Guofeng in 1978. Deng brought in new reforms that scrapped the communes and gave the peasants incentives to labor. Deng came up with the idea of Communism with Chinese characteristics.

I WAS INTERESTED in Chinese medicine, so I gladly accepted the doctor's offer to stop on the way to work, have tea, and talk. In addition, it would help Mr. Li. From my reading and talks with Mei, I had a little background in the topic but wanted to learn more about the fascinating subject. I was curious to learn more about Chinese medicine because I was sure Western medicine, with its emphasis on costly drugs, wasn't the only road to better health. There were just too many active, healthy seniors everywhere I went.

Chinese medicine was old when Christ walked the earth and many of the concepts used today are from medical books that have become timeless classics. These classics evolve around "yin" and "yang," concepts rooted in ancient Chinese philosophy. For example, yin is feminine, passive, soft, or the north side of the hill (in the shade). Yang is masculine, active, hard, or the south side of the hill (in the sun). Striking a fundamental balance between yin and yang is the most basic principle in Chinese medicine. For your house to be comfortable, there must be a balance between sun and shade. There are many differences between Western and Chinese medicine, and the idea of yin and yang is only one of a long list of things that make the Western version so different from the Chinese. Today in China, in most places, traditional Chinese medicine and Western medicine are practiced side by side, though I was told many Chinese prefer traditional Chinese medicine to Western. If it didn't work, why is it still around? In China everywhere you look differences abound, so why not in medicine?

The first morning after tea I learned that in traditional Chinese medicine there are four basic methods of treatment: food cures, herbology, acupuncture, and manipulative therapy. It also includes remedial exercises like *tai chi* and *qigong*. The doctor said he did not practice manipulative therapy or teach *tai chi* and *qigong*. For these things, he referred patients to colleagues of his. He did say he did *tai chi* every morning before work.

He said the Chinese do not draw a distinction between food and medicine and suggested we start with food. I knew what he meant because I have been to stores in Chinatown in Los Angeles where it is hard to tell whether certain shops sell more food than medicine or more medicine than food. We stopped during the discussion and talked about English, but, in general, the doctor spoke good English. The hour went by fast, and we were on the way to the bus station before I knew it.

Mr. Li went to the boatyard with me just three days a week, so the next day I was on my own. When I got there, I went up to the office to have a cup of tea and saw an example of food cures: one of the workmen had a bad cold and was making his tea with thin slices of raw ginger.

The day was spent working on a missing part problem. I found I had just forgotten to order the part and would have to order it when I got back to the hotel. After work, I walked to a small covered bus stop not far from the boatyard to wait for the bus, where there was a man with a young boy sitting on one of the wood benches. I sat down on the other bench and got out a book to read while I waited. It wasn't long before the little boy walked over and stood right in front of me. He stared at me like I was a strange creature from a *Star Wars* movie that had walked in to wait for the bus. I'm sure I was the first non-Chinese person he had ever seen. I got uncomfortable after a while. "*I wish I knew how to say, "Stop staring," in Chinese.*" I looked over at the father, and he had a broad smile on this face, so I gave the kid a big one of my own and went back to reading. The little boy just stood there watching me as I sat reading. I got saved when the dusty old bus arrived. I grabbed a seat in the back, away from the kid, and read my book, one of several Chinese poetry books I had brought with me. The next chapter presents a taste of Chinese poetry.

The next time we got together the doctor started out talking about food cures and food. He said he always asks patients about food preferences and eating habits in addition to taking their pulse, looking at their tongue, observing their complexion, and asking questions about their symptoms. He said he would come up with a diagnosis based upon these things and then decide whether they needed herbs or acupuncture. In addition, he would talk to the patient about how they might improve their diet. You can see from the start how different traditional Chinese medicine is from Western medicine, beginning with how the diagnosis is done.

In China, a balanced diet means two different things and is somewhat complicated. I will attempt a brief overview. He said people have a tendency to eat foods that are pleasing to the digestive system, like sweets. He stressed the need to also eat foods that are pungent, salty, sour, and bitter. Also, you must have a balanced diet based upon your physical constitution, since all people are not alike. They define six different types of constitution: cold, hot, damp, dry, excessive, and deficient.

For example, if you have a cold physical condition, you should eat more hot and warm foods. It takes knowledge of Chinese medicine to arrive at a diet that will maintain a balance in your system. We spent several sessions talking about food, food cures, and food illnesses (overnourished, intoxication, etc.). In the end, I believe connecting food and medicine makes good sense, and I better understand the Chinese connection between cooking and health. For instance, meat does not predominate, vegetables do; and if there is meat, it is used in moderation.

Work on the junk slowly progressed though I was still sure they would not finish all the work by March 15th. I think they also knew it was going to be delivered late, so my requests for them to amend their Letter of Credit went nowhere. They treated the matter as if the contract didn't exist.

After we finished talking about the importance of food in Chinese medicine, the doctor showed us his wooden cabinets full of herbs. The dried roots, weeds, and grasses were stored in well-marked drawers. He said diseases of the internal organs and most skin diseases were usually treated with herbs. If possible, he would use a food cure before using herbs. He said herbs are arranged in groups determined down through the ages and well-documented in Chinese medical journals. The doctor said in most cases the diagnosis would have more than one symptom and was not usually treated with a single herb. Usually, several herbs are used in the formulation like what he had prepared for Mr. Li's mother. Most of his formulas were not available in powder form, so it was necessary for the patient to brew a "soup" out of the prescription.

On our next visit, he showed us his poster and said, in general, muscular symptoms and pain are best treated by acupuncture; however, sometimes he uses both acupuncture and herbology. How it works is a mystery to Western medicine, so I won't attempt to explain it. Many of the concepts the doctor talked about have no true counterpart in Western medicine. Acupuncture works on the concept of *qi* (pronounced "chi") which, in Chinese medicine, is considered a vital force responsible for controlling the workings of the human mind and body. The doctor said that when he inserts a needle in an acupuncture point he can manipulate the needle to either build *qi* if there is a deficiency of energy or drain *qi* if there is an excess of energy. It is through this balancing that the patient's health is restored. Remember, it's all about striking a balance between yin and yang.

On one of my visits, I decided to ask the doctor about the eight wooden panels that were to be installed on each side of the main deck. I had seen the panels at the boatyard, containing carved images, such as a sword and a basket of flowers, and other panel designs I didn't recognize. The man working on the furniture had written out rows and rows of Chinese characters on a small slip of paper. I gave the slip to the doctor and asked him to explain about the Eight Immortals. He read it and with a big smile began explaining the mystery.

He replied that the Eight Immortals were popular figures of Chinese myths and legends, and revered by ordinary Chinese as they represent all the conditions of life. They signify male, female, old, young, rich, poor, and the humble Chinese. Each panel contained a symbol (like a sword or basket of flowers) and represented one of the Eight Immortals. He said there were many stories about them.

After about a dozen visits, our English sessions came to an end as I was leaving. Before I left, I took the good doctor a small can of fine green tea. I stayed a while, and we just talked and drank. As I got up to leave the doctor said, "I wish to thank you for spending time with me. I hope you have learned a little about Chinese medicine and the Eight Immortals."

I did and, dear reader, I hope you did, too.

CHAPTER THIRTY-ONE

CHINESE POETRY

China in the Twentieth Century - The New China

During 1978–79, Deng moved toward diplomatic relations with Japan and the United States and inaugurated an era of reform. It should be noted that Deng had authority in Chinese politics until his death in 1997, mainly because of his connections with the military and respect from others in the government he had earned over the years. Purged party members returned to take up the banner of economic development. Deng brought back men like Zhao Ziyang and Hu Yaobang to help stamp out the starvation, poverty, and backwardness created by the Cultural Revolution.

In 1978, Nien Cheng was declared "rehabilitated" and a year later Leo She and thousands of others were posthumously "rehabilitated" by the Communist Party, and Deng visited the United States.

CHINESE POETRY AS a literary tradition goes back to the ancient anthology *The Book of Songs,* gathered about 2,500 years ago. Those who have written books about Chinese poetry don't all agree on which dynasties since then represent the golden age of classical Chinese poetry, but most would probably agree that poetry by the twentieth century had exhausted itself.

A poet from the past could be an emperor, a scholar, a general, a civil servant, or a statesman; he or she was well-educated, but more than likely not just a poet. Back during the Tang Dynasty (618–907 AD), poetry was so important that its composition became one of the main skills needed to pass the imperial civil service examination to become an official in the government. During this period, all travel and communications were slow, so the emperor depended on thousands of civil servants in the large cities and villages to provide the glue that kept the empire together. This elite group was the creator as well as the audience for almost all the poetry that was written. Because of the long, sluggish travel over land and sea, exchanging poems between scholar-gentlemen became common practice. Trips on the thousands of junks in service at the time were long, especially when they traveled to ports as far away as India and the Persian Gulf to bring back traded cargo and Christian missionaries. Down through succeeding dynasties, writing poetry continued to be the sign of a well-educated man and a requirement on the imperial examination to become a scholar-official.

My favorite poet from the Tang Dynasty (618–907 AD) is Li Po. The following, titled "Ballad of the Voyager," is one of my favorites and is presented in the front of the book.

Ocean voyager, on heaven's wind,
In his ship, far wandering
Like a bird, among the clouds,
Gone he will leave no trace. [6]

By the late nineteenth or early twentieth century, the imperial examinations were gone, and poetry had changed radically. The guardians of Chinese culture were people like teachers, writers, and poets. Their poems represented the China they saw every day, and the people who wrote the poetry lived between the lines of every poem. They were a part of the bloodthirsty upheavals around them during that period.

One of the things I like best about Chinese poetry is that it provides a window through which to see an ever-changing China. In the next poem, called "The Soul of Shanghai," try and guess when it was written, and see if you don't agree that it is sort of like an old dog-eared, black-and-white photograph of Shanghai. The answer can be found in the Notes section.

I stand on top of a seven story-storied building,
Above, there is the inaccessible sky;
Below, the cars, telephone wires, and the horse race track.
The front door of a theater, the back view of a prostitute;
Ah, these are the soul of a metropolis:
Ah, these are the soul of Shanghai.
Here one need not fear the rain or the sun:
Or the autumn and winter of death, or the spring of life:
How can any fiery summer be warmer than the lips!
Here there are true illusions, false sentiments;
Here there are unsleeping evenings, smiling lights;
Come, then, here is your burial ground.

Shao Hsun-mei[7]

After the Communists took over in 1949, the government encouraged students, workers, soldiers, and peasants to write social realism (government-sanctioned literature) through mass poetry movements. These poets wrote more about the lives and activities of common people, using mostly proletarian folk song forms. When the Cultural Revolution arrived, reading and writing almost anything was out of favor, except for Mao's little red book, *Quotations from*

Chairman Mao Zedong, and his book of poetry, which sold over fifty million copies. Being an intellectual or writing poetry was hazardous to your health, and many writers were persecuted and died during the Cultural Revolution. Even though intellectuals were being victimized, Mao has probably had more poetry printed in newspapers and magazines and has sold more poetry than any other poet in the history of the world. His little red book ranks second in total copies sold in the world. In Chapter Nine see Chairman Mao's 1956 poem titled "Swimming."

After the Cultural Revolution and Mao's death, many poets started losing their jobs or "iron rice bowl" (a promise by the government of a salary for life) when Deng Xiaoping brought in the new money-driven, one-party dictatorship reforms and the economy started slowly shifting to the powerhouse we see today. The current poetry has an opacity that I think is brought on by present political culture in China.

Whether written by a bohemian poet during the Tang Dynasty (618–907 AD) or a Shanghai taxi driver, I like most Chinese poetry. I hope you enjoyed this brief introduction. Well, back to the story.

CHAPTER THIRTY-TWO

TOP OF THE MOUNTAIN

China in the Twentieth Century - Hu Yaobang Period

By the early 1980s, the countryside economy of small-scale industry and farming was on the move. Deng's new programs would maintain the Communist Party state with slight Confucian characteristics. Deng asked why Socialism couldn't have a market economy. Hu Yaobang worked as Deng Xiaoping's right-hand man and soon became the new symbol of liberalism. The government introduced the "one child per family" policy. Deng used the word "democracy" a lot, but in 1986, when students in Beijing began to criticize Deng and his policies, he ordered a crackdown. Deng and the old guard thought it was time to dump Hu Yaobang in 1987; they thought Hu had spread bourgeois liberalization ideas that had aroused the students. Deng replaced Hu with Zhao Ziyang.

CHANGSHU DIDN'T HAVE many places to visit. Do you remember what the bartender at the Hengshan Hotel told me about Changshu on my first trip? He said something like, "Not many visitors go to Changshu because it is mainly a manufacturing center." Well, the exception is Mount Yu. One Saturday morning during the trip Mr. Wen, Mr. Tao and I visited the mountain. When I asked where we were going, I was told, "To see the clouds, mist, rocks, and trees up on Mount Yu."

We started out from the hotel walking through town until we reached the base of a hilly area not far from the hotel. Once we entered the base of Mount Yu, it was like we were magically transported into ancient China—the kind of place depicted in Chinese paintings where the natural elements are big, and man is small. It wasn't long before civilization disappeared and there were no people, cars, noise, buildings, or any other signs of civilization. How was it possible to walk such a short distance and lose all the hustle and bustle of the million or so people living in the area? As they had promised, we traded it all for clouds, rocks, trees, bushes, and silence. While hiking up the hill, I was urged to enjoy the mountain haze, the rocks, the various vegetation, and maybe an occasional bird. They would stop along the way to examine an old pine tree or a rock outcropping. Many had names.

We stopped to rest and saw three older women slowly making their way down the trail. As they approached Mr. Wen walked over and started talking with them. They conversed for about five minutes and then continued their trek down the mountain.

After they left, I learned through Mr. Tao the women were Buddhists and had just come from a pile of stones where they had gone to pray. Before the Cultural Revolution, there had been a Buddhist temple on the site. It was just a temple that had gotten blown up (along with thousands of other temples all over China and Tibet); the incident was treated as nothing special.

We continued our walk, and I didn't ask any questions because I sensed they really didn't want to talk about it. We walked along in silence for a long stretch, and the mountain vapor continued to get thicker the higher we went. It wasn't until we were almost to the top when I saw the outline of a building. Only a piece of a carved railing and a curved tile roof stuck out of the mist. We walked through an opening in the dense shrubbery that surrounded the building and went up many stairs past a small pond drenched with mist to a tall door that was partially open. We proceeded inside and sat at a small table and ordered tea while the misty air found its way through the partially open door. When the tea came Mr. Tao poured; Mr. Wen responded by tapping the table with three fingers.

"It's silent thanks," Mr. Tao said, without being asked.

We chatted about our climb, and I told them it was the first time I had been invited to see clouds, mist, rocks, and trees. As they talked, I looked out the window into the mist surrounding the tea house and thought, "*I don't think I will ever see or experience a place like this again – this is like seeing an old Chinese painting right out the window.*" I think the concept of withdrawal into the natural world has always been a major thematic focus of the Chinese. Retreating to the mountains to find sanctuary from the chaos like I have outlined in the book is a long tradition in China. After a couple of pots of tea, we headed back down.

The next day, after our hike up Mount Yu and the chance meeting with the three Buddhist women, I began wondering why, down through the years, the Communists have been so against the Buddhist religion. I think I have found the answer right in Mao's little red book.

> *After the enemies with guns have been wiped out, there will still be enemies without guns; they are bound to struggle desperately against us, and we must never regard these enemies lightly. If we do not now rise and understand the problem in this way, we shall commit the gravest mistakes.* [8]

Mao's speech warning about enemies without guns was made in 1949. In 1951, the People's Liberation Army marched into Lhasa, the capital of Tibet, completing a "liberation" they started two years earlier. The destruction of Buddhist monasteries and the Tibetan culture continued during the 1950s; in the last year of that decade, the Dalai Lama fled to India. During the Chinese Cultural Revolution, the Chinese government stepped up its destruction of Buddhist monasteries and culture. Thousands of monks were persecuted and "reeducated." In 1995, the Dalai Lama selected a new Panchen Lama (second highest lama in Tibetan Buddhism). Two days later, the new Panchen Lama disappeared. The Chinese government destroyed many of the monasteries like the one I visited, and they still continue working against the cultural and religious life of all "enemies without guns" like the Dalai Lama.

On my trip to the top of the mountain that day I learned that it doesn't take much for atmosphere—a piece of a carved railing, a curved tile roof sticking out of the mist, misty air flowing through the partially open door, a bit of haze over a little pond, and the view of rocks and trees through a rustic window.

CHAPTER THIRTY-THREE

MARCO AND ME

China in the Twentieth Century - Tiananmen

Hu Yaobang died in 1989 and provided a reason to have another student-led protest. The students demanded political reforms and the end of corruption and inflation, and the cause soon spread to every big city in China. Millions of workers and ordinary citizens joined the students. When they staged a demonstration in Tiananmen Square, Deng called out the army and the demonstration ended in a hail of bullets. Zhao Ziyang lost his job and was replaced by Jiang Zemin. The event in Tiananmen showed that the leadership and the political structure ruled only through the power and consent of the army, just as it had when Marco Polo was in China, except now the army had tanks.

ON THIS TRIP, I finished reading *The Travels of Marco Polo*. I skipped over the parts of his book detailing his Eurasian travels and concentrated on his writing about China and her culture. After reading his narrative, it dawned on me that I had seen some of the same things that he saw over seven hundred years before. This is still possible because there is a part of China and Chinese culture that remains forever old. China appears to be rapidly changing, but underneath, away from the neon signs, is an old China that never seems to change.

I made notations in my journal about things he wrote about that I had seen and made a list of things I wanted see on this extended trip. What Marco and I saw in China is what this chapter is all about. But first, dear reader, let me give you a little background information.

Marco Polo traveled across Eurasia eastward along the caravan roads to China—then known as Cathay—and arrived during the Yuan Dynasty when China was part of the Mongol Empire. He was there from 1275 to 1292 and during that time traveled throughout parts of China in the service of Kublai Khan. Later in life, in prison, he wrote about his adventures in a book best known as *The Travels of Marco Polo*.

The remainder of this chapter presents some of Marco's vivid descriptions along with my observations and comments. Marco's observations are from *The Travels of Marco Polo*.[9]

Troops Used for Civil Control (from Book II, Chapter I, pages 154–55)

"It may be proper here to observe, whilst on the subject of the armies of the grand khan, that in every province of Cathay and Manji, [northern and southern China] as well as other parts of his dominions, there were many disloyal and seditious persons, who at all times were disposed to break out in rebellion against their sovereign, and on this account it became necessary to keep armies in such of the provinces as contained large cities and an

extensive population, which were stationed at a distance of four or five miles from these cities, and can enter them at their pleasure. These armies the Grand Khan makes it a practice to change every second year, and the same with respect to the officers who command them. By means of such precautions the people are kept in quiet subjection, and no movement nor innovation of any kind can be attempted."

Because of the television coverage during the Tiananmen Square incident in 1989, people throughout the world saw the lone Chinese man standing in front of a tank column as if to say, "Aren't we all Chinese?" As happened in other insurrections against those in power, the army prevailed, and many young protestors fled or joined the ranks of others in prison who dared rise up against established authority. The world was shocked at how Chinese citizens were treated by their government; however, the people understand well that the government and the army represent the real power in China.

If you go just a few pages back in Chinese history, you will find many uses of troops for civil control. As China grappled to form a republic, between the abdication of the Manchu dynasty in 1912 and when Chiang Kai-shek headed for Taiwan in 1949, armies were what determined the course of history, not constitutional procedures. Mao's army brought the next government into power, not the ballot.

Sudden arrest, prison, or executions are nothing new to a large portion of China's 1.3 billion people. What Polo and I saw in China were governments that would not hesitate to use troops for civil control.

Capitalism and the Army (from Book II, Chapter I, page 155)

"The troops are maintained not only from the pay they receive out of the imperial revenues of the province, but also from the cattle and their milk, which belong to

them individually, and which they send to the cities for sale . . . "

One day I was reading an English-language newspaper and was astonished to learn that the People's Liberation Army (PLA) at the unit level was involved in the farming business. I did further reading and discovered that the PLA has a huge business empire with many commercial enterprises and defense industries, as well as income from international arms sales.

So, just as when Polo was in China, the troops are still maintained not only from the money they receive from the state but also from all of the PLA businesses that contribute to the total budget of the Chinese military.

Cultivating Every Square Inch (from Book II, Chapter XX, page 209)

"With them no spot of earth is suffered to lie idle, that can possibly be cultivated . . . "

This is one of Marco Polo's comments that made me sure he had traveled to China. One day riding the bus to work with Mr. Wen I wrote in my journal, "As I rumbled along on the bus, from time to time I would see a small graveyard with vegetables growing between the gravestones."

Polo and I had noticed the same thing about China.

Rice Wine (from Book II, Chapter XXIII, pages 214–15)

"The greater part of the inhabitants of the province of Cathay drink a sort of wine made from rice . . . "

During my reading about China, I read a story about one of the most famous wine drinkers in Chinese history: the Tang dynasty poet Li Po. As the story goes, he was traveling down the Yangtze by boat and, as in many of his poems, he had too much wine to drink. Leaning out of the boat in order to embrace the moon's reflection in the water, he fell overboard and drowned.

On my first trip to China, I attended a banquet where it became apparent that the Chinese see drinking as one of the great pleasures of living, second only to eating. But I must explain that the wine Marco Polo was writing about, and the wine served at the banquet, was traditional Chinese wine, distilled from rice or other grains. My first taste had the mule kick of firewater. As the dinner progressed a person would stand and propose a toast, shout *"Ganbei!"* and then everyone would toss their wine down in one gulp. I knew I would never be able to drink a toast with every person around the table, so after the second drink I turned my glass over and asked for a beer. I'm sure this was against every Chinese drinking protocol, but at the end of the evening I thanked Li Po as I walked in a straight line out of the room. Like Marco and me, if you go to China and drink traditional Chinese wine, you might be advised to remember it, too.

The Extensive Use of Coal (from Book II, Chapter XXIII, page 215)

> *"Throughout this province there is found a sort of black stone, which they dig out of the mountains, where it runs in veins. When lighted, it burns like charcoal, and retains the fire much better than wood; insomuch that it may be preserved during the night, and in the morning be found still burning."*

If you are in a large city like Beijing, you don't have to look far to see the extensive use of coal—just look up. Beijing, like almost all big cities, has chronic air pollution. Coal is used extensively for heating homes, public baths, industrial boilers, and power generation. Many old factories have no pollution control equipment; there are even some coal-fired steam locomotives still in use. Adding to the gray skies is the rapid increase in the number of cars and trucks, power plants, and the extensive use of charcoal for cooking.

When the Olympics were held in Beijing in 2008, the government developed a massive program to relocate industries and convert to cleaner coal and natural gas. I'm sure the government's program to clean up the air in Beijing helped, but if you travel anywhere in China today, your eyes and nose will probably tell you they have a long way to go.

Public Baths (from Book II, Chapter XXIII, page 215)

> *"It is true there is no scarcity of wood in the country, but the multitude of inhabitants is so immense, and their stoves and baths, which they are continually heating, so numerous, that the quantity could not supply the demand; for there is no person who does not frequent the warm bath at least three times in the week, and during the winter daily, if it is in their power. Every man of rank or wealth has one in his house for his own use; and the stock of wood must soon prove inadequate to such consumption; whereas these stones [coal] may be had in the greatest abundance, at a cheap rate."*

Public baths are still in use in China. In large cities, there is usually one every few blocks, easily recognizable by the steam and the pile of coal outside.

Gambling (from Book II, Chapter XXVI, page 221)

> *"The present grand khan has prohibited all species of gambling and other modes of cheating, to which the people of this country are addicted more than any others upon earth . . . "*

I think I agree with Polo, that the people of this country are addicted to gambling "more than any others upon earth." Gambling was popular in ancient China and has remained so throughout Chinese history. Many of today's favorite card games are thought to have been invented in China. As when Polo was in China, gambling is officially banned in China . . . well, almost. The government allows gambling in Macao and Hong Kong, but it is banned elsewhere in China. This ban has resulted in a large, illegal underground gambling network. All the various government campaigns have not had much luck stamping out gambling; however, billions of dollars are raised yearly through a number of government-sanctioned provincial social welfare lotteries.

When I was in Shanghai sometime after buying my pet cricket, I read that the police broke up a large organized cricket gambling ring, so I think Polo got it right once more.

The Grand Canal (from Book II, Chapter XLIX page 267)

"They are subjects of the Grand Khan, and his paper money is current among them. . . . This city [Hangchow] has many towns and castles under its jurisdiction: a great river flows beside it, by means of which large quantities of merchandise are conveyed to the city of Kanbalu [Beijing]; for by the digging of many canals it is made to communicate with the capital."

The threats of war brought about the building of the Great Wall of China, but few know it was also the threat of war and the accompanying food shortages that could befall Beijing that made the Chinese build the Grand Canal. The southern and central parts of China are the "rice bowl" of China. Long before the Grand Canal, fleets of large, sea-going junks carried this rice north up the coast of China, exposing them to attack by pirates.

The Grand Canal became the answer to transporting large amounts of grain and merchandise North in a more secure way. It was started in 486 BC and modified and added to until it stretched a total length of twelve hundred miles, from Hangchow in the south to Tientsin in the north. The northern portions of the canal, in the area between Beijing and Tianjin, have fallen into disrepair.

It was in Suzhou, during the second trip—where I went to discuss testing the junk—that I first saw the Grand Canal. The canals in and around Suzhou date back to the eighth century BC; these canals and beautiful arched bridges were in Suzhou long before Polo visited China and saw the canal he later described in his book.

They Don't Care For Red Wine (from Book II, Chapter LXVIII, page 294)

"Grapes are not produced there, but are brought in a dried state, and very good, from other parts. This applies also to wine, which the natives do not hold in estimation, being accustomed to their own liquor prepared from rice and spices."

On the last trip to China, I took two bottles of very good red wine with me that came from the Napa Valley in northern California, thinking I would celebrate my birthday with whomever I happened to be with when the day rolled around. Several days before my birthday, the Chinese at the boatyard found out that I was going to have one, and planned a small party to be held at the restaurant not far from the boatyard where we ate lunch. I thought it would be a gracious gesture to share my wine during my birthday party, so I took the bottles to work with me. After lunch, they set off a string of firecrackers attached to a long pole, hung out the second-story window. After the explosions ended and the smoke cleared, and the evil spirits had departed, I opened the two bottles. I proposed that we have a toast and poured everyone a glass, using the small glasses they normally drink Chinese wine from.

After the *"Ganbei!"* I learned that what Polo had said was true: there were no smiles or favorable opinions about my offering of California's finest. This is changing in places like Beijing and Shanghai, where incomes are high enough for some people to afford French and American wines.

Construction of Wooden Vessels (from Book III, Chapter I, pages 321–2)

"We shall commence with a description of the ships employed by the merchants, which are built of fir-timber. They have a single deck, and below this the space is divided into about sixty small cabins, fewer or more, according to the size of the vessels . . . They have four masts, with as many sails . . . Some ships of the larger class have, besides (the cabins), to the number of thirteen bulk-heads or divisions in the hold, formed of thick planks let into each other . . . The crew, upon discovering the situation of the leak, immediately remove the goods from the division affected by the water, which, in consequence of the boards being so well fitted, cannot pass from one division to another. . . . The ships are all double-planked; that is, they have a course of sheathing-boards laid over the planking in every part. These are caulked with oakum both withinside and without, and are fastened with iron nails. . . . The people take quick-lime and hemp, which latter they cut small, and with these, when pounded together, they mix oil procured from a certain tree, making of the whole a kind of unguent, which retains its viscous properties more firmly, and is a better material than pitch."

Regarding wooden ship construction, what Marco Polo saw is almost exactly what I saw during the period the *Mei Wen Ti* was being constructed. The only real difference was that the *Mei Wen Ti* and the fishing boats I watched being built and repaired were smaller. What he described were large ocean-going junks used for commerce between faraway places and China.

The planking on the *Mei Wen Ti* is fir-timber. It has a single deck, and below deck the space is divided into eight divisions of the hull, created by thick athwart-ship planks forming watertight compartments. The junk is double-planked, fastened with iron nails, and caulked inside and out.

The Chinese building the junk made the iron nail fasteners and the caulking material at the boatyard. The nails were made by hand in a blacksmith shop.

The caulking was made by a man in another small shop. He took quicklime and camphor oil (procured from a certain tree, as Polo says) and pounded the mixture over and over to form a thick paste that became the caulking material. The caulkers would then rub this into strands of hemp with their hands. Using special tools they pounded it into the cracks between the planks. This was allowed to harden, and then the boat would be caulked all over, again and again. As Polo observed, the junk was caulked from the inside (withinside) and from the outside (without). This continued until the caulking material completely filled all the spaces between the planks.

Because of his many omissions, tall tales, and errors in his book, there has been long-standing debate over the validly of what Marco Polo wrote. Some even say he never traveled as far as China. I think we must remember that Polo dictated his travels to someone in prison six years after returning from his twenty-plus years of travels, so it is easy for me to understand how some of the details got left somewhere in the far reaches of his mind or twisted in the many translations. I also believe he added the many tall tales to juice up the story. For example, he wrote about a bird large and strong enough to carry off an elephant, yet went on to say, "Not the twentieth part have I described." Had he left out parts like elephants being carried away by giant birds and added, say, a tenth of what he really saw, I'm sure there would be fewer detractors.

These few examples allow me to conclude that his story is more factual than not and that he definitely must have traveled to China in order to write his (imperfect) account of what he saw.

Now that you have read the chapter, what do you think: did Marco Polo visit China?

CHAPTER THIRTY-FOUR

STILL A LOT TO DO

China in the Twentieth Century - The Jiang Zemin Period

Jiang assumed the leadership in 1989, but Deng still held the real power, like Mao before him. Jiang did not slow China's rush to capitalism; however, Deng's economic program slackened in the aftermath of the Tiananmen Square massacre. The Tiananmen Square demonstration leaders had scattered or were in prison. Ah, stability.

Since you can't have capitalism without hamburgers, McDonalds opened its first fast food restaurant in Beijing in 1991 as the Soviet Union collapsed.

That same year, I took my first trip to China to investigate the possibility of building a Chinese junk.

THE BOATYARD HAD worked every day, including Sunday, since I arrived trying to get the junk finished by March 15th. I informed Don early in March that I did not think they would be done by the 15th and not to plan on flying over for sea trials. The date came and went, and there was still a lot of work to be done. Every time Mr. Chao came to the boatyard I would remind him the contract required them to update their Letter of Credit and keep the junk insured. I thought it would be a waste of time to go to their office in Nanjing and tell his boss the same thing. I was sure the import-export company had made a decision to do just what they were doing. They were sure there was going to be a delivery problem, or there was some other problem they weren't talking about.

Every day I went into the boatyard to help in any way I could. They lifted the engines aboard the boat one hundred and sixteen days after they picked up the engines in Shanghai, yet the contract required the junk to be delivered ninety days after receipt of the engines. Mr. Wen and Mr. Li continued to go with me three days a week, and we continued to work on Mr. Li's English. One day after work, as the three of us walked down the dirt alley toward the bus stop, I pulled out my handwritten list of slang terms.

"Here's an easy one: 'quick buck'," I said.

"Fast dollar."

"Good. 'All the tea in China.'"

"Not do it for any price."

"Good. 'I wouldn't do it for any price' might be better."

Walking along we continued through my list until I came to a new word: "Instead of saying, 'Let's stop for a beer,' you can say, 'Let's stop for a brewski' or 'a cold one,'" I said.

"Let's stop for a brewski."

"Good. When we get off the bus, why don't we?"

"I think was a trick," he said with a big smile.

Mr. Wen picked up his bicycle at the bus station and headed for home. Strolling toward the hotel, we stopped at a small store Mr. Li knew about that sold beer and a little bit of everything else. I bought two bottles of Tsingtao, and we went outside the back of the store and sat on short stools to drink and chat. Since we were alone, Mr. Li talked freely about his present situation at the hotel and said he thought it was a worthless experience and a waste of time. He said if the schools had not been closed during the Cultural Revolution, he would be better educated and able to get a much better job.

"I would like to share with you a Chinese short story I just read," I said in response. I paraphrased a short story from a book I had been reading by a Chinese philosopher named Lin Yutang. "An Old Man was living with his son at an abandoned fort on the top of a hill, and one day he lost a horse. The neighbors came to express their sympathy for this misfortune, and the Old Man asked, 'How do you know this is bad luck?' A few days afterward, his horse returned with a number of wild horses, and his neighbors came again to congratulate him on this stroke of fortune, and the Old Man replied, 'How do you know this is good luck?' With so many horses around, his son began to take up riding, and one day he broke his leg. Again the neighbors came around to express their sympathy, and the Old Man replied, 'How do you know this is bad luck?' The next year, there was a war, and because the Old Man's son was crippled, he did not have to go to the front.[10]

"I tell you this story because you said your present situation was worthless and a waste of time. You see, good things can happen unexpectedly, and you really don't know what life has in store. What you now see as worthless and a waste of time may be something good in disguise."

We finished our beer, walked back out on the busy street, and headed for the hotel. Before we parted, he said, "Thanks for brewski, English lesson, and good old Chinese story."

After dinner, I had just returned to my room when there was a knock on the door. I opened it, and Mr. Ru and Mr. Tao were standing in the hall. "*I wonder what this is all about,*" I thought.

"Please come in. I'll make us some tea." There was always a tall thermos of hot water and cups in my room. I had my own teapot and a large box of green tea I had bought in a small store not far from the hotel. From the somber look on their faces, I was sure the visit was about a serious matter concerning the junk; to cover my nervousness I made small talk while making the tea. I started by pouring hot tap water in the teapot and cups. After a few minutes I poured the water out of the teapot, added a small amount of bulk tea, and then filled it with hot water from the thermos. As the tea brewed, we made more small talk. After a short while, I poured the hot water out of the cups and filled them with green tea.

After I served the tea and we talked a while before they got to the reason for their evening visit to my hotel room. They said both of the new engines for the junk had been damaged—the boatyard people had started them without connecting them up to cooling water, so the raw water pump on each engine had been damaged. They assured me the engines had only been run a short time and had not overheated. After listening to their story, I was sure it was only a minor problem. Back on my third trip, five months ago, there were many questions related to the engine cooling system. Maybe I had not made it clear how the engine cooling system worked, or should have cautioned them against running the engine without external cooling water connected. I felt partially responsible for the screw-up.

"Mei we ti. When they ran the engines without the cooling water hooked up, they damaged the rubber impeller inside the raw water pump. We will just order two more from the Yanmar dealer down in Hong Kong. I will take care of ordering the parts when I get home. You must make sure they check the engines to ensure there are no pieces of the rubber impeller inside the cooling system on each engine," I said.

Their faces brightened as their fears evaporated: the mistake wasn't going to sink the project or cost a vast sum to fix. I filled the pot with more hot water, and we had another cup of tea, which tasted better. Mr. Tao said he was going to be in town for a few days, so we made arrangements to have dinner together. They thanked me, and I noticed a bit of a smile on their faces as I closed the door.

Several days later, Mr. Tao and I met one evening after work and went to a small restaurant not far from the hotel. Perhaps the most remarkable thing about China is the food, and I always looked forward to sharing a meal with someone. This meal was memorable.

"What is that dish?" I asked.

He looked at his plate and said, "I don't know how say in English."

"Is it chicken?"

"No, it not chicken. It four-legged creature. Four-legged creature eats worm."

I still couldn't guess.

"Have big eyes," he said.

"Are you sure these are not just in China?" I couldn't guess what he was describing.

"Oh, no, America have, too. You know: they hop."

"Hop?" I thought and thought about such a creature, rejected a rabbit since I didn't think they ate worms. Then it dawned on me.

"You mean jump—it's a frog!"

"Yes, yes, they frog legs."

The next day, I asked to have a meeting to talk about what remained to be done, since they now said they were not sure when the junk would be ready for sea trials. My best guess was in about a month. With so much work yet to be accomplished, the engines out of commission, and my visa about to expire, I got my ticket changed to fly out on March 23rd. During the days before leaving I did what I could to help out. I told Mr. Li I would probably be back in a month or so, and he agreed to act as my translator again.

I left the hotel early the next morning. I wanted to check in early and get front-row or exit door seats on the China Eastern Airlines flight to Los Angeles. In the van on the way to the airport I got out my passport. The Chinese consulate in Los Angeles had given me a visa to stay in China for thirty days, and I decided to see how long I had stayed.

I checked the date stamp on the page showing when I had entered and counted off the days. "*Uh-oh, I have overstayed my visa!*" I arrived at the airport extra early and had no choice but to proceed. Inside the airport, I got into a long line to show my passport.

No one jumped the line that day. I slowly made my way forward, and soon there wasn't anyone to stand behind. "*I hope they don't look too closely,*" I thought when I got to the front of the line. I handed my passport to a uniformed man in a tall booth. He thumbed through it rapidly until he came to the page stamped with my entry date. He looked at the page intently for what seemed like a long time. He looked down with a little smile and asked me to step aside. He turned and motioned to an older woman standing a short distance away who also wore a uniform.

"You should not stay longer than visa allows," she said after studying my passport for a short while.

"I assure you, it was an oversight," I said. "*I hope I don't get sent downtown to straighten this mess out. I'll miss my flight.*"

"There is penalty for overstaying a visa. Please come with me."

By this time, everyone in line was looking at me and probably thinking I was a spy or criminal who had just been nabbed. I followed her into a small office, which contained a well-used desk and one filing cabinet. She shut the door and asked me to have a seat. Opening the desk, she took out a small pad of paper. "*Is this going to be an interrogation?*" I wondered. Looking at my passport, she began writing on the pad.

After what seemed like an eternity she looked up and said there would be a fine. She gave me the fine amount in *renminbi,* and I couldn't believe my ears. I wouldn't miss my plane, and there would be no questioning, only a very small fine. I paid her, and she wrote something in the pad, stamped the page, and then tore out a thin, tissue-paper receipt. She stamped the receipt and handed it to me with my passport.

"Thank you. No one is allowed to come and go as they please. Please be more mindful next time you visit our country," she said.

"I will." *"America should have such a policy. No one knows how many people are in the country with expired visas or who crossed our borders illegally,"* I thought as I picked up my bag and rushed out the door.

CHAPTER THIRTY-FIVE

YOUR REQUEST IS RIDICULOUS AND IMPOSSIBLE

China in the Twentieth Century - Southern Journey

In 1992, Deng decided to tour southern China to try and reinvigorate the economy and push his reforms, which he feared would go the way of the old Soviet Union.

Deng ended the peasants' ties to their villages, giving workers greater labor mobility and providing a ready workforce in the non-state sector. By 1996, profits from state-run companies represented less than one percent of gross domestic product.

THE FLIGHT HOME was my eighth trip over the dark blue Pacific in my quest to build the junk, and I had another round trip to go. My plan was to return as soon as they finished with the remaining work that should take about a month. I was going home without an amended Standby Letter of Credit or an updated copy of the builder's insurance policy, but I was sure the trip had been a success. I had been able to answer many questions, help solve many problems, and had learned a lot about the junk.

When I got back, I ordered the raw water impeller and sent Mr. Chao a fax asking them (for the hundredth time) to update their Letter of Credit and send me an updated builder's insurance policy. As usual there was no reply; it was as if we didn't have a written contract.

Once the junk arrived I'd need a slip for it, so I spent my weekends looking. My search began in Dona Point in Orange County, and I worked my way north. After looking at about a dozen marinas, I visited Ventura, just slightly south of Santa Barbara. I fell in love with the old town section of the city, and the harbor had several good marinas with slips available. I rented a fifty-by-twenty-foot one and made plans to move to Ventura until the junk arrived. A week later, I found a great apartment in a 1920s apartment house high on a hill, overlooking the old part of town. I could walk down a long flight of stairs into town, and the market was only a block away.

Not long after I moved in, I saw a poster in town advertising a reading of Percy Bysshe Shelley's poetry at a little theater-in-the-round not far from my apartment. I was distantly familiar with his work and decided to attend. The clock on the mantel said it was time to go, so I took the last gulp from my glass of Chardonnay and headed for the stairs. When I got to the theater, I paid my four bucks and walked in. I was early, so I picked out a folding chair in the second row and sat down and waited for the room to fill with strangers. The first poem on the program was "Ode to the West Wind."

Finally, an older gentleman stood and said, "Would someone please close the door?" His accent made me think he might be from Vienna. The racecars at the fairgrounds could be faintly heard in the distance even with the door closed. He started reading.

O wild West Wind, thou breath of Autumn's being,
Thou, from whose unseen presence the leaves dead
Are driven, like ghosts from an enchanter fleeing,

Yellow, and black, and pale, and hectic red,
Pestilence-stricken multitudes: O thou,
Who chariotest to their dark wintry bed[11]

In between each long poem, there was a little Beethoven or Chopin with faint racecar sounds superimposed. After the last poem, they played a beautiful Chopin ballade, and it was all over; the man next to me clapped with a glove on one hand. I didn't care for the poetry, but it wasn't a bad evening for four bucks.

The next day, a fax dated April 5, 1993, arrived from the import-export company. Not having the amended Standby Letter of Credit and an updated copy of the builder's insurance policy were mere snowflakes compared with the blizzard this message blew in.

It read: "I have been informed that the Junk will be launched for the first sea trial on April 9th, 1993. This is very good news, but we have not got the rubber impellers from Yanmar. I am sure that you already knew the rubber impeller damaged in test, and we need other one as replacement. If Yanmar would not deliver the parts in time, I suggest you bring two pics of the part to the shipyard when you come China to speed up the sea trial. The sea trial will be finished before April 20th, 1993. The delivery time could be arranged around April 30th, 1993.

I have contacted many shipping Co. and found that there is only one that agree to ship your junk so far. The freight charge is USD65,000.00. It is too high to accept. The reply from shipping Co. listed as follows.

Shipping Co. Reply:

1. *AMERICAN PRESIDENT LINES:*
   They have never done business like that and refuse to do.
2. *CHINA OCEAN SHIPPING CO:*
   Transfer via Kobe, cost too high.

3. KAWASAKI KISEM KAISHA LTD:

No experience and refuse to do.

4. MAERSK LINE:

Refuse to do.

5. MITSUI O.S.K. LINES LTD:

No experience and refuse to do.

6. OVERSEAS CONTAINERS LTD:

Refuse to do.

7. SEA-LAND SERVICE INC:

They promised to undertake this business and offered us the cost two years ago. But they change ideas and refuse to do.

8. UNITED STATES LINE INC:

Refuse to do.

9. SINO-TRANS, SHANGHAI:

No direct vessels and refuse to do.

10. SINO-TRANS, JIANGSU:

They agree to do this business, but they offer high price.

Also be noted that the recent advance in price of raw material has made the shipyard suffer some loss.

*Based on above mentioned facts we have to adjust our price for Junk. That means you must add **USD45,000.00**. We are sorry to say so. But this is only way to resolve the problem. Awaiting for your reply."*

I sat down and read the message over several times. It was pretty simple: all they needed were two rubber impellers, forty-five thousand dollars, and my reply. I believed the message confirmed that they knew there was a shipping problem a long time ago (from the number of shippers contacted), and that was the reason they had not added funds to their Standby Letter of Credit. They knew if they didn't deliver the boat to Los Angeles as agreed to in the contract, I would have the right to demand and get all my money back.

The majority of the money I currently had was the other half of the purchase price, which was due when the junk was delivered; I had set aside a small amount of funds for projects after it arrived. Back in early 1992, I had started reducing the cost of the project because my projections showed I might run out of money. The first major thing I did was to remove the generator and all associated equipment from the requirements. I knew that when the junk was delivered I would need money to purchase a stove and refrigerator, install propane tanks, and do several other small jobs. I did not have an additional forty-five thousand dollars. I barely had enough money to finish the project. What was I going to do?

I contemplated calling Don, but I didn't since I was sure he would advise me to go to arbitration like he did before. I needed to try and solve the problem before doing that. I needed to *think*. I made myself a pot of tea and went out on the balcony where I had a small table and chair. Sipping my drink and looking out at Santa Cruz Island, I let my mind wander back over the project. "*What could I do?*"

I looked at my teapot, and it reminded me of the time I had tea with the business attaché at the Chinese Embassy in Los Angeles before my first trip to China. He had advised me about doing business in China; "Americans are always in a hurry," he said. "It is better to have a cup of tea and visit first. When you go to China, try to slow down and remember this."

"Slow down, don't be in a hurry. Maybe I should simply do nothing. Could doing nothing be a strategy?" I thought so.

I went inside, turned on my computer, and wrote Mr. Chao a reply. The short message read, "Your request is ridiculous and impossible." I knew by now short messages worked best. To drive the point home, I faxed the same message for the next two days. The ball was now in their court.

CHAPTER THIRTY-SIX

WHAT TO DO—ARBITRATION IN CHINA?

China in the Twentieth Century - China Loses Deng

In 1997, Deng died. Since Jiang and his colleagues had ruled under Deng for about eight years, the transition of power went much smoother than in the past. There was no one to assume Deng's position as paramount ruler. Under Jiang, there would be no political reform.

Hong Kong was restored to China and became a Special Administrative Region. In 1999, Macau was also returned to China, bringing to an end to 442 years of Portuguese colonial rule. In 2001, China gained entry into the World Trade Organization.

I SENT DON Mr. Chao's message and my reply, waited a while and then called him. From the way he greeted me I figured he had spent too much time in China to be surprised. After talking, I made it clear that I did not have the money. We agreed that they had knowledge about the shipping problem for quite some time and so had not updated their Letter of Credit. I told him I did not want to negotiate their request for more money. I promised to call back as soon as I came up with a plan ... which I didn't have. For now doing nothing was my strategy.

What I lacked at this point was leverage in the negotiation. How could I get them to do what the contract required? Weeks went by, and I just couldn't come up with a starting point. Then one day the solution just came to me. I turned on my computer and wrote Mr. Chao a short, clear message.

"If you do not intend to honor the contract and deliver the junk, I plan to submit the matter to arbitration immediately. In arbitration, I will not ask for the junk because I do not have the money to ship it. Instead, I plan to ask the arbitration commission for all the money I have invested to date in the construction of the junk. The total amount includes the down payment, cost of the engines, parts, engineering services, commissions, travel expenses, and all my arbitration expenses."

Don was getting ready for a trip to China, so I asked him to stop at the boatyard and tell the management the project was headed for arbitration and to read them my last message to Mr. Chao. I thought this move might get the boatyard's attention since it represented a lot more money than I had given them for a down payment. The boatyard had by now spent the down payment and probably had a bit of their money invested in the project. Mr. Chao's fax said that the cost of raw materials was causing the boatyard a problem. Maybe this tactic would cause the boatyard to put pressure on the import-export company to figure a way to ship the junk. I also asked Don to stop at the American Consulate in Shanghai and see if there was anything they could do to help us.

After Don left for China, I wrote the business attaché at the People's Republic of China Embassy in Los Angeles and updated him on the project, telling them we were going to arbitration over nondelivery of the junk. I thought the embassy might be required to keep the trade officials in Beijing informed about problems involving trade and hoped that someone in Beijing would call the import-export company to make an inquiry about the project.

Next, I sent a message to the China International Economic and Trade Arbitration Commission (CIETAC) in Beijing and requested information about the arbitration process.

A few days later I got a message from Mr. Chao. "Honoring the contracts is basic principle we do business and would never break it," the message began. It went on to tell me I needed to pay the additional forty-five thousand dollars and ended by saying it would be better to solve the problem through friendly negotiations.

Really? Before the contract was signed, I had spent many days in friendly negotiations. After all of that, I had put together the contract, and everyone had signed it. I was not going to negotiate another one at this late date. In my response, I told Mr. Chao I had no intention of paying them one additional dollar for the junk, much less forty-five thousand dollars.

A few days later, the American Consulate in Shanghai sent me a fax saying they did not get involved in trade disputes. They did, however, include a list of lawyers in the Shanghai area. I immediately mailed out nine inquiry letters asking about arbitration experience, an estimate of their fee, and an approximation of how long the arbitration might take.

Sometime later, I received a letter and the booklet I had requested from CIETAC, which detailed all the rules of arbitration. They said my application for arbitration should be sent to their office in Shanghai and that they would hear my case. The proceeding would be in Chinese, and they had the right to ask me to provide translated copies of all my documentation. This would mean hiring someone to translate all my documentation, and since I knew there was multiplicity of meaning attached to certain Chinese characters, it wouldn't help me present an unambiguous case. After reading the booklet, I thought my chances of prevailing in the arbitration were slim to none.

I just couldn't forget the time in Changshu, on the third trip, when I ask Mr. Li to find out what it would cost to ride a pedicab to the bus station. When he returned after talking to the pedicab drivers, he said, "I don't know how you say, but fare not same for me-you."

"You mean because I am bigger and heavier the fare is more?" I replied.

"No, it's you foreigner and me Chinese."

When I returned from my last trip at the end of March, my plan was to return in about a month for sea trials. Instead, here I was in June working on an application for arbitration. My best guess was the whole arbitration process would take six months minimum, cost a bunch, and the outcome was anyone's guess.

The business in Pasadena had been sold, so during this period, I only worked at the store in Montrose part-time. This left me time to work on the arbitration document, get acquainted with Ventura, and go to Mexico once a month with the Flying Samaritans.

The import-export company claimed they had the shipping problem because we were late delivering the engines and parts. This was simply not true. In early February 1993—at the beginning of my last trip—when I first saw their parts storage area at the boatyard, I noticed that very few parts had been installed on the junk. The main power panel and the engines remained to be installed. I had shipped the parts to them in mid-October 1992. Later in the trip, the engines were finally hoisted aboard the junk one hundred and sixteen days after they were signed for. I had signed and dated documents showing when they picked the engines and parts up in Shanghai, most of the time long after they had arrived.

If the case were to be solely decided on fact, I would easily win. But would the truth be enough to win? I didn't think so. I was sure the truth would be factored because I was a foreigner. To compound the matter, I knew facts get lost or changed in translation. Also, many times when translating the main point would get lost. Translating English into Chinese was not precise. In the end, I believed the arbitration commission would tell me to pay the forty-five thousand dollars and tell the boatyard to have sea trials and then ship the junk to Los Angeles. At best, they might ask me to pay half. Whatever their decision, it would be final, and I could not bring a suit before a law-court or any other organization. In either case, I would also be out the cost of the arbitration. Even though I thought the deck was stacked against me, I was determined to give it my best shot.

While I waited to hear from the nine lawyers, I worked on building a case with airtight documentation. My plan was to have it finished along with all the supporting documentation by the time I heard back from the lawyers. The focus of the document was an attack on their contention that the delivery of the engines and parts caused the problem. In addition, it would present their other contract violations.

One day while I was working on the case, I received a call from the Flying Samaritans coordinator, wanting to know if I was going to Mexico on our monthly trip. I was a regular volunteer and had several jobs in process that needed to be finished. He wanted to know if I was available on a Friday, Saturday, and Sunday. I told him to count me in.

The primary mission of the Flying Samaritans is to provide medical assistance and education to people in the rural areas of Mexico. The small group I worked with went to two clinics monthly in Baja Norte, California. One clinic was in Punta Prieta and the other in Bahia de Los Angeles. Punta Prieta is approximately 400 miles south of the border, along the highway that runs the length of the peninsula, and Bahia de Los Angeles is to the east on the coast of the Sea of Cortez. The group was made up of pilots, doctors, chiropractors, dentists, nurses, translators, and guys like me who did maintenance. On my application, where it asked what service I could provide I wrote, "I can fix anything." If you have ever been to Mexico you know, there is an abundance of things just waiting to be refurbished, repaired, or painted. The two facilities I went to were full of worn-out medical and dental equipment; and a variety of other things like generators, air compressors, toilets, and windows that needed to be mended.

On a typical three-day trip, I would meet the pilot at an airport somewhere around the Los Angeles area on Friday morning. I've gone on trips where I was the only passenger, but on most there is a pilot plus two or three passengers. En route, we would stop to clear customs and immigration. The flight time was about two hours (depending on the plane) to Punta Prieta and sometimes, if we were the first plane to get there, we might have to buzz the runway to scare off cattle that liked to hang out there. I ate my bag lunch while we were checked out by the local Mexican military. The clinic, located in a building that once housed construction workers back when the highway that runs the length of the peninsula was being built, was only a short walk from the airfield.

On this particular trip, I worked on two old-style dental chairs that were donated to the Flying Samaritans after first spending a lifetime in some dentist's office up in California. On the previous trip, I had removed a large amount of the old wiring and plumbing from inside the pedestal of each chair. On this trip, I finished converting the chairs to operate with new high-speed, air-driven drills. By the end of the workday, I had completed all the modifications and the chairs were ready to be used—time to get rid of those old regular chairs. Since there are no landing lights on the runway at Bahia de Los Angeles, we had to leave in the late afternoon and fly the short distance over to the coast.

We checked into a small hotel not far from the landing field and had a wonderful fish dinner with plenty of Mexican beer. The Flying Samaritans shared a small government clinic that had a full-time, resident Mexican medical doctor. On Saturday morning, I got there early to set up our generator and air compressor before everyone showed up to start work. I labored all day Saturday and half of Sunday completing modifications to another dental chair. In the early afternoon, we took off and flew out over the pristine shoreline of the Baja peninsula, heading north. Flying out over the beautiful blue-green water of the Sea of Cortez toward the States, I didn't think about my Chinese arbitration.

When I got home, though, several messages hung out the back of my fax machine. I had responses from two of the lawyers I had contacted. Over time, more messages arrived until I had nine responses. It was time to make a decision. I first put all the messages that used really poor English, I couldn't understand, or had not answered the three simple questions in my inquiry into one pile. I figured if they couldn't write a clear response to a simple letter they would be no help to me. This left me with two choices. After reading both over, I had to discard one because at the end of the letter it said, "If the legal fee is paid by cheque it is for your interest to indicate on the cheque 'To the order of (letter writer's name)' instead of the name of our law firm, because of the large difference of exchange rate between the individual's foreign currency and that of organization." I wasn't sure what that meant and didn't want to find out. The last letter was from a small law office in Shanghai. The letter was on good-looking stationery and answered all my questions. At the end it said they had "rich experience in commercial arbitration." I was sure I was going to need all the "rich arbitration experience" I could get. I had found a law firm!

I finally finished the arbitration document, withdrew ten thousand dollars, made out an application for arbitration, contacted the law firm, and packed my bag. I was all ready to go. And then I thought of something. I got out my old Chinese amulet and stuck it in my pocket. I had a feeling I was also going to need a lot of calm wind and good fortune and maybe a little luck on my fifth trip to China.

CHAPTER THIRTY-SEVEN

LAST TRIP TO CHINA—FIFTH TRIP

China in the Twenty-First Century - China's Rising Star

In 2001, under Jiang, entrepreneurs were admitted into the Communist Party. Mao's worst dreams were coming true as China passed Japan as America's biggest supplier.

China was selected to host the Summer Olympics in 2008, and America's trade deficit headed off the scale.

AND THEN SOMETHING unexpected happened. I received a strange message from Mr. Chao that read in part: "I got news that there will be a direct vessel to US. But the destination port of this vessel is NEW YORK and whether it will stop over at LOS ANGELES was not decided yet. I have already booked shipping space on this vessel. If we are lucky, all the problem regarding shipment will be settled this time. The vessel will left JIANGSHU port around the end of this month according to schedule." The message went on to say they did not want the final payment debited because of late delivery. There was no mention of more money. It was like a message from Alice when she was in Wonderland.

I responded with a note of my own saying I did not understand and asked for clarification. How could he book space on a ship if he didn't know whether it was stopping in Los Angeles or not? The most important thing in the message was what was missing: they had not asked for more money. Why had they dropped their demand for an additional forty-five thousand dollars? Was it the letter I wrote the business attaché at the People's Republic of China Embassy in Los Angeles? Had someone in Beijing called them? Was it my threat to ask the arbitration commission for all the money I had invested in the construction of the junk? Was it Don's visit to the boatyard to tell the management the project was headed for arbitration? Had the boatyard put pressure on the import-export company? Whatever the reason, one thing was clear: they were trying to get the junk shipped.

Days went by, and I heard nothing back. Were they going to just ship the junk? I sent another message saying if the junk was not going to be shipped to Los Angeles they should cancel the space they had booked and we should proceed with the arbitration. I received no response to that one, either.

More days went by—nothing. It wasn't until late July that I received communication saying in part, "The business regarding transportation is under negotiation. Please come China this week!!! There will be a lot of jobs to do if you want to make a sea trial."

I remembered earlier in the year when they told me they would *for sure* have the junk ready for sea trials my March 15th. Would they be ready this time? Would they ask for the money when I got there? Since receiving CIETAC's booklet, which detailed all the rules of arbitration, I had done more investigating and found that Chinese arbitration had even more pitfalls than I had originally thought. I found out CIETAC could use their own personnel as arbitrators, and one of their personnel might even be appointed as the presiding arbitrator. I didn't like the fact that the arbitration organization played such an important role in the hearing and thought it made it harder for me to receive a reasoned and fair decision. Most of all, I still believed the truth would not be enough to win.

I wasn't sure the Chinese had their act together regarding shipment of the junk, but the fear of arbitration and its cost drove me to reluctantly make the fifth trip to China. I sent them a message inquiring about the status of any work remaining to be done on the junk, saying it was impossible to leave for China on such short notice, and as soon as I had made arrangements I would notify them. I contacted the law firm and told them I was coming to China and wanted first to meet with the boatyard to see if the shipping problem was truly resolved and if they had really dropped their demand for more money. If the two issues were not settled, I would come to Shanghai and work with them on the arbitration. I contacted Don and told him about my decision and said I couldn't be sure there was going to be a sea trial based on what happened on the last trip. We agreed that I might very well spend the trip in Shanghai at the lawyer's office. We decided there was no need for him to make the trip.

Prior to leaving I sent Mr. Li (from the Yushan Hotel in Changshu) a message saying I may need him for a few days to act as my interpreter. The last thing I did was get Mr. Wen a carton of Marlboro cigarettes and some Gillette razor blades.

My cricket, Pu Yi II, and I zipped through customs like seasoned China travelers. The cab at the head of the line was new, and the inside was clean and didn't smell. "*Things, they are a-changing,*" I thought as I got in. The driver had on a clean shirt (washed and ironed), spoke good English, and knew exactly where the Hengshan Hotel was. Pictures of neither Mao nor Li Feng were to be seen. He didn't smoke or spit out the window on the way to the hotel and was interested in what I was doing in China. His conversation sounded just like a cab driver you might meet in San Francisco's Chinatown.

"Welcome, Mister Walt, good you back," the old clerk said as he handed me the familiar registration card.

"You alone again?"

"Yes, except for my pet cricket."

He laughed as he handed me a pen.

"How many times stay here?"

I thought about it for a minute. "Let's see . . . this is my fifth trip to China, and I stay here every time I am in Shanghai, so that makes it nine times."

"*Chuan* finished?"

"Yeah," I said, giving him the short answer.

Just like on all the other trips, Mr. Wen and a driver arrived on time in the same old work van. I piled in with my bag, and we headed out into the heavier-than-ever morning traffic. The highway infrastructure around Shanghai was still going through a massive renaissance that has made room for more cars and trucks. On the long ride to Changshu, I just looked out the window and listened to an unending conversation I didn't understand.

Mr. Wen and I got to the boatyard early the next morning because I always tried to arrive early when there was a meeting scheduled; it showed respect to my host. Everyone greeted me with a quick handshake and each other with a nod of the head or a slight bow. There was the usual tea and a lot of small talk and questions about my trip or the weather. Everyone was polite and gracious. Once the meeting started there was no mention of money or shipping problems. I knew it was important that everyone maintain face, so I didn't push for an explanation. It was as if it was April instead of August and I had just returned to take the junk on sea trials as we had discussed last time we all talked together. It seems as if there was a real aversion about talking about negative matters I had noticed many times before. After a meeting with little substance, we walked down to the canal so I could inspect the junk and see for myself that it was ready for a sea trial.

I saw the junk tied outboard of a wooden fishing boat parked on the canal. We walked across a long wooden gangplank, boarded the fishing boat, and then crossed the main deck to board the junk. There were tires hanging between the two vessels to keep them from being damaged when they bumped each other. There were workers aboard stringing up colorful flags and finishing up last-minute details before the sea trials tomorrow. Most of the boatyard personnel slowly disappeared, and I spent the rest of the day looking the junk over. Since I had written every page of the design document, I used a copy as a sort of check-off list. I went into every space including under all the floorboards. I could see nothing wrong—we were ready.

The next morning when I got to the junk it was ready to go with small flags flying from one end to the other.

As the morning passed, the junk accumulated a large crew aboard consisting of managers, boatyard workers, Mr. Wen, Mr. Ru, Mr. Tao, Mr. Chao, a Chinese captain, and others I assumed were involved with the Chinese test document. The workers had brought a number of watermelons. In the background, I heard Chinese music from someone's portable radio.

The canal beside the boatyard was bustling with morning boat traffic in both directions—it looked like a boat freeway, and I sure didn't understand Chinese rules of the road. I was relieved they had brought along a Chinese captain to take the junk out on sea trials. He had all the windows in the steering station open and was yelling commands to those handling the lines. He maneuvered the junk out into the thick traffic on the canal, yelling at his crew and at those on passing boats.

The junk attracted much attention as we cruised down the canal toward the mighty Yangtze River. There were boats of every size and long trains of barges snaking slowly along. Along the canal, workers would stop to look and wave at the strange new boat all decked out festively. A well-used Chinese flag flew proudly from a teak flagpole on the stern. The traffic thinned as we approached the Yangtze. We went by a large ship graveyard where a huge old oil tanker was being cut into pieces by a small army of workers. Pieces of machinery from the ship stood on the bank awaiting a new home. The traffic got thinner and thinner.

We turned right when we hit the Yangtze and headed toward Shanghai and the East China Sea. Now out of the traffic, the captain turned over the helm to me, and I held a steady course down the river.

In the picture notice the celebration watermelon on the main deck. The Yangtze was nearing the end of its 3,900-mile trip down from the Tibetan plateaus in the west when I turned and headed back upstream toward the boatyard. As we headed back, I couldn't help but feel as if, like the Yangtze, my project was nearing the end.

As the traffic got thicker the captain took the helm—thank God. I think to be a Chinese boat captain you need to speak Chinese, have good seamanship skills, have a loud voice that travels, and know a long list of good slang words.

As we headed back, I stood next to the captain checking to make sure the multipurpose Global Positioning System (GPS) was working properly. It had been turned on since we left the boatyard and was a big hit with everyone because they had never seen one before. I'm sure the builders of the GPS system never envisioned it being used on a Chinese junk cruising the Yangtze River.

Not only did the system on the junk show the current longitude and latitude, it displayed current depth, along with a picture of the bottom (with fish sometimes). The system had also drawn a real-time plot of the track of the boat since we left port earlier in the day. I could see we were headed back not far off the outbound image. The trip back up the canal was over before I knew it. The captain eased the junk back alongside the fishing boat while yelling at the line handlers and all nearby vessels. We tied up again outboard of the fishing boat. After checking to see all was secure, the captain smiled at me and after a thumbs up, shut off both engines—the sea trial was over.

I went in the next day and said good-bye to all the people who had worked on my boat and all the management people in the front office. They made it a special occasion when they handed me the key to the junk. It was an old-style door key just like they still used at the Hengshan Hotel in Shanghai. As I left the boatyard, I stopped and said good-bye to the old man who staffed the front gate. He smiled, bowed, and shook my hand. As I turned to leave he took a Chinese coin out of his pocket, pointed at it, and then pointed to me. I don't know why, but

I understood. I reached in my pocket and found a dime amongst all the change. I handed it to him; with a big smile he took the dime and said, "*Sha-sha*" (thanks). I bowed slightly and left the boatyard for the last time. It was a sad walk to the bus stop knowing I would never see any of these wonderful people again.

After paying my bill at the Hengshan Hotel I reached over and shook hands with the old desk clerk and told him it was my last trip to his hotel, the project was finished, and the new junk would soon be leaving China. His face seemed a bit sad when I said goodbye in my bad Chinese. "Have a good trip," he answered as I walked toward the door.

I went across the street to say goodbye to the shopkeeper who had sold me the old teapot. As I walked in he rose from his old wooden stool and said, "First, we have cup of tea."

CHAPTER THIRTY-EIGHT

THE JUNK ARRIVES

China in the Twenty-First Century - Hu to Xi

In 2003, Hu Jintao became China's new leader in a smooth transition. Hu and those now governing China lack the authority of Mao's or Deng's regimes. The new leadership has had to deal with new problems such as increasing economic inequities, pollution, energy, and human rights issues.

On November 15, 2012, Hu stepped down, and Xi Jinping became the new General Secretary of the CPC Central Committee and Chairman of the Central Military Commission (CMC).

History has a habit of repeating itself. Remember back during Pu Yi's time when the dynasty was corrupt, ineffectual, and weak? In the future, will Xi see the dragon run wild once again? In Chinese history, there is still plenty of time.

DEAR READER, THE story has come full circle. We return to that December day in 1993, right after the monster gantry crane had softly landed the junk on the pier, not far from *Empress Heaven*, in Los Angeles Harbor.

Right after the junk was placed on the pier, a crew of longshoreman disconnected it from the crane. As soon as it was disconnected, the longshoreman started rerigging the crane to finish lifting the remaining shipping containers from the ship. I walked over to look at the junk. It had been five long months since the sea trials in China. As I approached, a longshoreman in khakis and a hard hat walked up next to me and stood quietly looking up at the junk.

He joined me as I walked around inspecting the hull for any signs of damage from the long trip and all the handling. His name was Duke, and he looked as if he had spent his youth on the docks. We walked around the junk together and talked as I inspected.

We walked and talked several revolutions around, and then he stopped and said, "Mind if I ask you a question?"

"No," I replied, anticipating that he was going to ask how much it cost.

"How can I get one of these?"

"Well," I said, "it's kind of a long story—a very long story."

There was yelling from across the pier. "I'm sure, but I'm being yelled at and gotta get back to work," he said. He turned and looked back toward the person waving at him.

"It's my boss—I gotta go. Good talking to you and good luck with your new boat." He turned and began a slow jog back across the pier toward the *Empress Heaven*.

I had made an appointment with a marine surveyor to meet me on the pier to begin a survey of the junk. When you buy a new boat or purchase any used vessel, it is customary to do a comprehensive inspection, referred to as a "marine survey." Most insurance companies will not provide insurance on a vessel without a current survey. The plan was to inspect the hull out of the water and then complete the survey once the junk was in the water. His report would also include the fair market value, replacement cost, and general remarks regarding the overall condition. I currently had insurance coverage but needed to send the insurance company the final report after correcting any recommendations.

While I was waiting for the surveyor, I decided to go aboard to continue my inspection. I climbed up on the cradle and managed to get aboard the junk. Gone were all the festive flags, sails, and masts. No old pieces of watermelon were to be seen. Everything was dirty, and the giant canvas cover was torn and hanging down from the huge bamboo poles they used to hold it up. The masts were lying on the main deck along with crude wooden boxes that held the sails. I walked up a short ladder to the main deck aft. Reaching into my pocket, I retrieved the old-fashioned key given to me after the sea trials and unlocked the entry leading below. There was a small anchor on the key. "*Wonder where they got this key with an anchor on it?*" I went down the steep ladder backwards into the steering station. It seemed only yesterday when I had steered the junk down the Yangtze on sea trials. I remembered everyone staring at me through the open windows and the rocking watermelon rinds. Before I could look around, I heard a knock on the hull.

"Anyone aboard?"

"Be right up," I yelled as I scurried back up the ladder.

I looked over the side and saw a not-quite-retired guy in work clothes looking up at me. "My name's John. I'm here to do your survey. You must be Walt."

"Yeah, I'm Walt. Come aboard."

We shook hands and talked a bit about where the boat was built. I sensed he wanted to get on with his work, so I gave him a well-used copy of the specifications that contained some of the information I knew he would need for the survey like the engine manufacturer, horsepower, etc. "How about I walk you around first, for starters?"

"That would be great. After that I will go through the boat—I mean junk—and take notes to use when I type up the survey. I just got several pictures of the boat." (I've included a picture taken that day in this book.)

"Let's go up to the bow and start there," I said. "The basic design of this hull was lifted from an ancient fishing-boat hull design. This first hatch leads into the chain locker. Water that may get into the chain locker drains into the next compartment that contains a bilge pump. There are six bilge pumps in the junk because there are six athwartship watertight bulkheads."

As we moved along, I explained that most of the construction techniques he was seeing were old when Marco Polo visited China. "The vessels he described were caulked with a caulking make of quicklime and tung oil. This caulking material, along with hemp strands, were pounded into the cracks to seal the junk just like the seams you see everywhere you look," I said, pointing at a caulked seam.

"This anchor windlass was manufactured in the boatyard. Everything I didn't send to China was made by the boatyard." As I walked him around, I continued to explain those things that I knew were different from boats he normally surveyed. After a quick introduction, he began his survey by going through the junk in detail. Since part of the survey needed to be done in the water, when he finished I explained that I had made arrangements to lower the junk into the water the next day. I had also made arrangements for a sea-going tugboat to arrive at that time to tow the junk up the coast to Ventura Harbor. In addition, the tug had large pumps aboard in case there was any flooding. We made plans to meet the next day.

The following day the surveyor arrived early, and we both watched from the main deck of the junk as the longshoreman rerigged the enormous gantry crane to lift the junk from the pier into the water. Once they had connected the cradle to the crane high above us, the junk was gently lifted and set into the water. While the operator waited, I inspected all the bilge areas for water and didn't find a drop. The cradle was then lowered further down into the water, and the junk was moved clear and tied up to the pier. The cradle was then lifted out of the water and put back on the pier. I had made arrangements with a company that moved boats to have the cradle picked up from the pier before the next ship arrived.

After John completed his work, he shook my hand and said, "You will have my survey in a few days. This is an amazing boat and it is the first wooden boat that I have ever seen that didn't leak after being out of the water as long as this one has."

The tug had arrived earlier and moved into position alongside the junk. The junk was secured directly alongside the tug and moved across the harbor in preparation for the trip to its new home up the coast in Ventura Harbor.

That evening, as I headed alone on the junk toward Ventura under tow, I began to think about the times where events had set a completely new direction to my life. Sometimes they were planned and sometimes they weren't. "*This is another monumental, life-changing event,*" I thought as I watched the swells between the two vessels cause the tug's many lights to rise and fall as we moved along the coast. "*Here I am, at fifty-eight years of age, no longer adrift because of my son's death, ready to pursue my dream of living on a boat.*" But not just any boat.

EPILOGUE

In 1996, eighteen years ago, I was living on the junk in Ventura, California, as I had planned. For some reason, in May of that year I was in Laguna Beach, which is one of my favorite places to visit. As you may recall from Chapter Two, I had owned an art gallery in Old Town Pasadena and consequently had many artist friends. That day I decided while I was in Laguna to visit one of those friends named Andrew Stanley Wing. A few years older than me, Andy had come to Laguna Beach in the 1950s and had been a constant presence in the city, and in its art scene.

Andy lived in Laguna Canyon, in an area called Sarah Thurston Park. So, to get to his one-of-a-kind house I needed to find a parking place and then because there were no streets connecting the many lots in the area, walk on paths to his house. I got there, parked, and started walking, but couldn't find his house. I asked the first person I met and got directions. Everyone knew Andy.

As I recall, he was working outside on a painting under a tall eucalyptus tree when I arrived. He was in the process of incorporating a small piece of debris that had fallen from the tree into his painting. He stopped, and we went into his small kitchen, and he put on an old teakettle. After the tea was made, we talked for quite some time about the junk and what I had been doing since we last spoke. I paused to sip my tea, and Andy started recounting one of the many stories from his past. Sometime in the 1970s, the city council proposed getting rid of Andy and his hippie artist friends who had constructed a rather unorthodox community of small houses using their own building code. Andy said he responded by circulating a petition in opposition to the city council's plan. After collecting a pile of signed petitions, he said he decided to connect them all together (I think he was fond of painting on scrolls). Andy taped all the signed petitions together, making a very long scroll that he unrolled from the back to the front of the council chambers, where it was presented to the City Council. Because of this, the council voted to delay their plans. He said in time the city council voted to support the neighborhood and installed water and sewage lines.

Smiling broadly, he said everyone in his little community was so happy that he became the unofficial mayor. It was getting late, and I figured it was time to leave. Andy wouldn't let me go until I picked a picture to hang on the junk. After telling him several times that all his pictures were too large to hang on the junk, he just wouldn't take no for an answer, so he took me into his bathroom and there, next to his mosaic bathtub, hung a small painting. He took it down, wrote something on the back and handed it to me. During the period, he worked on the painting he had kept a log of his progress on the back.

Here is what Andy wrote on the back of the picture that day in Laguna:

Spring – Seed – Sown (title)

1967 – 1985 – 1993 (26 years)

Inks, Pencils, on paper mounted

For Walter 5/96

The next year I met a wonderful woman named Virginia (she had a boat next to mine in Ventura Harbor) and I remarried in 1997. Today, Andy's picture hangs by the front door in our home in Bakersfield. Through the years, I would often look at Andy's picture and wonder if my book (started around 2003) wasn't a bit like Andy's painting. Would I ever get it done? Well, here I am in 2014 writing this epilogue, and, like Andy's painting, there were a few stops along the way, but 2014 will be the year the book hits the street.

On one of the stops along the way, we sold the junk to my daughter, Lynn. In 2008, she sold the junk, and its new owner took it back to Los Angeles Harbor, not far from where it was put in the water from the main deck of the *Empress Heaven* back in 1993. Not far at all from the pier where I walking around inspecting the junk with a longshoreman named Duke and ended our conversation with, "It's kind of a long story—a very long story."

PEOPLE

Bartolomeu Dias: Portuguese explorer who sailed around Africa, 1488

Chen Ho [Zheng He]: admiral who the world explored during Ming dynasty

Chiang Kai-shek [Jiang Jieshi]: Nationalist politician, 1888–1975

Confucius: philosopher, 551–479 BC

Deng Pufang: Deng Xiaoping's son

Deng Xiaoping: leader and de-facto leader of the PRC, late 1979s to mid-1990s

Dr. Sun Yat-sen [Sun Zhongshan]: father of modern China

Hu Jintao: General Secretary of CPC

Hu Yaobang: his death triggered 1989 Tiananmen protest

Lao She: novelist and dramatist, died during GPCR

Lao Tzu: philosopher, 570–490 BC

Li Po [Li Bai]: Tang Dynasty poet

Lin Biao: Mao's successor who attempted a coup and died in a plane crash

Liu Shao-chi: led for a while with Deng Xiaoping

Mao Zedong: Communist politician, 1893–1976

Nein Chen: writer, in prison during GPCR

Peng Dehuai: first Long Marcher to fall

Prince Chun: father of Pu Yi

Pu Yi: the last emperor

Sun Yat-sen: first president of the Republic of China

Tu Fu [Du Fu]: Tang Dynasty poet

Tzu-His [Ci Xi]: Dowager Empress, 1835–1908

Wang Wen: Tang Dynasty poet

Yuan Shi-kai: Manchu general and briefly president, 1912–1916

Zhou Enlai: Mao's right-hand man

Zhu Di: Ming emperor

Zhu Gao Zhu: son of Emperor Zhu Di

PLACES

Beijing: capital of PRC

Chunking [Chungqing]: Chang Kai-shek's provisional capital, 1937–1945

Canton [Guangzhou]: capital of Guangdong Province, near Hong Kong

Changsha: Mao began his career here, and it was once a big tourist location

Changshu [Changzhou]: city in Jiangsu Province near boatyard

Comintern: the Communist International, Comintern was an international Communist organization initiated in Moscow during 1919.

Forbidden City: Imperial Palace or Palace Museum or Gugong

Formosa: old name for Taiwan

Grand Canal [Da Yunhe]: ancient canal system

Hangchow [Hangzhou]: 110 miles southwest of Shanghai

Hong Kong [Xianggang]: transferred to China in 1997, now the Special Administration Region

Jiangsu Province: Province near Shanghai

Jining: Grand Canal navigable from Hangzhou to Jining

Macao: near Hong Kong

Manchuria [Manzhou]: large area in northeast China

Nanking [Nanjing]: city in China, infamous incident committed by Japanese here 1937–1938

Shanghai: largest city

Shensi [Shaanxi] Province: Northern Province at the end of Long March

Suzhou: city in Jiangsu Province

Szechwan Cuisine [Sichuan]: Cuisine originating in southwest China

Taiwan: Republic of China

Tiananmen Square: vast square in the center of Beijing

ABBREVIATIONS, DEITIES, AND OTHER WORDS

Baozi: steamed bun

CPC: Communist Party of China

***Congee* [xifan] (*jook* in Cantonese)**: rice gruel

GPCR: Great Proletarian Cultural Revolution

Fu: happiness or blessing

Inverter: a piece of equipment used to change DC into AC.

Kitchen god [Zao Jun]: deity who reports on family to heaven

KMT: National People's Party or Kuomintang

Kuan Yin [Guan Yin]: deity also known as the goddess of mercy

Lai see: little red envelopes that contain good luck money

Lu Pan: The Builders' God also known as the carpenter god

Renminbi: Chinese currency or people's money

Sha-sha: thank you

Tsingtao: a popular Chinese beer

Wei wu wei: to do without doing, or to act without action

DYNASTIES AND PERIODS

Shang: 1766–1122 BC

Chow [Zhou]: 1122–770 BC

Spring and Autumn Annals: 770–476 BC

Warring States: 476–221BC

Chin [Qin]: 221–206 BC

Han: 206 BC–220 AD

Three Kingdoms: 220–265 AD

Jin (Tsin): 265–420 AD

Southern and Northern: 420–589 AD

Sui: 618–907 AD

Tang: 618–907 AD

Five Dynasties and Ten Kingdoms: 907–960 AD

Sung [Song]: 960–1280 AD

Yuan: Part of the Mongol Empire: 1280–1368 AD

Ming: 1368–1644 AD

Qing (Manchu): 1644–1911 AD

Republic of China (not Taiwan): 1911–1949 AD

Nationalist-Communist Civil War: 1927–1949 AD

People's Republic of China: 1949–present

ENDNOTES

[1] The Buddha, *Dhammapada: The Sayings of the Buddha*, trans. Thomas Byrom (Boston: Shambhala, 1993), 1–2.

[2] G. R. G. Worcester, *The Junks & Sampans of the Upper Yangtze* (Annapolis: Naval Institute Press, 1971), 29.

[3] Mao Tse-Tung, *Poems of Mao Tse-Tung*, trans. Hua-Ling Nieh Engle and Paul Engle (New York: Simon and Schuster, 1972).

[4] ———, *Quotations from Chairman Mao Tse-Tung* (San Francisco: China Press, 1990) 11–12.

[5] Nien Cheng, *Life and Death in Shanghai* (New York: Penguin Books, 1986), 37.

[6] J.P. Seaton, trans., ed., *The Shambhala Anthology of Chinese Poetry* (Boston: Shambhala, 2006).

[7] Kai-Yu Hsu, trans., ed., *Twentieth Century Chinese Poetry: An Anthology* (New York: Anchor Books, 1963) 127–28. Answer: Shao Hsun-mei wrote this poem as part of a collection of his poems that were published in 1928 as "The Flowerlike Sin," 29–30

[8] Mao Tse-Tung, *Quotations from Chairman Mao Tse-Tung* (San Francisco: China Press, 1990) 16.

[9] Marco Polo, *The Travels of Marco Polo* (London: J.M. Dent & Sons, 1975).

[10] Lin Yutang, *The Importance of Living* (New York: William Morrow, 1965) 159.

[11] Percy Bysshe Shelley, "Ode to the West Wind," verse I, lines 1–3.

ABOUT THE AUTHOR

Author Walt Hackman is a retired computer executive, art gallery owner, philanthropist, Navy serviceman, father, husband, and world traveler.

Walt joined the Navy in 1954, where his attachment to the ocean began. The next four years were filled with electrical and electronics training and an international tour aboard the USS *Kermit Roosevelt* ARG-16. While stationed aboard the *Kermit Roosevelt*, Walt traveled extensively throughout Southeast Asia and developed an ardent and abiding interest in Asian and Pacific Rim culture.

After his discharge, Walt attended Glendale College, where he studied electronics, and then went to work for Singer-Librascope, a subsidiary of the Singer Company, which primarily developed and manufactured computer systems for the US Navy. Walt started as an Incoming Electrical Inspector and worked his way up to Field Engineer. In the early 1960s, he was sent to Mare Island Naval Shipyard where he worked on the latest computer system aboard nuclear submarines.

In 1962, Walt married Diane Magrina and they moved to Hawaii where Walt had been transferred for work and continued his travels throughout the Pacific. His daughter, Lynn (who would later own the *Mei Wen Ti* from 2000 to 2008), and son, Walt, Jr., were both born in Oahu. The Hackmans eventually returned to Glendale, California, and in his early forties, Walt pursued his bachelors and master's degrees at Pepperdine University, graduating with a BSAS with honors and his MBA. For a while, Walt was a partner in a small computer company that specialized in third party maintenance (before the Geek Squad).

In 1980, Walt and Diane purchased a local art gallery and custom frame shop. By the middle of the '80s, they had successfully expanded into an additional operation in Old Town Pasadena. Perchance, it was at the Pasadena art gallery that Walt met Don, a modern-day China trader, and his Chinese wife, Mei. They became friends, not realizing at the time that they would later share a life-changing adventure as they traveled back and forth to China together. In 1989, life as they knew it dramatically changed forever when the Hackman's son was tragically killed.

The Hackman's marriage fell apart, and by 1992, they had sold their businesses and home, and both were set adrift in sorrow and the uncertainty of new beginnings. It was then, in his early fifties, that Walt Hackman decided to pursue his dream of living on a boat. Not just any boat, as it would turn out. Thus began his adventure of building a boat, rebuilding a life, and discovering China.

The *Mei Wen Ti* would become Walt's phoenix rising, and the happy beginning of a life filled with adventure, discovery, and love. Walt met Virginia Harmening, who had a boat right next to the *Mei Wen Ti* in Ventura Harbor, and they married in 1997.

A Note of Thanks

Publish Authority

Thank you for reading

If you enjoyed *No Problem, Mr. Walt,* we invite you to share your thoughts and reactions.

iA goodreads

For more, the adventure continues at www.MrWalt.com